The Stars Bear Witness

DATE DUE

JUN9 '49	FEB 14 '50	
JUL 1 '49	FEB 24 '50	
GIFT BRANCH		
AU 26 '49	13 '50	
AUG 15 '49		
West		
JUL 6 '49		
SEP 9'49	NOV 17 1961	
SEP 24 '49		
OCT 25 '49		
NOV 12 '49		
NOV 19 '49		
DEC 7 '49		
JAN 27 '50		

We swear we will battle for freedom and right
Against all the servants of tyrannous might.
We swear we will conquer the darkness of night,
Or with courage, we will fall in the fight.
On this oath we pledge our lives
Heaven and earth will hear us,
The stars will bear witness for us
A pledge of blood, a pledge of tears,
We swear, we swear, we swear

*From the Anthem of the
General Jewish Labor Union of Poland (the Bund)*

THE STARS
BEAR WITNESS

by
BERNARD GOLDSTEIN

TRANSLATED AND
EDITED BY LEONARD SHATZKIN

The Viking Press · New York

1949

PRINTED IN U.S.A. BY AMERICAN BOOK–STRATFORD PRESS, INC.

PUBLISHED ON THE SAME DAY IN THE DOMINION OF CANADA
BY THE MACMILLAN COMPANY OF CANADA LIMITED

TO MY BELOVED AND UNFORGETTABLE
COMRADE, FRIEND, AND TEACHER,
SHLOIME MENDELSOHN

ABOUT THE AUTHOR

EVER since I was a boy I have heard about "Comrade Bernard."[1] To me he was always an almost legendary hero, a sort of Robin Hood or Jesse James. To the hundreds of thousands of Jews of Poland he has for many years been a real champion, fighting against very near and very unromantic enemies

My father left Poland at the end of the First World War to avoid military service against the young revolutionary regime in Russia. He brought with him to America the spirit of the Jewish Socialist movement which had been his life in the old country. In the evenings he and his fellow immigrants would gather to sing the old revolutionary songs, to talk about the old days, the illegal political activity, the narrow escapes from the Czarist police. The name of Comrade Bernard always figured in their conversations.

The interest of the Jewish Socialist immigrants was not entirely nostalgic. They kept very well informed of events in their former homeland, and especially of the activities of the General Jewish Socialist Labor Union—the Bund. From time to time the Bund would send a delegate to the United States, usually to raise money for a new printing plant, for equipping a theater, for expanding the Medem Sanatorium for children, or for some other of the organization's many projects. These visits were always holidays

[1] Much of the information in this preface is taken from the short biographical sketch by J. S. Herz in the Yiddish edition of this work, *Finf Yor in Warshaver Ghetto.*

for me. I was allowed to stay up late and to sit at the feet of our guest as he told about the Jews of Poland.

Again and again the talk would turn to Comrade Bernard, and I would listen in wide-eyed wonder to the stories of the wonderful things he did. For me they were glimpses into an exciting world; the most lurid tales of cowboys and Indians paled before them. And they were also glimpses into a real world, where real people struggled for their lives.

Bernard Goldstein was born in Shedltze, just three hours from Warsaw, in 1889 His was a generation destined to contribute its best sons to the mounting revolutionary tide in Eastern Europe, and he joined the stream early. At the age of thirteen his imagination was already fired by stories of anti-Czarist agitation in Warsaw brought home by his two older brothers. He began to read forbidden revolutionary literature and attend the meetings of underground youth groups. At sixteen he had his baptism of fire. In May 1905, during Russia's war against Japan, four hundred people gathered secretly in the Yugan Forest near Bernard's home. The meeting was organized by the Bund, at that time a young Jewish political party.

Suddenly the group was surrounded by a large contingent of cavalry and foot-soldiers.

"Who is the speaker?" the commander, Officer Kosakov, demanded angrily.

No one answered.

"Give him up!" he shouted. The crowd maintained its stubborn silence.

"Swords out!" Kosakov ordered.

The people moved closer together, locked arms, and defiantly began to sing revolutionary songs. The horses plowed into the crowd. Swords and bayonets were wielded without mercy. When Kosakov finally called a halt, eighty people lay wounded.

The entire assemblage was then arrested. At the Shedltze jail

2

they were made to run between two rows of soldiers who beat them as they passed. For the rest of his life Bernard was to wear the scar of a saber cut on his chin. He, a sixteen-year-old boy, ran the gauntlet and was sent to the hospital with the badly wounded. Almost immediately he escaped. Under his bloody clothing, wrapped tightly around his body, was the red flag of the Bund, which must never fall into the hands of the enemy.

Late in 1905, Bernard quit the village for Warsaw, the great boiling center of East European Jewry and the focus of anti-Czarist agitation. There, as a member of the Bund, he plunged into the crest of the revolutionary wave.

In 1906, Bernard was sent from Warsaw to help the striking fur workers of near-by Kalushin. As he and the strike leader sat at the negotiating table with the employers, the police entered. The two men were arrested, bound, and paraded in an open cart through the city while the whole town watched.

In prison they were deliberately thrown among the criminals who hated the revolutionaries more fiercely than they did the corrupt police, for the radical workers were much more energetic in fighting crime. In the prisons the criminals found their opportunity for revenge against the "politicals." A group of thugs backed Bernard into a corner, pummeling and kicking him. Then one of them, Piesak, a thief, took a good look at the victim's face.

"Let the boy alone!" he ordered sharply. The men backed away. Piesak's skill with the knife had made him a law among the lawless.

Piesak recalled that, a year before, this boy had been his cell-mate in the Shedltze jail. A sentimental attachment led him to protect Bernard.

Bernard's arrest led to a boycott of the Kalushin furriers. No wagons from Kalushin could enter Warsaw with their furs as long as Bernard and his comrade were in jail. The Kalushin furriers felt compelled to intervene, and they did it in a direct and simple way: they bribed the authorities to release the prisoners.

3

In 1907 and 1908 the revolutionary wave receded. After the abortive uprising of 1905 thousands were sent to prison, and many more were frightened by the Czarist reign of terror. The workers were discouraged and apathetic. On May Day of 1908 Bernard was sent to address a factory meeting of shoe workers at 14 Leshno Street. As he mounted the platform he was greeted with a volley of wet rags and shouts of "Enough strikes! Enough revolution!" Bernard wept. He had not wept in the Yugan Forest or during the beatings in the Kalushin prison, but this desertion by the workers moved him to tears.

But he refused to give up. He organized the painters and was arrested for leading a painters' strike. When he organized the ironmongers and the carpenters, he was arrested again. This time, after serving his prison sentence, he was exiled to a remote Polish village.

Finding banishment unbearable, he escaped and returned to Warsaw. The revolutionary movement was beginning to revive. Bernard was active in organizing the youth and the garment trades. In 1913 he helped to organize the general protest strike against the infamous trial of the Jew, Mendel Beylis, for ritual murder.

Bernard was one of two delegates elected by the Warsaw Bund to the projected Socialist convention in Vienna in 1914, but the outbreak of World War I disrupted the convention plans.

In 1915, at a secret meeting of trade-union leaders in Warsaw, Bernard was arrested again. As the Germans approached Warsaw, the Russian government evacuated its prisoners, and Bernard was removed deep into Russia, first to Moscow and then to Tver, where he was released on parole. He fled to Moscow and from there to Kiev on a false passport to continue his revolutionary activity. In Kiev the police caught up with him. For violating his parole he was condemned to exile in Siberia.

The journey on foot to Siberia was long and difficult, lasting several months, with stops at many prisons along the way. Finally

4

Bernard reached his place of exile, the town of Lukyanova in Yenusseisk. After a short time there, he became ill. The closest doctor was at Pirovsk, fifty miles away. But no exile was permitted to leave his place of residence without permission. Bernard went to the local police commissioner for authorization to make the trip.

The commissioner examined the prisoner, pushing back his eyelids to see whether he was malingering. Bernard was annoyed. "Are you a doctor?" he asked ironically.

Such lack of respect on the part of an exile was unheard of. The official answered with a resounding smack in the face. Bernard reached across the desk, picked up the ornate kerosene lamp, and smashed it over the commissioner's head.

Several orderlies dashed in to avenge the dignity of the Czar's representative. They beat up the ailing prisoner, bound him hand and foot, and carried him back to his bed.

The incident raised a storm among the political exiles. From Lukyanova to Pirovsk to Yolansk the news traveled, creating a sensation. The exiles sent angry petitions to the governor at Krasnoyarsk, protesting against the inhuman treatment of a sick prisoner by the authorities. After three weeks word came from the governor that Bernard was to be taken to the doctor at Pirovsk.

At Pirovsk Bernard learned that he was suffering from a serious case of pneumonia. The doctor, an exile himself, ordered Bernard hospitalized. His fellow-exiles made it a point of honor to care for the comrade who had reacted so proudly to the insult of the police commissioner. They considered his action a defense of the dignity of all the prisoners.

When Bernard was discharged from the hospital the police commissioner repeatedly demanded his return to Lukyanova. But the doctor stubbornly refused to admit that his patient was well. Bernard, supposedly convalescing, hunted and fished at Pirovsk.

One day an excited peasant arrived from Yenusseisk with the

5

news that the Little Father was no longer Czar and that there were disturbances. Sadly he advised the village to pray for the health of the Little Father. The Russian Revolution was ten days old.

The political exiles in Pirovsk went into action. Armed with hunting rifles, they rounded up the five policemen, disarmed them, seized the post office, and raised the red flag. Then there was nothing more to do.

Unaware of the change in his political fortunes, the Czarist police commissioner, accompanied by two guards, arrived in Pirovsk for a routine visit. His handsome sleigh, drawn by three horses, was ordered to halt. The revolutionaries in Pirovsk had taken a rich prize.

The exiles held a council of war to determine the prisoner's fate. Many of them had suffered at his hands and wanted revenge. The commissioner was condemned to die. Of course the honor of carrying out the sentence belonged to Bernard Goldstein since he, of all the prisoners, had suffered most.

The police chief was tied to a tree. Bernard, armed with a revolver, stood facing him. But the man's terror at the prospect of death was so abject that Bernard refused to shoot. When his fellow-exiles criticized his weakness, he declared that the victorious revolution must show a humane attitude even to an evil servant of the Czar.

The exiles journeyed home in triumph, greeted at every railroad station by happy singing demonstrators. In Russia's capital city a great crowd led by a delegation from the Petrograd Soviet waited to parade with them through the streets.

Bernard did not rest long. He returned to Kiev, where he volunteered for the army to defend the infant revolution. His fellow soldiers elected him to the Ukrainian Soviet. He participated in the seesaw battle between the revolutionaries and the Ukrainian reactionaries who were allied with the Germans. In Kiev he organized a militia among the Jewish workers which participated actively in

6

the overthrow of the reactionary government of Hetman Skor-padsky.

In 1919, when clouds were already beginning to creep across the revolutionary sun, Bernard's homesickness took him back to his beloved Warsaw. There, in the new independent Poland, he took his old place in the Jewish labor movement. The events of the preceding few years had brought great numbers of workers into the revolutionary ranks. The Bund and the trade-union movement were once again strong.

Almost immediately Bernard was elected to the praesidium of the Warsaw Bund and to the executive committee of the trade-union federation. He was assigned to work particularly in the most poorly organized trades.

He was active among many workers, but the bakers, the transport workers, and the butchers—considered tough, uncohesive elements, difficult to organize—were his principal concern. His achievements and influence among them were to be crucial in the difficult years that followed. His stubborn honesty won the devotion of men used only to force or cunning.

The transport workers were a very important group. In Warsaw thousands of Jews made their living as porters, draymen, droshky drivers, and, later, chauffeurs. The human back was the most important means of transport and the bearers were the best paid, the aristocracy of the trade. Physically they were strong; culturally and intellectually they were backward.

The transport workers were very close to the underworld. They lived on the same streets, in the same buildings, were often close friends of criminals, even members of the same family. There was always the danger that the ephemeral boundary between the heavy workers and the easy earners would disappear altogether. Bernard had always to be on guard to see that a wall was erected between the two elements.

Bernard was also active among the meat workers. They, too, were a strange and curious world unto themselves, with a social scale of their own. The slaughterhouse workers dominated the butchers and the workers in the wurst factories.

The slaughterhouse workers, Poles and Jews, were often slightly drunk. They found it difficult to work on a sober stomach Always smeared with blood, they were easily roused to a fight, but they never lost their heads. The sign of an impending brawl was the clanging of their bloody knives on the stone floor as they pulled them out of their boots and tossed them away. No one wanted to kill a comrade in the heat of the fight.

On the job they were divided into partnership groups of sixty or seventy, and were paid collectively. Jews and Poles worked side by side and the relations between them were good, despite the fact that both were strongly nationalistic, unruly, and impulsive. They had frequent conflicts over working conditions, but they always managed to settle them in comradely fashion. They drank and played cards together, living in friendly harmony.

All these rough unpolished workers had to be taught the most elementary things. They had to be reared like children. The unions had to break their habit of taking disputes to the strongest member of the group for adjudication. The hierarchy of toughs who ruled like petty tyrants had to be deposed.

For serious moral offenses, members were expelled from the unions. In each case it was necessary to convince the people that the offender had committed a wrong and that expulsion was necessary. By example and by patient understanding, Bernard acquired great authority among the meat workers and porters, gave them some understanding of right and wrong, and showed them how, even under conditions of extreme poverty, they could live in dignity.

Bernard was more than a political officer; he was a father confessor and a court of domestic relations.

As a result of his administration, union members were increasingly concerned with keeping their reputations spotless. Little by little they established better habits. When a member died, they offered his job to his son, or helped the widow and the family financially. They uprooted the practice of extorting large sums from workers seeking admission to the partner-group. They no longer permitted the strongest to take the largest share of the group's earnings.

An embarrassing incident which characterizes Bernard's position among these men occurred with a young porter from the market. He was called "Little Mother" because his mother was very short. He resembled her, being very short, extremely broad, and exceptionally strong. He would lift the heaviest weights and throw them over his head on to his broad back with ease.

The well-paid meat workers and porters liked to live on a grand scale. They often celebrated marriages, circumcisions, fetes of all kinds, with great banquets to which they invited large crowds and sometimes even the union brass band. "Little Mother" gave a big party at his home on Krochmalna Street to which he invited Bernard. When Bernard arrived at the entrance, he was greeted by an orchestra which played the Bundist anthem. With great pomp he was escorted to the apartment of "Little Mother," where the table groaned under bottles of whisky, fish, geese, and mountains of other food.

Bernard surveyed the table, the walls of the room, the floor, the wife of the porter and their child, turned silently on his heel, and left. The crowd was in consternation. The celebration was completely spoiled.

"Little Mother" was a member of the Bund militia. He refused to attend the next meeting. He paced back and forth on Pzheyazd Street in front of the headquarters. At the meeting his friends created a storm, shouting demands that Bernard explain this insult to a party comrade.

Bernard rose to answer. "When I came into the apartment, I saw that the walls were filthy and covered with cobwebs, the floors were thick with dirt; even his wife and the pretty little child were unwashed and dressed in soiled, sloppy rags. If some-

9

one can afford such a grand celebration, he should first see that his home and family are properly cared for."

Everyone was still. The meeting adjourned.

A few weeks later "Little Mother" again invited Bernard to a party—in his freshly painted, well-scrubbed apartment. The wife and child were freshly bathed and radiantly dressed in white. This time there was no gloom. "Little Mother" beamed among his happy guests and laughed with unalloyed pleasure. Krochmalna Street buzzed with the story.

"I could have talked about hygiene until my voice gave out," Bernard said later. "They would not even have understood what I was talking about. But I spoiled a *simcha*, and that set them thinking."

While Bernard gave much time to trade-union organization, he was also active in Bundist party work. He was in charge of all large political demonstrations. During the twenty-year period between the wars there was not a single Warsaw Bund mass meeting or street demonstration of which Bernard was not the responsible organizer.

Because of his extensive political and trade-union activity, he was constantly in contact with Polish labor leaders and other Poles prominent in public life. In the years 1920–21 the Warsaw Bund found it necessary to set up special defense groups to protect public demonstrations from attacks by Polish hooligans, and to maintain order in the crowded union halls. Shortly after their organization, Bernard was placed at the head of these groups.

Besides the street hooligans, and in later years the organized fascist bands, the militia often found it necessary to resist Communist terror. In their campaign to split the labor movement and to destroy the Socialists, the Communists stopped at nothing. They used intimidation freely. They would often send groups armed with revolvers to break up workers' meetings. Once they even attempted to disperse a national convention of the Jewish Transport Workers' Union with gunfire. They did not shrink from a shooting attack on the famous Medem Sanatorium for Children at Myedzeshyn, near Warsaw. The attacks were carried out by toughs who received from the Communists an ideological justification for their own predilection for violence.

The Bundist militia was angry enough and strong enough to give the Communist attackers a lesson which would have driven from their minds any desire to continue their disruptive activity. But this could have been done only by a blood bath, and Bernard refused to permit it.

Despite the fact that Bernard kept the militia strictly on the defensive and was careful to avoid killing, the Communist press carried on a scurrilous personal campaign against him. But some of the most important Communists maintained the closest friendly relations with him. The Communist Sejm deputy, Stefan Kruhkovsky, for example, after his wife died, placed his young daughter in Bernard's care. Many more thoughtful Communists realized that if Bernard were killed it would remove the most important barrier to a bloody campaign of revenge against them. That explained in part why Bernard could show himself openly in the most dangerous situations without being shot.

However, an attempt on Bernard's life, resulting from a formal sentence of death passed on him by the Communist party, was actually made in 1929. Returning home late one night, he had reached the closed courtyard gate, when several men sprang out of a parked automobile and began shooting at him. He returned the fire and one of the attackers fell. The others threw the wounded man into the car and drove away. Bernard was unharmed. After that no further attempts were made to carry out the sentence.

Many people came to the Bund for aid and protection against injustice. It seemed to them in their helplessness that the Bund could accomplish anything. Such petitions were usually handed over to Bernard. Many people went directly to him.

After Hitler came to power in Germany, anti-Semitism in Poland took a more severe turn. The reactionary anti-Semitic

Endeks (National Democrats) and the fascist Falanga (Narodova Mlodshesh) had long striven to ride to power on anti-Jewish slogans. Now they had a concrete example of how to deal with the Jews. The Polish government, composed at that time of Pilsudski's followers, also took an anti-Semitic course, partially to counteract the propaganda that it was a government of "Jew-lovers." The anti-Jewish campaign became more and more poisonous. The Falangists and Endeks, moreover, did not content themselves with propaganda. They immediately translated their words into deeds.

In Warsaw attempts were made to drive the Jews from public parks and gardens. On the eves of national holidays pickets paraded in front of Jewish stores to prevent Poles from entering. At the beginning of the school year Polish students were stopped at the doors of Jewish bookstores. In the University, the Polytechnic, and other higher schools, the Jewish students were not allowed to sit with the Poles. Jewish pedestrians were attacked on the open streets.

The Jewish press protested these outrages as loudly as the censor would permit. Jewish representatives appealed to the government. It was no use. The Warsaw committee of the Bund discussed the problem more than once and finally concluded that the only recourse was active resistance. The Bund was the only organization which undertook to carry on an active fight against the anti-Semites. And the main burden fell on Bernard Goldstein as leader of the militia.

Bernard often sought and received help from the organized Polish workers. He was particularly concerned that the conflict should not degenerate into a fight between Jew and Gentile. Just as Hitlerism was a deadly danger not only for the Jewish people but for all workers, so too was Polish anti-Semitic fascism. The active participation of the Polish Socialist workers in the defense of the Jewish population pointed out that lesson and kept sections of the Polish youth from joining the ranks of the Fascists.

Most of the time, however, the Bund fought alone. More than once militia groups went to Warsaw University and to the Polytechnic to protect the outnumbered Jewish students from the inflamed anti-Semites. Bundist students, led by Michel Klepfish, distributed leaflets at the school gates protesting against the ghetto benches and the attacks of the hooligans, while in the classrooms the Jewish students would remain standing, refusing to sit on the benches set aside for them.

The leaders of the fascist Falanga knew that the center of the resistance was 26 Dluga, the headquarters of the Bund. They wrecked the building with a time-bomb.

Such arrogance could not go unanswered. Bernard organized a group of Bundists and Polish Socialists who went to the Falanga headquarters on Bratska Street in the heart of the Polish district and smashed it to bits. Everyone found there was soundly beaten.

The Falanga, which, together with the Endeks, had sought to create the impression that Jews were helpless and could be tormented with impunity, learned that such acts would not go unpunished. If the official organs of justice were passive, the Jewish workers would undertake to protect the Jewish population and punish the guilty. At the Bund headquarters the phone would ring constantly as now from one section, now from another, would come appeals for help against anti-Semitic attacks. Flying squads were always rushed to the scene.

Bernard's activity was concentrated in Warsaw but from time to time he had to go to the smaller towns to bring assistance.

In 1930 anti-Jewish excesses broke out in Minsk-Mazovietsky In such cases the censor strictly forbade the word "pogrom." It was true that no Jews were killed, but many were badly beaten and the windows of many Jewish homes were smashed. Some houses were set afire.

The pogrom was touched off when a mentally sick young Jew from the neighboring village of Kalushin shot and killed a sergeant of the Polish Army. The Endeks proclaimed the slogan,

"Blood for blood!"—all Jews must suffer for the crime of spilling the blood of the higher Slavic race.

Several days later the funeral of the murdered sergeant was to take place and there was danger that it would be the signal for a new pogrom. The central committee of the Bund sent Bernard Goldstein and Yosef Gutgold to Minsk-Mazovietsky, where they contacted the local organization of the PPS (Polish Socialist party). With the help of the Polish shoe workers they organized a campaign to counteract the anti-Jewish propaganda among the Polish population.

In the tense hours preceding the funeral the Endeks set fire to a Jewish house which had been abandoned by its frightened tenants. The fire was not content with Jewish walls and spread to a neighboring Polish house. No one did anything to stop it. The assembled crowd watched indifferently as the flames began to eat at the roof of the second house.

Suddenly a man broke from the crowd and dashed into the burning building. He carried out the small children and led out a feeble old woman. He climbed to the roof and called for water to fight the blaze.

Then the crowd came to life. Someone shouted, "Look! Endeks set fire to a Polish home—and a Jew is fighting the flames."

There were shouts from many throats, "Down with the Endeks! Down with the hooligans!"

The Jew on the roof was Bernard.

The crowd was exclusively Polish workers and ordinary villagers. The story of how the Endeks had set fire to a Polish home and a Jew had risked his life to save the Polish children raced through the village. The mood of the people changed immediately. Bernard and Yosef Gutgold hurried through the town, driving the frightened Jews out of their barricaded homes into the streets to take advantage of the new atmosphere and re-establish friendly relations with their Polish neighbors.

14

In 1936, Bernard was sent on a difficult mission to Lodz. The greatest industrial center and the second largest city in Poland was holding elections for the City Council that year. In Lodz the Endeks, under the leadership of Kovalski, were bolder than elsewhere and aped Hitler's methods more closely. At the beginning of the election campaign they posted placards warning the Jews not to appear at the polls and to stay in their homes on election day.

The Endeks had large well-armed bands in Lodz, and Bernard, who was delegated to foil their plan, knew that the organized Jewish workers did not have sufficient strength to pit against them. Everyone knew what it would mean to all the Jews of Poland if the first attempt to prevent Jews from exercising their rights of citizenship were to succeed. The Lodz experiment would spread like an epidemic through the land. Extraordinary measures were required.

Bernard arrived in Lodz two weeks before the elections and looked up a short thin wizened little Jew who called himself Mendele. Others had nicknamed Mendele "King of the Strong," for he ruled a small empire of thieves and petty gangsters. Bernard went to him to convince him that his help was necessary to protect the Jews of Lodz. At first Mendele refused to discuss it. He didn't know anything about any elections; he had his own problems and he wasn't going to get mixed up in any political squabble that was no concern of his.

Bernard finally persuaded him to telephone Warsaw and consult with some of his important friends there. After the telephone conversation, he was a changed man; his Warsaw connections knew Bernard well.

He organized a group of toughs, both Jews and Christians, and put them at Bernard's disposal. He insisted they would be enough to handle any situation, but Bernard brought reinforcements from the Warsaw militia.

The Endek hoodlums, many of whom were sidekicks of

Mendele's coterie, were informed in good time that things would be hot on election day. Their enthusiasm for the holy war sagged. Face to face with a group that knew them and could meet them on equal ground, their love of battle cooled. Except for a few normal scuffles, election day in Lodz was peaceful and serene.

In the evening, after the election, Mendele called his followers together to celebrate the victory with food and drink. Bernard was there to thank them and bid them good-by. Happy and proud, Mendele delivered a long speech, spiced with rich and pungent expletives. He told them what a fine thing they had done in preventing a bloody pogrom. As he spoke, his enthusiasm mounted and the crowd listened attentively.

They did not even lose their spirit when Mendele, throwing wide his puny arms, shouted, "There will be no pay for today's work. We have done a great *mitzvah*, and for doing *mitzvahs* there is no pay!"

Bernard's broad activity in the defense of the Jewish population was, naturally, no secret from the authorities.

Once, when he was arrested during a fight in the Warsaw streets the Federal Governor for Warsaw, Yaroshevitch, and the Chief of the Security Police, Captain Runge, threatened to send him to the notorious concentration camp, Kartuz Bereza. The leader of the Bund, Henryk Erlich, went to Runge and demanded that Bernard be freed. Runge ordered Bernard brought to him in Erlich's presence.

As Bernard was led into the room, Runge, beside himself with rage, demanded, "Who is the boss of Poland's capital, you or I?"

Bernard answered quietly, "As long as you refuse to protect the Jewish people, I will do it. If I am to get Kartuz Bereza for that, go ahead and send me there."

The most difficult task of Bernard Goldstein's long political career was setting down the story told in the following pages.

For a long time he refused to undertake it. Only after repeated pleadings from his comrades, particularly the late Shloime Mendelsohn, did he agree to attempt it.

His active leadership before the war and his position in the Jewish underground during it qualify him as the chronicler of the last hours of Warsaw's Jews. Out of the tortured memories of those five and a half years he has brought forth the picture with all its shadings—the good with the bad, the cowardly with the heroic, the disgraceful with the glorious. This is his valedictory, his final service to the Jews of Warsaw.

The appeal to his sense of duty reversed his early stubborn refusal to write this book, but nothing could shake his modesty. The complete story of Bernard's activity during the occupation will not be found here. We know from other sources that there were bloody encounters in which Bernard was an organizer and active participant. He refuses to speak of them. For him, the heroes of the Warsaw ghetto died in battle. Let no one presume to strike a pose upon their ashes.

L. S.

THE STARS BEAR WITNESS

ONE

IN THE tense years before the outbreak of the Second World War, the peoples of the countries soon to be a battleground watched in disbelief the events unfolding toward the already inevitable catastrophe.

Perhaps no group watched more closely and more fearfully than we, part of the greatest concentration of Jews in Europe, citizens of Poland and Socialists. Hitler had doomed us thrice—to subjugation as Poles, to liquidation as Socialists, to extermination as Jews.

The years that followed fulfilled every promise, realized every fear. Our wildest nightmares became terribly immediate reality. Murder and bestiality became familiar companions.

Some of this had been broadly anticipated in the coolly reasoned warnings of our political writers and in the almost prophetic dramatics of calamity howlers, but no one could have predicted the tragic march of individual events, nor the heroism born of desperation that drove our docile people, already persecuted for generations, to battle with their fists against one of the mightiest military machines the world has ever known.

After Hitler had defeated our comrades of the German Social Democratic party in 1933, we felt increasingly that the double threat of a world war and an extension of Hitler's policy of violence and anti-Semitism hung over us. Each successful fascist defiance of world opinion made the anti-Semites in Poland more

audacious. The semi-fascist government of Poland closed its eyes
to the activities of the anti-Semitic gangs. Their attacks on Jews,
which reached the scale of pogroms and became increasingly frequent, had to be met by our own physical resources, for the
official organs of police power usually looked the other way.

In the face of the growing danger we worked at home for the
social, economic, and political rehabilitation of the Jews, for a
more democratic organization of the nation's economy, and for a
more equitable distribution of the fruits of that economy. We
struck back at every action of the Polish anti-Semites, believing
that the Jews would retain their civil rights only if they showed
that they could protect themselves. On the international plane
we used what influence we had to support a system of collective
security which would contain the aggressor nations before war
became a reality. But our efforts were too puny to turn back the
powerful forces that were pushing an indifferent and unresisting
world toward the precipice.

When I say "we," I mean primarily the great mass of Jews
who lived in Eastern Europe, the cradle of modern Jewish culture
and, before Hitler, the greatest center of Jewish population in the
world. In Poland, which was the focal point of this great Jewish
community, there were many towns and cities in which the Jews
were the majority. We were a nation within a nation, formed and
tested in a thousand years of struggle, cherishing our heritage and
the rights that we had wrested from our unfriendly hosts, cemented by our own language, culture, schools, trade and labor
organizations; cemented even by our own internal conflict over
Jewish clericalism.

In the second place, and more specifically, when I say "we,"
I mean the members and supporters of the General Jewish Labor
Union of Poland, *Der Allgemeiner Yiddisher Arbeiter Bund*, more
familiarly known as the Bund.

In America, I have discovered, "the Bund" usually means the
German-American Bund, the fortunately insignificant fifth col-

22

umn Hitler attempted to organize in the United States. It is ironic that a gang of preposterous strutting hoodlums should create such a connotation for a name that in Poland represented exactly the opposite. There the Bund was the most important expression of the modern Jew emerging from the centuries-old darkness of the Middle Ages. In the belated assertion of the Jew's right to national recognition, the Bund was not only a political force, it was a cultural, educational, and economic force as well.

The Bund was organized in Vilna in 1897, only a few years after the first national stirrings among Eastern European Jews. Partly because of their own ignorance and superstitions, and partly because of the unfriendliness of their neighbors, the Jews experienced their Renaissance many years after the Christian nations of Europe. Like popular movements in other nations to which the Renaissance came late, the Bund combined the philosophy of new national awakening with a working-class socialist philosophy. It was organized to fight both against Czarism, which was oppressive to the Jew as a worker and as a Jew, and against the feudal elements in the Jewish community itself.

From its very beginning the Bund was much more than a political organization. Even in the early days it undertook, in addition to its political functions, the educational function of establishing Jewish schools and of raising the vernacular Yiddish to the status of a recognized language. It undertook the cultural function of encouraging the new poets, dramatists, and novelists who were using the Yiddish language, refining it, and making it a literary tool. It undertook the function of organizing the Jews into trade unions to defend their economic interests against Jewish or Christian employers. It also set up trade schools to win for the Jews a place in the national economic life. It established health resorts and recreational facilities. In the sense that it taught a new ethics of the brotherhood of man, of mutual respect, and of the dignity of the individual, it also carried out a spiritual function; it substituted these concepts for ancient religious superstitions.

23

The Bund almost immediately became an important factor in Jewish life. With the outbreak of the revolution of 1905, only a few years after its formation, it threw itself into the struggle against the Czar. The great numbers of us who sat in Russian prisons and Siberian camps in the years immediately following were evidence of the widespread influence of the Bund among the Jews. Even then one could see that the devotion of its followers to the Bund was different from the attitude of followers of other political parties. The Jew who came to the Bund found it not only a political medium but also the expression of his national pride and of his way of life, so that the loyalty which in other peoples is divided among political parties and church and nation was, for us, concentrated entirely in the Bund. Perhaps it was unique among parties because the Jews of Eastern Europe, scattered yet together, a nationality without a nation, were unique among peoples.

With the end of World War I and the establishment of an independent Poland, the Bund became a force on the Polish political scene. It was the most active and energetic fighter against the anti-Semitic elements of the Polish people. This was natural, since the Bund believed that the only hope for the Jews was to win their rights in Poland, and that the only way to win them was to fight for them. We looked upon ourselves, not as transients waiting to be taken to some distant promised land, but as citizens of Poland who would have to build a better life there for our children and for the generations to come.

I know it must be surprising to Americans that the Bund, which was the most important Jewish political organization in Poland, was opposed to Zionism. The Bund conceived as its purpose the winning of political, social, and economic rights for the Jew where the Jew was—in our case, in Poland. This seemed as natural to us as it does to the American Negro to fight for his rights in the United States rather than to accept emigration back to Africa as a solution to the problem of racial inequalities in America.

24

Until the early thirties, the Bund concentrated its political activity in the Polish arena, remaining aloof from the Kehilla, or Jewish Community Council, which was recognized by the Polish government as the guardian of Jewish religious affairs. The Kehilla had official status. It collected taxes from all Jewish citizens and was responsible for the maintenance of the Jewish cemetery, Jewish religious instruction, and so forth.

A few years before the outbreak of World War II, the Bund entered the Kehilla elections with the avowed purpose of transforming it into a secular organization and of winning from the Polish government the right to expand its functions With the growth of European and specifically of Polish fascism, and with the recognition of the increasing danger to Poland's Jews, the strength of the Bund grew by leaps and bounds. It became not only the most important Jewish spokesman in Poland's legislative bodies, but also the most powerful group within the Kehilla itself. After the 1936 elections, in which the Bund received a plurality, the Polish government dissolved the Warsaw Kehilla to forestall the passage of a Bund resolution that the Kehilla should undertake civil as well as religious functions. In 1938, in country-wide elections to city legislatures, the Bund received an outright majority of all Jewish votes.

Paralleling the growth of the Bund in those last few years was the growth in stature of the Jew himself. There was no mistaking the fact that the Polish Jew was a new man, who for the first time walked with his head erect and with pride in himself. This was the culmination of long years of struggle for the right to learn a trade and to practice it, to enter the professions, to educate his children as he saw fit, to attend colleges as freely as other citizens without being confined to "ghetto" benches.

It was at the highest point in the Jew's climb toward recognition as a human being with national and social rights that Hitler struck him down.

To us, the German attack on Poland was not unexpected. The innocent man who stands before a firing squad is not surprised when bullets hit his body. We had all hoped against hope that something would save us at the last moment, but the logic of events was too clear. We had pleaded with the Polish government to make more adequate preparations for defense. We had asked for the arming of the population and the organization of volunteer companies to defend the country and to act as partisans if necessary. Within the limits of government policy we had done everything we could to strengthen the defense of the country.

We hoped, also, that the logic of the situation would convince the Russians that they must come to our aid. Of course Poland's strength alone could not stop the German Army. No one even dreamed that the Polish Army could do more than harass and slow up the invaders, giving our more powerful allies time to throw in their might.

But the crushing strength of the panzers was greater than military strategists or popular opinion had imagined. So swift was the advance of the German war machine into Polish territory that only a few days after war broke out Warsaw was face to face with the problem of defending the city. After some hesitation the Polish government announced that it would declare Warsaw an open city. This decision was based on the opinion of the military command that a stand along the Vistula was hopeless and would only expose the civilian population to all the horrors of modern mechanized warfare. All men capable of bearing arms were ordered to leave the city, to avoid falling into the hands of the enemy, and to proceed in the direction of the new defense line along the Bug River. At the same time the government began to evacuate all important national institutions and the city garrison. One after another the important organizations, including all political parties, evacuated their key personnel, leaving behind skeleton staffs to await the entrance of the German Army. Even the fire department moved out, with all its equipment.

We called an emergency meeting of our central committee on September 6, 1939. It was a solemn session, permeated with anxiety and foreboding. We were trapped completely and hopelessly.

The decision by the Polish government to abandon Warsaw to the Germans had not been taken lightly, to be sure, but whatever Warsaw's Poles might suffer under Nazi occupation could not compare with the disaster confronting the Jews. Was it not better for us to fight to the last breath rather than permit five hundred thousand Jews to be handed over to the fate which Hitler had promised? We knew that the Jews of Warsaw, of all Poland, looked to us to make our decision. We felt that the eyes of the entire world were upon us as we squirmed helplessly in our dilemma.

What would happen if we attempted to organize popular resistance in spite of the decision of the Polish authorities? How would the Poles react if we insisted on precipitating a situation which would condemn their capital to destruction and would send thousands of unwilling and innocent civilians to their deaths? Even among the Jews of Warsaw, had we any right to expect popular support for a desperate adventure which would ignite a fierce blaze of anti-Semitism throughout Poland and would invite the Germans to answer with savage reprisals? Warsaw's Jews had given us seventeen out of twenty Jewish representatives, but they would not follow us into what would seem to them mass suicide.

We were trapped utterly and irretrievably. Reluctantly, we concluded that we had to submit to evacuation. We appointed a skeletal organizational leadership to remain, and directed all able-bodied members of the party and the central committee to follow the government east.

On September 7, in the company of Victor Alter and several other comrades, I left Warsaw on foot and headed toward the Bug River. With some difficulty, because of the congestion and confusion of the military and refugee traffic on the highways, we reached Myendzyzhetz in the vicinity of the proposed Bug River defense line. There we heard the radio announce that the evacuation orders had been countermanded, that Warsaw was being defended, that volunteer companies were being formed and armed, and that the city would resist to the very end.

We called together the members of the central committee to consider the sudden change in the situation. All agreed that Victor and I should return to Warsaw as quickly as possible.

This was much more easily decided than accomplished. All the main highways were blocked by the military and closed to civilian use. We decided that the long road, through Lublin, was the only practical way back.

We got to Lublin on September 11 and found the city a mess. Devastating German bombardment had spread destruction and chaos. The hysteria of the population seemed to reach even to the garrison; military police were stopping people in the streets at random and forcing them into labor gangs to clear the wreckage. The attitude of the military served to increase the population's terror.

We offered the commandant our help in organizing voluntary brigades of workers to clear the wreckage and to get essential services operating if he would stop the terrorizing activities of his soldiers. He agreed, and we set our comrades to work to do what they could. We also managed to get out one issue of our Lublin newspaper, which did something to help the morale of the Jewish population.

But the problem of getting to Warsaw remained. Alter and I agreed that we had better separate, to double the chance that one of us would reach the capital.

We had been friends for a long time. He had joined the Bund in 1905—a year after I had—while still a student in Warsaw. We had both known the inside of Czarist prisons and the barren wastes of Siberian exile. Victor had always been a dynamo of

28

activity. Besides being a member of the central committee, he had sat on the Warsaw Board of Aldermen, had edited a Bundist newspaper in Polish, had been chairman of the Jewish Trade Union Federation, was on the praesidium of the all-Polish Trade Union Federation, was a leader of the cooperative movement, and had managed to find time to write books on a variety of subjects in Polish, French, and Yiddish.

He was a rare combination, a brilliant, profound thinker, a lovable friend, and a devoted servant of his people. His tall handsome figure, shock of black hair, and blazing dark eyes were familiar to every Jewish and Polish worker. In a nation more favored, more powerful, than the Jews, he would have risen to great political heights, perhaps to international eminence. But he had no personal ambition and was content with what his own poor people showered upon him—sincere love and gratitude for such a champion.

It was hard to say good-by to Victor. This was our last farewell.

I left Lublin and proceeded east, getting as far as Vlodava, where I learned that Lublin had fallen to the Germans. Since I was now cut off from Warsaw, there seemed nothing else to do but get behind the German lines and wait for the city to fall. I therefore returned to Lublin.

There I got my first taste of life under the German occupation, as Nazi soldiers spread terror through the Jewish community. With the exuberance of victorious hoodlums they looted, pillaged, and terrorized the Jewish section of the city.

Our spirits rose temporarily when we heard that the Red Army had crossed the eastern frontier and was advancing into Poland. Then the German radio announced that the Russians were coming as German, not as Polish, allies and that Poland was being partitioned between the two.

Optimism could not be completely extinguished, even under

this great blow. We heard rumors that the line of partition was to be the Vistula, with Lublin in the Russian sphere. But we lost even that small comfort when the Russians retired to the Bug River, handing over Vlodava, which I had left a few days before, to the Germans with a great show of friendly ceremony.

I heard that Victor Alter had been arrested behind the Russian lines. This was not the first time the Bolsheviks had arrested him. In 1921, when the Bund was considering joining the Third International, he had gone to Moscow to negotiate with the Bolsheviks. While there, he was handed letters of protest written by friends of socialist and democratic anti-Bolsheviks who were already languishing in Russian prisons. Victor made no secret of the contents of the letters, but he refused every demand by the Communists that he reveal their source. Incensed at his refusal to betray other comrades, his hosts threw him into prison. He was released after an eight-day hunger strike and escorted to the Polish border.

Bolshevism had developed since 1921. This time Victor was not released. Along with the great and beloved Jewish Socialist Henryk Erlich, Victor Alter, secretly and without trial, was put to death in the cellars of the NKVD.

When Warsaw finally fell to overpowering German might, after a heroic and stubborn defense by its citizens, I was able to carry out my instructions and return to the city.

I had begun to grow a mustache as soon as I had left Warsaw. Although it was still somewhat thin, it already helped to discourage recognition. I continued to cultivate it and somewhat later I sported a beautifully thick mustache, beard, and side whiskers, worthy of a Polish major-general. It was an effective disguise, and in the right direction too—it even helped me to pass as a Christian.

I re-entered Warsaw on October 3, almost a full month after I had left, to begin in earnest my life under Nazi occupation.

30

TWO

Warsaw was a shambles. After Lublin, I was prepared to find it considerably damaged, but the ruin so surpassed my expectations that I was staggered.

Everywhere there was evidence of the pounding the city had taken from German artillery and the Luftwaffe. Everywhere were bombed-out and gutted buildings, their walls leaning precariously over the city sidewalks. One could hardly find a window with an unbroken pane of glass. Warsaw had paid dearly for daring to resist, and the Germans had deliberately made the price high. Warsaw was their dramatic warning to the world that resistance was hopeless and costly.

Comrades told me about the terrible days of the siege. At the very last moment, after all the important government institutions as well as the Warsaw garrison had already been evacuated, the Polish Socialists Niedialkovsky and Zaremba went to General Tshuma, the military commandant, and to Starzinski, the Mayor of Warsaw, to demand that the city be defended. Partly as a result of their intervention, the plan of surrender was abandoned.

Whatever arms were available were distributed among the volunteer defense companies. Barricades were erected, first-aid stations set up, food distribution organized, and the city prepared hurriedly for the siege. Soldiers from the general area of Warsaw were brought in to take the place of the evacuated garrison.

The Bund joined with the PPS (Polish Socialist party) to form fighting companies, which, like the other volunteer units, were placed under the command of the Polish Army Our comrades threw themselves into the work, goaded by the knowledge of the fate that awaited them under the Germans.

The spirit of popular resistance kept the Germans outside the city gates long after the Polish military had decided the fight was hopeless. An armed populace organized by the political parties and the trade unions, just as we had demanded when war broke out, was the backbone of the city's defense.

Victor Shulman, a staunch revolutionist, and Artur Ziegelboim, who had arrived from Lodz only a day before the outbreak of the war, reconstructed the editorial staff of the *Volkszeitung*, our daily newspaper. Loeser Clog, president of the Jewish section of the Printers' Union, spark-plugged the technical staff and managed to get the paper out in a reduced format. Among Warsaw's Jews, the regular appearance of the newspaper under such difficult conditions helped to stiffen morale. On days when the bombardment was light enough to permit the distribution system to function, circulation reached from ten to twelve thousand copies.

When the gasworks were destroyed and the linotype machines could no longer function, the paper was set entirely by hand. A few days later electricity was disrupted, and printing had to be done on a handpowered press. Finally, a few days before the fall of the city, when every utility, including the water supply, had ceased to function, the newspaper suspended publication. Before that happened the group was able to issue, on the insistence of the Bundist youth, one edition of the youth newspaper, *Der Yugendwecker*.

But Warsaw was destined to fall. The first thing the Germans did on entering the city was to demand twelve hostages for the good behavior of the population, and Mayor Starzinski requested that the Bund supply one of them. After some discussion, the Bund appointed Artur Ziegelboim for this hazardous role.

Artur's absence from Warsaw for several years would, it was hoped, make him safer as a hostage than some of the better-known Warsaw comrades. He had joined the Bund after World War I and had crammed a whole lifetime of political activity into the years that followed. He came from a poverty-ridden working-class family and had been a glove worker. He had been active in Warsaw for many years, reaching the position of secretary of the Trade Union Federation, and was a member of the central committee of the Bund. In 1937 he had moved to the industrial city of Lodz where he was elected to the Board of Aldermen, serving until the outbreak of the war.

When the Germans crossed the Polish frontier, Artur had rushed to Warsaw. Although he was certainly among those who should have left the city, perhaps the country, to work at a safer distance, he remained, devoting his considerable talents to mobilizing the Jewish organizations to withstand the siege. In the chaos and uncertainty of those first days, his quiet, efficient determination was an inspiration to the disoriented Jewish workers It was characteristic of Artur that he did not shrink from the task of being a hostage to the Germans. He placed no limit on his loyalty to his cause and his people. Later, in London, he was to prove that to the hilt.

Fortunately the hostages, Artur with them, were soon freed. But the Gestapo immediately began a hunt for well-known Socialists. They searched in vain for Henryk Erlich, the acknowledged leader of Jewish socialism in Poland and one of the most important figures in the Socialist International. No one guessed then that Henryk was already in a Soviet prison awaiting the pleasure of his Communist executioners.

I returned to my old apartment at 12 Novolipya Street to find that my brother Laeb had moved in with his wife and two young sons. His house had been burned out in the bombardment. We boarded up the windows to keep out the cold and made ourselves as comfortable as possible.

The city emerged from the destruction with great difficulty. The utilities were repaired very slowly. People had to carry water from the Vistula after waiting in long lines for an opportunity to dip their buckets into the river. The fuel shortage was so severe that it did not permit boiling of water for drinking purposes. To minimize the danger of epidemics, the dead who littered the streets were buried in the city squares and small public gardens as quickly as possible.

The difficulties of living in a badly bombed city were multiplied a thousand times for Warsaw's Jews. The Germans did not wait long to spread terror through the Jewish neighborhoods. Soldiers went from house to house and from store to store, supposedly looking for hidden weapons but seizing anything that took their fancy. Trucks and small carts stood along the curbs ready to receive the spoils, and passers-by were commandeered to help load them. German soldiers stopped Jews in the streets and emptied their pockets, then beat them up for sport. After the seven P.M. curfew, when all courtyard gates were locked, the Germans broke into apartments, plundering and smashing furniture. For clearing wreckage and other heavy work they relied upon roving press-gangs who seized Jews on the streets and dragged them off to forced labor. To alleviate the terrible food shortage and to win the good will of the population, they set up mobile soup kitchens—for "Aryans" only. The Poles were quick to point out any Jew who tried to sneak into the lines.

The atmosphere was so saturated with fear that people were afraid to leave the illusory security of their own homes and went out on the streets only when necessary.

The Germans proclaimed the revival, with new functions, of the Kehilla or Jewish Community Council, which they rechristened the Judenrat. It was no longer a religious institution but a racial one and must assume jurisdiction over all matters affecting

34

the Jewish "race." Even converted Jews or persons with a strain of Jewish blood were now included in the Jewish community.

Adam Cherniakov, a member of the old Kehilla, was appointed president of the Judenrat and undertook the task of preparing for the Germans a list of twenty-four members. Before the war, Cherniakov, an engineer, had been a little-known leader in the Artisans' Union. Politically he considered himself a Zionist, although he had never played an important role in Jewish life. He spoke Polish exclusively, which in the Jewish community was a mark of "assimilationist" tendencies.

Cherniakov demanded that the Bund, which had been the largest Jewish party, supply one member. Artur Ziegelboim, who, having been a hostage, was already in an exposed position, agreed to serve.

Under the chairmanship of Cherniakov, the Judenrat undertook such new duties as the registration of Jewish citizens, issuance of birth certificates, issuance of business licenses and permits, collection of government taxes from Jews, issuance of and collection of payment for ration cards, registration of workers, and so forth. From the registrants, Jews were drafted for forced, unpaid labor for various periods.

The organization of forced labor was the first major action of the Judenrat and undertaken on its own initiative. In an attempt to mitigate the terror aroused by the press-gangs which seized people at random in the streets, the Judenrat offered to provide labor battalions at specified times and in specified numbers for the use of the German authorities. The Germans agreed to this plan. Although the Judenrat set it up in what appeared to be a fair way, serving subpoenas on the list of registered Jewish citizens in rotation, the operation very quickly became corrupt.

All of its functions were sources of revenue for the Judenrat. The most important was the labor registration, for rich Jews paid fees running into thousands of zlotys to be freed from forced labor. The Judenrat collected such fees in great quantity, and

35

sent poor men to the working battalions in place of the wealthy.

From the outset the Nazi racial policy was a hardship for all Jews, but the wealthy found they could soften its effects. They were able not only to buy themselves out of forced labor but to get black-market food and to buy other favors, while the poor in some cases could not even afford to pay the few zlotys required to register for a ration card. Some families even found it necessary to sell the ration cards of some members in advance so that they might have money to buy cards and food for the others.

Aside from the taxes which it collected and passed along to the government, the Judenrat used its funds for relief, for maintaining the Jewish cemetery, and for meeting the new responsibilities now thrust upon the Jewish community—support of the Jewish hospital, organization of soup kitchens, to mention only the most pressing One-third of its budget was spent on the forced labor battalions—providing food on the job, caring for the families left behind, salaries of office personnel, and so forth

One community expense which had previously been an important part of the budget of the Kehilla no longer existed. That was the cost of maintaining a Jewish school system The Germans forbade the education of Jewish children in any form whatever.

In spite of the wishes of its members, the Judenrat was forced to become an instrument of the anti-Jewish repression policy of the authorities. The blows of the Nazis were struck at the Jews through the Judenrat, which acted as the involuntary agent of the occupation in the Jewish community.

In October the Gestapo officials called the Judenrat together and ordered it to set up a Jewish ghetto. For several days the Judenrat debated the question, but the result was never in doubt. Most of the members had already acquired the habit of obeying orders. When the vote was taken, the majority consented to carry out the command of the Gestapo.

At this point Artur Ziegelboim made the following statement: "You have just taken a historic decision. I have been, it appears, too weak to convince you that we cannot permit ourselves to do this. I feel, however, that I have not the moral strength to take part in this action. I feel that I would no longer have the right to live if a ghetto were set up and my head remained whole. I therefore declare that I lay down my mandate. I know that it is the duty of the president to inform the Gestapo immediately of my resignation. I am ready to accept the personal consequences of this action. I can act in no other way."

His declaration startled the Judenrat, and they agreed to re-open the question. The debate had been carried on in secrecy, and the members felt uneasy about what might result when the Jewish population compared their decision with Artur's intransigeance.

After some further discussion, the Judenrat agreed on a compromise: It would take no responsibility for setting up the ghetto, but would inform the Jews of what was being planned so that they could prepare to move out of the proscribed sections of the city.

That night the rumor that there was to be a Warsaw ghetto spread through the Jewish neighborhoods. The following morning thousands of Jews appeared in panic before the Community Building at 26 Grzibovska Street, clamoring for information. Before a crowd of more than ten thousand people, Artur was lifted to the shoulders of two comrades. In the name of the Jewish trade unions and the Bund, he told the people to keep up their courage, to refuse to go into a ghetto, and to resist if they were forced to do so. The substance of his defiant speech spread quickly through the city by word of mouth Such boldness in the face of the Germans was unheard of; it acted as a tonic, strengthening the spirit of resistance among the Jews.

The obvious approval with which the Jews greeted Artur's audacity had its effect upon the Judenrat. A delegation was sent to the Warsaw commandant of the Wehrmacht to appeal for a reversal of the Gestapo's orders. The Army was still supreme in Warsaw, and the commandant, who professed never to have heard of the Gestapo plan, issued the necessary instructions to nullify it. For a time the threat of a ghetto receded

It was obvious that Artur Ziegelboim's speech was the equivalent of his death warrant. He had to go into hiding immediately. We kept him concealed until December. Then, after forged documents had been prepared, we smuggled him across Germany and into Belgium with the help of Paul Henri Spaak. He arrived in Brussels dramatically, just in time for the meeting of the executive committee of the Labor and Socialist International, to which he reported on the situation in Poland.

We were of course overjoyed when word came that Artur was safe. After a short stay in Brussels he went to the United States and later to London, where he represented the Bund in the Polish parliament-in-exile. During the terrible days of the ghetto uprising he was to go from office to office in London pleading for aid for the embattled Jews. He got nothing but diplomatic expressions of sympathy. When it became clear that neither the British government nor any of the embassies in London was very much interested in the plight of the Jews of Warsaw fighting their last battle, Ziegelboim committed suicide as a protest against the callous attitude of the entire Allied world toward his comrades in the burning ghetto. His eloquent farewell letter, addressed to the conscience of the world, is one of the great documents of all time and will be enshrined forever in Jewish literature, as his heroic memory is enshrined in Jewish hearts.

In the first weeks of the war the ruined city of Warsaw was the goal of tens of thousands of Jewish refugees who streamed in from all over the country. They swelled the normal Jewish population of 350,000 to more than half a million. Terrorized, bewildered, and helpless, they rushed to their brethren in the capital city, hoping that among the great numbers of Jews there they would find anonymity and peace. Many came in caravans from villages destroyed by the war or from sections from which the entire Jewish population had been expelled by the Germans.

The refugee problem was a severe burden for the Jews of Warsaw. The food shortage was so severe that it was difficult to maintain life. There were no apartments for the great influx of new people. The refugees filled every vacant building, moving into the synagogues and schools and into every office belonging to the Judenrat. A few wealthy refugees paid fancy prices for apartments; others were fortunate enough to settle with relatives. But the overwhelming majority were poor and hungry and wandered from place to place seeking help. Many died daily of hunger and disease

The Jews of Warsaw, particularly those of the working class and lower middle class, who had no money or negotiable valuables, were themselves hard hit. The first to suffer were the white-collar workers—clerks in banks, offices, and government bureaus. They were fired immediately after the occupation. Every Jew connected in any way with the printing, paper, or publishing business was also discharged. The Germans prohibited the production of shoes, clothing, metal goods, or textiles for the Jewish market. The workers whose industries had formerly supplied Jewish consumers were left jobless. The Jewish food industry was hard hit due to the extremely low ration allotted to Jewish citizens.

To meet the scarcity of essential goods and the sudden mass unemployment the Jews resorted to all sorts of improvisation, some legal, some illegal. In place of leather shoes, the shoemakers, with the permission of the German authorities, created an entirely new industry. They manufactured shoes with uppers of fabric and soles of wood. Since the Germans had cut off the

39

clothing supply completely and had excluded Jews from the textile and clothing industries, Jewish tailors developed methods of extracting the last bit of wear out of a piece of cloth—patching, repairing, and even resewing the suit inside out to make it look less shabby.

The city slaughterhouse was closed to Jewish workers, who had been a large part of its personnel. Many of them established small illegal slaughterhouses which depended upon the cooperation of peasant smugglers. Although Jews were not permitted to have either soap or candles, illegal factories were soon making them out of fat procured from the clandestine slaughterhouses. The shortage of sugar created an illegal saccharin industry.

An illegal cigarette industry provided work for a large number of unemployed Jews. Some tobacco was smuggled in by peasants and some was bought from Christian tobacco workers, who found it very profitable to steal tobacco from the factories in which they worked. In secret, workers cured and shredded tobacco and manufactured the finished cigarettes. To extend the tobacco supply, it was liberally mixed with beet leaves and other adulterants.

Salvage reached new levels of importance. Many Jews earned their livelihood by collecting rags, paper, bones, tin, and other metals from garbage cans or burned-out buildings to sell to the Germans.

To meet the need to repair the broken windows of the city's buildings thousands of Jews became glaziers. Since there was no glass, windows were repaired either by boarding them up with wood, which kept out the cold but made the house dark and unpleasant, or by piecing together small bits of glass with putty to make larger panes. In a short time there were experts whose trade was making big panes of glass out of thousands of little ones in a mosaic pattern.

The lack of electricity, gas, and kerosene brought forth a lighting substitute—calcium carbide lamps These were made by mounting two small metal pots one above the other. The lower one contained lumps of calcium carbide. The upper contained water, which was allowed to drip on the calcium carbide drop by drop, releasing acetylene gas which was the fuel for the flame. The use of these lamps spread quickly, and they soon became a commonplace in every Jewish home.

Despite the severe personal competition for even the barest necessities, there remained a certain feeling of social responsibility, and even in the first catastrophic days organized relief began to function. As before the war, the most important instrumentality for relief and self-aid was the American Joint Distribution Committee (JDC). It provided funds for many organizations, primarily for Toz (medical aid and hygiene), Centos (aid for poor and orphaned children), and the ORT (trade schools and training centers). Although money was also collected from other sources, the JDC remained the most important source of financial aid.

Toz, the organization for Jewish health, took over the task of improving hygienic conditions in the Jewish districts. It set up medical clinics, children's homes, communal kitchens, and public baths. It distributed vaccines and operated a service for nursing children. In view of the great need, the effect of all this effort was pitifully small.

Centos, the center for orphans' help, maintained orphanages and also took care of children whose parents had been sent to the labor camps. It contributed to the Jewish Children's Hospital on Shliska Street and supported homes for deaf and dumb children and children of refugees. It also organized day camps during the summer. Since leaving the city was now prohibited, the day camps pursued their activities in vacant lots and in unused Jewish school buildings. In general, Centos was responsible for the care of all Jewish children. It found adult patrons to contribute money and supplies to supplement the funds provided by the JDC.

The ORT continued to run its trade schools. In addition, it established several small factories which operated under subcon-

41

tract with Polish and German firms. Together with the JDC it opened centers for repair of shoes and clothing and collected clothing, food, and other necessities for distribution among the needy.

The JDC operated special soup kitchens throughout the Jewish quarter for feeding adults, particularly refugees. Here the hungry were registered and waited in line each day for a plate of soup and a piece of black bread. The JDC also provided funds to help artisans who had lost their tools.

Jewish political and social organizations also established feeding centers for their members and sympathizers. The Bund had seven soup kitchens and two tea rooms. Each served as a meeting place for members of a different trade or profession. Other political groups, the Orthodox, the Zionists, the Poale Zionists, had their own kitchens. All of these received help from the JDC to supplement what each organization was able to raise.

At first these relief measures were intended largely for refugees. Later, the entire Warsaw Jewish population had to depend on such facilities.

Late in October, shortly before Artur Ziegelboim's historic speech at the Judenrat, we held a meeting of the central committee of the Bund to consider how we would carry on our work under the occupation The committee at that time consisted of Sonya Novogrodsky, Abrasha Blum, Loeser Clog, Artur Ziegelboim, Berek Snaidmil, and myself. It was obvious that in time our activities, already forced underground, would become extremely difficult. We decided to create a skeleton underground organization as quickly as possible to prepare ourselves for the days ahead.

We set up three commissions to carry on organizational work. The first was a relief commission to organize and operate soup kitchens, collect and distribute food, and generally to mitigate the great distress. The second was a trade-union commission to restore contact with key people in the prewar trade unions and to establish an illegal trade-union organization. The third was a political commission to organize an underground political organization.

I presented a peculiar personal problem to the central committee. My work before the war had made me a familiar figure among large numbers of Jewish and Polish workers, and I was well known to almost every policeman and plainclothesman in the city. While my wide acquaintance could be put to good use it also represented a danger, for a chance recognition by the wrong person would put a quick end to my career. The central committee instructed me to do undercover work only. I was to work with the trade-union and political commissions, but completely behind the scenes. I was forbidden to participate in any activities with legal organizations or to appear before government bureaus when delegations were sent to request this or that. I was not to enter a café under any circumstances. I could leave my apartment only when absolutely necessary and was to operate as much as possible through trusted intermediaries who would communicate for me with comrades in open organizations.

We got to work immediately on the trade-union problem, which we considered second in importance only to the pressing need for relief. I appointed a confidential agent for each of the old unions. He was given the task of choosing from among the comrades in the unions a group of the most trusted, excluding former leaders who were registered in the government files or who were generally well known. After being approved by the central committee, these comrades set themselves up as an organization committee for their particular trade.

The first undertaking of each of these committees was the organization of a soup kitchen. The kitchens filled two functions. They supplied nourishing food at low prices. But they also served as centers where members of the trades could meet and

43

maintain their old contacts and through which the small, select, illegal group could broaden its activities.

From the skeleton organization in each trade a delegate was sent to a city-wide trade-union committee. Three members of the city-wide committee acted as an executive committee to carry on the work between the extremely rare occasions when the entire committee could meet. The three were myself, Laible Kersh, an active garment worker; and Mirmelstein, a bookkeeper who had formerly been president of the Lodz white-collar-workers' union.

As soon as the trade-union organizations had begun to function we started to build a political organization. First we set up small groups within the trade unions. Each group consisted of five or ten people. The organizer of each group submitted its list of names to the central committee for approval before the members were admitted and the group permitted to function. In so far as possible each person knew only the members of his own "fiver" or "tenner." As the organization grew we placed several groups of ten under one comrade. He maintained contact among the groups, who were not permitted to know each other, and between them and the central organization. These groups were generally organized by trades, so that one comrade was responsible for all the groups within the metal industry, another for all in the garment industry, and so forth. The responsible comrades formed the "collective," which considered political problems as they arose, made the necessary decisions, and informed the "fivers" and "tenners," who translated the decisions into action.

Once these organizations were well under way we turned our attention to the establishment of an illegal press. Every Jewish printing plant of any description, including the smallest and most insignificant, had been confiscated by the Germans. One small press was allotted to the Judenrat. Our underground press therefore consisted of two mimeograph machines which far-sighted

44

comrades had removed from institutional offices and hidden. After the small initial supplies of ink, paper, and stencils had been used, we acquired new supplies only with great difficulty. We worked in constant fear that if copies of our newspaper fell into the hands of the Gestapo they would be able to track us down through discovering our sources of paper or ink.

For safety, the editorial work and the technical work were completely separated One person was delegated to maintain contact between the two. Distribution was completely divorced from the printing. If any distributor fell into the hands of the Germans he could not, even if he wished, endanger the plant.

In the early stages of the press we distributed copies of the literature only to contact men who were permitted to read them and to let certain others read them. They were then returned to the central organization, which maintained a record in cipher of all copies issued. Later, as our organization expanded, we were able to distribute larger quantities of material.

We also set up a Socialist Red Cross, whose work was carried on under three divisions. One took care of the needy and sick, organized medical aid, procured drugs, and made clothing and food collections. The second arranged for hiding places and for care for comrades who had to become "illegal" The third was responsible for providing clothing and food for, and maintaining contact with, those who were arrested or in labor camps.

Finally, we organized an underground militia in the same manner in which we had organized the underground Bund, taking in only trusted members of our prewar militia. I assumed my old position of commandant. We added Berek Snaidmil, who had been a commander of the Youth Militia before the war, and Abrasha Blum, to form a command junta of three.

Berek was a young reserve officer of the Polish Army. Because of the chaotic inefficiency of the government he had not been mobilized before the occupation. Before the war he had attended the law school of Warsaw University but had had to abandon his studies for lack of funds. His thin, wiry frame radiated energy. He did everything with enthusiasm—party work, studying military strategy and tactics, mountain climbing. There was a cynical twist to his witty, carefree, bantering manner, but at the same time he was an incurable romantic. Some years before the war a street argument with a fellow Polish officer had resulted in a challenge to a duel. Although Berek's good judgment and the advice of his comrades convinced him that it was cheap feudal bravado unworthy of a Socialist, his romantic pride could not permit him to ignore the challenge. Fortunately, neither party was injured.

His socialism, too, was romantic. He had no interest in weighty Marxist economic doctrines.

He had left Warsaw with the evacuees. In Vilna, Noah Portnoy, our old and beloved leader, called Berek to him and instructed him to return to Warsaw to join the illegal organization. Berek stood stiffly before him. He spoke slowly and dramatically to the patriarch of Jewish socialism who had earned his place through a lifetime of revolutionary activity "I shall serve you," Berek said and kissed Noah's hand.

Twice Berek had tried to cross the demarcation line into German territory and failed. Each time he was badly beaten by the border guards. The third time he succeeded and made his way to Warsaw. You could depend on Berek.

Abrasha Blum was a different personality—a tall, slim, quiet intellectual. His eyeglasses and thinning hair were hardly characteristic of a militia commander. He was a wonderful writer and speaker. Originally from Vilna, where his parents had owned a candy factory, he had studied engineering in Liége, Belgium. Before being co-opted into the underground central committee, he had been a leader of the youth movement, Zukunft, and a member of the Warsaw city committee.of the Bund.

He was one of the most beloved of the underground leaders. His friendly manner, his air of quiet dignity, his self-control

46

even in the most perilous situations, gave everyone around him strength and courage. He suffered severely from a stomach ailment which kept him in great pain under the difficult ghetto conditions, but he never complained.

He was more humanist than Marxist. He saw not only the mass but the individual, and he was always ready to help. People would bring him their personal troubles, and he always tried in his patient, sympathetic, friendly way to help them. In the ghetto he was to be separated from his two children for weeks at a time, but when he came home, he would sit on the floor with them and play like a carefree child.

Both of these men, Snaidmil and Blum, were destined to play leading roles in the life and death of the Warsaw ghetto.

After our Warsaw organizations were functioning fairly well, we sent agents to other towns and cities in Poland. There they set up similar organizations, distributed literature, and doled out supplies and money.

We established a courier service to maintain contact and exchange information among the organizations throughout the country. Before the end of the first year of the occupation our couriers were tying together groups in sixty Polish towns and villages. We were also able to set up illegal counterparts of our prewar youth organizations, Zukunft for youngsters of sixteen to twenty-one, Skiff for children of twelve to sixteen, and of the women's organization, Yaff.

· Because of the Nazi ban on the education of Jewish children, an illegal school system was essential. This was our most difficult undertaking because children could not be depended upon to maintain the necessary conspiratorial secrecy. Nevertheless, we were able to organize several underground grade schools and high schools. For the most part, we used the communal kitchens as an excuse to bring children together in groups. In addition to their other troubles, our teachers were plagued by the extreme shortage of textbooks and writing paper. Great sacrifices were neces-

47

sary on the part of both teachers and parents to continue the education of the children.

It was absolutely essential that we establish regular contact with the Polish underground. At first our contact was limited to the trade unions and the two wings of the Polish Socialist movement, but later we were in close touch with other political groups, as well as with the underground Polish government One of the most important individuals in helping us break out of our isolation was Antoni Zdanowski, the general secretary of the Polish Trade Union Federation. Many years before, when I was a raw youth in the revolutionary movement under the Czar, Zdanowski and I had met in prison. We had spent many hours together in political discussion as he waited under a sentence of death which was finally commuted.

Later, in the years of Polish independence, Zdanowski, who achieved great prominence as a labor leader, publicly credited his conversion to socialism to those prison talks. We were fast friends and good comrades, and our friendship helped to act as a bridge between the Polish and Jewish workers.

After Poland's liberation by the Russians, Zdanowski was arrested by the Communists. He died in prison.

The monotonous daily struggle of the individual to sustain life in his body was occasionally interrupted by some crisis like the one that Artur Ziegelboim had met so superbly in the Judenrat.

Shortly after the Germans entered Warsaw an underworld character, who we later discovered was in the pay of the Germans, shot and killed a Polish policeman. The Germans executed fifty-three Jews whom they took from the apartment house at 9 Nalefky Street, including some who were visiting at the time. A short time later the Germans discovered a radio in the home of a Polish intellectual on Uyasdovsky Boulevard. As punishment

48

they arrested several hundred Polish and Jewish professionals and shot them.

Thus did the Germans impress on the minds of the population their doctrine of collective responsibility: for the crime of one, many would suffer.

Slowly but methodically the Nazis began to collect the important cultural treasures of Warsaw and to ship them to the Fatherland. They removed the entire contents of the City Art Museum, of the Jewish Art Museum, and of the several-hundred-year-old Judaica Library. We were afraid that the same fate would befall our own Bronislaw Grosser Library, which had been built with so much difficulty and sacrifice by the Jewish workers of Warsaw. The library had been closed and sealed by the German authorities, and by December 1939 it was clear that soon it would be looted like the others. We resolved to recover our books at any cost.

We delegated some comrades to work under the direction of Moishe Suffit, the librarian. He had worked in the library since it was founded in 1915, during the first German occupation. From the cellar of a tenement building at 13 Leshno Street adjoining the library they tunneled into the building. For a week they carried out stacks of books camouflaged with potatoes, vegetables, coal, and other items less dangerous than books. Suffit drew up a list of priorities, to make sure that the most valuable items were taken out first. He did not overlook the important records, including a card file of names and addresses of library members.

At the end of that week the Germans broke the seal and began to remove the library. The tenement house watchman, who had been bribed to keep his mouth shut, was alarmed and demanded that we cement up the hole in the cellar wall immediately and remove all traces of the tunnel. Naturally we had to do so.

The books we salvaged were used to set up small libraries in various homes. The largest collection was put in the home of a

49

comrade named Shur, who later died in Treblinka. He was a linotype operator and at one time had been a partner in a Vilna publishing house. He cared for his treasures with great love and respect, lending them out carefully to a secret library circle. Hundreds of people were thus able to take advantage of these books. They helped many forget, if only for a moment, the painful realities of their life.

By February of 1940 we felt strong enough to issue a semi-monthly newspaper to supplement the handbills issued from time to time. There was some discussion as to whether this newspaper should proclaim itself the official organ of the underground Bund. Prudence won, and the paper appeared anonymously with the simple title *Bulletin*. Each issue was ten or twelve—much later, sixteen—pages of typewritten copy. At first the editors were Abrasha Blum and myself. Later we added Morizi Orzech, after he returned from Germany, and Berek Snaidmil.

Our distributors were mostly women because they were less likely to be stopped by roving press-gangs. After the second issue we began to receive voluntary contributions for our press fund, although we had made no appeal for help. The newspaper elicited great interest. People outside our regular readership offered as much as twenty zlotys a copy.

The same technical organization also handled the publication, once a month, of the *Jugendstimme*, organ of the youth group, Zukunft.

A pressing and ever-present problem was the procuring of funds to carry on our activities. We collected dues from our members, but these could not begin to supply the money necessary to carry on the work under the conditions with which we had to cope.

One important resource was the "money transfer." Our comrades in America raised money by various means. We received money from individuals in Poland and wrote to our comrades in

New York to pay out an equivalent amount to a person designated by the one from whom we got the money. The individuals in Poland thus accomplished their purpose of getting money out of the country, and we received funds to carry on our work.

We were able to borrow amazingly large sums of money. The Bund's reputation was sufficient guarantee that, if anyone lived through all this, the money would be paid back. In the meantime, the money was safer as a debt of the Bund than in the pocket of the owner.

Without let-up the Germans maintained a barrage of propaganda to stir up hatred against the Jews. In this they received the wholehearted cooperation of those groups of Poles for whom anti-Semitism had always been a political stock in trade. The Jews were depicted as filthy, lousy, diseased, scabrous, as bearers of sickness and epidemics. Again and again the propagandists demanded that they be isolated because they represented a danger to the health of the entire Polish population. And of course the Jews of Poland were accused of being allies of the international Jewish plutocrats who had brought on the war and all its attendant tribulations. The Germans forced the Jews to wear identifying arm bands to make it simpler for the Poles to concentrate their hatred.

This propaganda had its effects, and incidents began to multiply.

Early in April 1940, just before the Easter holiday, a Polish hooligan attacked an old religious Jew on a Praga street and began to tear out his beard and sideburns. Comrade Friedman, a husky, well-built slaughterhouse worker, happened by. He came to the defense of the helpless old man and gave the Pole a thorough beating.

A crowd gathered quickly, and a street battle broke out between Jews and Poles. German police arrested Friedman and shot him the following day. The Jews of Praga waited in terror for the consequences of Friedman's boldness.

But the pogrom that followed had obviously been organized long before this incident. Groups of hooligans, mostly youths, stormed through the Jewish sections of Warsaw. They charged down the streets shouting, "Beat the Jews! Kill the Jews!" They broke into Jewish homes and stores, smashed furniture, seized valuables, and beat the occupants. In the district near the Polish Handicraft High School at 72 Leshno Street the older students joined the pogrom as soon as school was out.

All over the city Jews barricaded their doors and hid in cellars and attics. Panic spread throughout the Jewish community.

The Germans did not intervene. They neither helped nor hindered the pogromists. We saw many smiling German cameramen recording the scenes with relish. We later learned that the pictures appeared in German magazines. They were also shown in movie theaters as graphic evidence that the Poles were winning their freedom from Jewish domination.

We were immediately besieged by requests from comrades that something be done. An emergency meeting of the Bund collective was held in my apartment at 12 Novolipya, and we discussed the possibility of active resistance. Over us hung the danger of the German doctrine of collective responsibility. Whatever we might do to hinder the pogromists could bring terrible German vengeance on all the Jews of the city. Despite that danger, we concluded that we had no choice—we must strike back.

We decided to fight back with "cold weapons"—iron pipes and brass knuckles, but not with knives or firearms. We wanted to reduce the danger that a pogromist might be killed accidentally. We hoped in this way to teach the hooligans a lesson and to minimize the possibility that the Germans would inflict some terrible punishment on the entire Jewish community.

Every fighting contingent was mobilized—slaughterhouse workers, transport workers, party members. We organized them into three groups: one near the Mirovsky Market, another in the Franciskanska-Nalefky-Zamenhof district, and the third in the Leshno-Karmelitzka-Smotcha district.

When the pogromists appeared in these sections on the following morning they were surprised to find our comrades waiting for them. A bloody battle broke out immediately. Ambulances rushed to carry off wounded pogromists. Our own wounded were hidden and cared for in private homes to avoid their arrest by Polish or German police. The fight lasted for several hours against many waves of hooligans and raged throughout a large portion of the Jewish quarter.

The battle kept shifting to various parts of the city. Our organized groups were joined spontaneously by other workers. In the Wola district, our comrades received help from non-Jewish Socialist workers to whom we had appealed for aid. Many Christians tried to persuade the pogromists to stop. Many Jews, afraid of the dangers of "collective responsibility," tried to keep us from hitting back.

The fight lasted almost until the eight o'clock curfew. The following morning it was resumed. At about one o'clock in the afternoon the Polish police finally intervened and dispersed the combatants.

The expected retaliation against the entire community did not come. The Jews of Warsaw breathed easier. This dramatic demonstration that the Jews need not accept every blow helplessly gave them renewed courage. On all sides the Bund received expressions of thanks. Many former members and friends of our prewar organization requested that they be admitted to the underground.

We were afraid that a large influx of new members would make it possible for police agents to infiltrate. We exercised great care in choosing from among the new applicants. As an additional screening measure we instituted a solemn oath for all new members that they would be loyal unto death and would never betray the organization or any of its members. So far as we know no one ever broke that oath.

But this taste of victory over the Polish hooligans and their German senior partners turned sour in our mouths. Denmark and Norway, countries we had always esteemed for their healthy native Socialist movements, collapsed beneath the Nazi onslaught. We were disturbed not only by the triumph of German arms but by the seeming strength (exaggerated, of course, in the official press) which the Nazi ideology found among the conquered populations. I recall the hours we spent discussing how a man like Knut Hamsun could join with the oppressors of his own people. The Nazi press kept reminding us, too, how wholeheartedly Stalin endorsed the specious justification for the invasion of Denmark and Norway.

We encouraged each other with the hope that this defeat would shock the Allied world into greater effort and would strengthen it against the next German blow. But in June the French Republic fell. Jews wept openly in the Warsaw streets. What could save us now? The German war machine seemed as invincible as its propagandists claimed. We could find nothing to brighten the darkness of our helpless hopelessness.

The only cheerful moments during those days, when our dreams of ultimate liberation suffered one heavy blow after another, were personal. Some comrades whom we had long given up as lost returned to Warsaw. Among them was Morizi Orzech.

At the age of fifty, Morizi had behind him a lifetime of valuable service to the Jewish working class. Although he came from a very wealthy family, he had joined the Bund at the age of sixteen while still attending a Russian high school. He had immediately thrown into our work all the energy of his temperamental nature. During the First World War he had been a member of the Warsaw Board of Aldermen. An economist and journalist, serving both the Jewish and Polish Socialist press, he was noted for his forthright, forceful articles, his factual knowledge, his common sense, and his gift for rhetoric. Not the least of Morizi's contributions was his effectiveness in binding Jewish and Polish workers together. He combated prejudice on both sides and tried to pound home the idea that both had a common destiny. He came to the Poles, not as a petitioner, with hat in hand, but as an equal speaking to equals.

Orzech had left Warsaw for Kaunas at the outbreak of the war. The Germans demanded that the Lithuanian government surrender him because of a sizzling dispatch he had written to the *Jewish Daily Forward* in New York, detailing the Nazi treatment of Jews in the occupied areas. Orzech was brought to the frontier, but thanks to the strenuous efforts of comrades in Lithuania, he was saved at the very last moment.

Later he was arrested at sea aboard a neutral ship. The German officers did not realize the identity of the man they had in their grasp. As a Polish citizen of military age, he was taken off the ship and sent to a German concentration camp for Polish prisoners of war.

Orzech had written to us from his German prison, but we never expected to see him again. Early one morning in April 1940, shortly after the three-day battle with the anti-Semites, we received word that a transport of Jewish prisoners of war had arrived in Warsaw. Among the group was our own Morizi Orzech. We did not realize then that the Germans were sorting out all Jews from among the Polish military prisoners and returning them to their homes in accordance with the long-range plan for total extermination of the Jews.

Orzech had always been the dandy of the movement. In contrast with the "old-fashioned" Socialists, whose disregard for fashion was part of their revolt against convention, Morizi was always neatly and elegantly dressed, his suit pressed and his shoes shined. But the Orzech who stepped from the line of returning prisoners was not recognizable. His cheeks were sunken and his tattered clothing was dirty and crawling with lice. We understood now why in his letters from prison he had asked for a bottle of eau de cologne. At the time we had taken it as simply a good-natured joke at himself.

The day after his arrival, he came to see me at my apartment at 12 Novolipya. He was the same old Orzech, elegantly dressed, smoothly shaven, full of life and vitality.

With me at the time were Abrasha Blum, Berek Snaidmil, Loeser Clog, and Sonya Novogrodsky. Orzech fired lively questions at us about the general situation, the organizational work, and the personal situations of the comrades. What had we accomplished? What were our prospects? What was the attitude of the Polish workers?

We made plans for the future: how to get money from outside the country, how to establish our contacts throughout Poland, and so forth. Orzech insisted that we proceed immediately to issue a Polish-language publication to keep the Poles informed of what the Jews were thinking and doing and living through.

Soon it was past curfew and no one could go home, so we talked and planned throughout the night. With great interest we listened to Morizi recount his adventures, life in the prisoner-of-war camps, his observations of life in Germany, his conversations with people he met. For us, who had been completely isolated from the entire outside world for eight months, his story was a refreshing experience.

Orzech's considerable talents were soon put to work. He became our principal editor for Jewish and Polish papers and bulletins. He constantly reminded the Polish underground, particularly the Socialist sector, that the fight against anti-Semitism was not being pushed sufficiently. He urged the underground to fight not only against the occupier and for the independence of Poland but also for the higher goal of a better world, democratic and Socialist. He raised our underground press to the level of earnest journals which dealt profoundly with all important political and economic problems. He studied the German press and literature very carefully, turning the Nazis' statistics against them to expose their policies in the occupied countries.

How fortunate we were to have Orzech back with us! He maintained steady contact with the Polish underground and, through it, with the outside world. He had no equal when it came to raising money for our political work, for cultural institutions, for soup kitchens, for the Red Cross. His prestige and his sound common sense enabled him on occasion to influence decisions of the Judenrat and the Joint Distribution Committee.

In the darkest ghetto days and after, his enthusiasm never flagged, his courage never faltered, his fighting spirit never wavered.

Our action in the April 1940 pogrom strengthened our organization tremendously and also won for us a great deal of respect in Polish underground circles. The Polish Socialist and democratic underground press severely criticized the pogromists and insisted that the pogrom had been organized and instigated by the Germans.

After April there was a period of "quiet" while the Jews waited for the next blow to fall.

During the first few months, the Poles felt the effects of the Nazi terror much less than the Jews. No mass arrests, mass shootings, mass robberies, or mass impressments took place in the Polish districts. In the early period many Poles, for example, did not even bother to comply with the order for the surrender of radio sets, though the penalty was death.

The Germans did close the University, as well as the schools and cultural institutions which had survived the bombardment. To a certain extent, all social and cultural life had to go underground at first, later the Germans relaxed these restrictions somewhat. In any event, the atmosphere of ruin and death, of total disorder and total fear, which pervaded the Jewish districts, was not at first evident in the Polish areas.

But before long the mass terror began to be felt even there.

Just before Easter 1940 a German gendarme who had distinguished himself by his cruelty was murdered in a saloon between the suburban towns of Waver and Anyn. Immediately the Nazis descended on the two towns, dragged more than a hundred guiltless people from their homes, and shot them. Hundreds of others were arrested and brought to Paviak Prison in Warsaw.

This brutal act of vengeance created panic among the Poles in the surrounding area. The neighboring district of Grochov was almost completely emptied of its inhabitants, who rushed to the vicinity of Warsaw.

In the meantime the underground continued to grow. Many illegal publications appeared. Every political group issued its own organ. The underground press warned women not to fraternize with the Germans, called on the people to boycott the movies, theaters, and concerts which the Nazis had organized especially for the Poles, and to stay out of cafés patronized by Germans. Its widespread influence is illustrated by the fact that on September 1, 1940, the first anniversary of the Nazi attack on Poland, in response to an appeal of the underground press, hardly a person showed himself in the streets of Warsaw between the hours of two and four P.M. The eerie, empty stillness had dramatic impact.

A characteristic method of boycotting and annoying the Germans was used on the streetcars. The passengers paid their fares but refused to accept receipts. To prevent the conductors from pocketing the money, the Germans sent out checkers to force acceptance of receipts, but they were not very successful.

But such measures were only irritants to the Germans. More effective was the sabotage carried out by Polish railwaymen. Munition and supply trains were derailed. Though many railroad workers were shot, the sabotage continued.

58

In 1941, the popular stage star, Igo Sym, who had been working closely with the Gestapo, was condemned for treason by the underground and shot. In reprisal the Germans arrested and killed some two hundred intellectuals, including many professors, scientists, and, particularly, theatrical people.

This was the first step in the uprooting of Polish intelligentsia all over the country. College professors, including almost all of those at Cracow University, teachers, lawyers, and especially clergymen were seized and shipped off to Dachau and Oswiecim. Thousands of priests were arrested.

To tighten their control over a reservoir of possible future resistance, the Germans ordered the registration of all former Polish army officers. It was quickly evident that registration usually meant being sent to one of the various labor camps, so the order was widely ignored. Tens of thousands of former officers who had to rely on illegal or forged documents filled the ranks of the underground military organization.

To maintain their labor supply the Germans called upon the Poles to register for work "voluntarily," with the promise of good pay and working conditions. The underground press carried on an effective campaign against registration. The result was the appearance in Polish districts of the German press-gangs which had earlier terrorized the Jewish districts.

On Sundays and holidays, the press-gangs would descend on churches and pick up as many workers as they required from among the worshipers.

The labor hunts were carried out with particular brutality in the villages. If a village failed to supply the specified number of workers, it was suddenly surrounded by the military, every nook and cranny searched, and everyone, without regard for age or physical condition, dragged off to the labor battalions.

THREE

THE SEPARATION of the Jewish population from the non-Jewish was accomplished gradually. During the first six or seven months of the occupation, the Jews were driven out of the better districts in the southern part of the city. Their apartments in these areas were already overcrowded by the addition of relatives and friends who had descended on Warsaw.

In desperation, uprooted from communities which had been their homes for generations, they nestled among the hundreds of thousands of their brothers in misery and suffering. Submerged among such great numbers of unfortunates, they at least felt more anonymous and more secure. They filled every cranny of the ruined city.

The Jews were eliminated first from one, then from another desirable section and forced into the progressively more crowded slum districts.

The Germans carried out the expulsions of Jews from the more pleasant and attractive parts of Warsaw in much the same manner they had used in some of the small towns. The janitors received orders not to permit Jewish tenants to leave the buildings with large packages. Everything had to remain in the apartments—furniture, dishes, clothing, linens. The expulsions came suddenly and without warning. It was not uncommon, after an absence of only a few hours, to return to an apartment already sealed or even occupied by a German with all the legal papers properly filled out. Such expulsions were carried out sometimes in an entire apartment house at one time, sometimes in an entire block of houses.

For great sums of money, particularly for gold and foreign exchange, it was possible to "buy" from the Nazis entire buildings, or blocks of buildings, which had been singled out for "Aryanizing." At this time there appeared on the scene "fixers" who had connections with various levels of the Nazi apparatus. The Judenrat—not officially, of course—used them to rescue some Jewish districts. The inhabitants could thus remain in uneasy residence, under constant threat of new expulsion orders and other unforeseeable miseries.

Through fixers, parts of Zlota, Chmelna, Shenna, and Sosnova Streets were ransomed. The inhabitants of the threatened houses gave up everything to pay the Nazis. The bribes ran into millions. Blackmail flourished, feeding on the desperation of the unnerved Jews. The field was wide open for the high officials of the Gestapo and for the civilian branch of the military authority headed by Herr Fischer. All of them must have known already what was being planned for the Jews, but in the meantime they filled their pockets with Jewish "war booty."

Breathing space for the Jews became more restricted and more congested. They were forbidden to go into Sachsen Park or to show themselves near Pilsudski Square, now renamed the Adolf Hitler Platz. Separate streetcars, carrying a Star of David on the front instead of the customary route number, were instituted for Jews. Along such cars, on both sides, there was a sign in German and Polish, "For Jews Only." The ghetto-feeling became more intense, saturating the atmosphere, oppressing and breaking down the spirit.

On October 16, 1940, the Nazis promulgated the decree establishing the Warsaw ghetto. It was placarded in German and Yiddish all over the city. The ghetto was to consist of an inadequate, congested slum area of the city, populated predominantly by Jews but with a generous sprinkling of Polish poor. It was to run from Shenna, Shliska, and Twarda Streets to Djika, Stavki, and Niska Streets on one side, and from part of Leshno Street, Novolipya, Novolipky, and Shwentoyerska Streets to Pavia, Djelna, and Okopova Streets on the other.

The Mirovsky marketplace was deliberately excluded from the ghetto area. There Jewish poverty had always been arrayed on pathetic little stands to catch the eye of the passing buyer. For generations Jewish peddlers had eked out their precarious living on its cobblestones. It was cut off on three sides by high brick walls and barbed wire. No entry to this former heart of Jewish petty trade was permitted.

All the Jews from the districts of Praga, Grochov, Wola, Mokotov, Povonzek, Zholibosh, Solets, Povishle, Staremyasto, and Peltzowisna, where Jews had lived for hundreds of years, had to find new homes in the small area allotted to the ghetto.

October 31 was set as the deadline for the complete exchange of populations. In the space of two short weeks all the Jews—about 150,000 of them—who lived outside the ghetto area had to move into it, all the Gentiles, about 80,000, who lived inside the fatal boundary had to move out. Actually, although the laggard Jews were severely punished with German promptness and Nazi brutality, the deadline for the non-Jews was extended several times.

Officially the Jews had permission to take their businesses, small shops, and other commercial establishments with them into the ghetto. Actually, most of the Jewish businesses were sealed long before the deadline of October 31. The Jews had to leave their possessions and enter the ghetto stripped of their property. There was also supposed to be an exchange of goods between the arriving Jewish merchants and the departing Gentiles. It was usually one-sided, however. Many Jews who left their merchandise for a Gentile failed to find the promised goods waiting for them.

The Poles who left the ghetto exchanged their small, crowded tenement apartments for the bright airy rooms of the well-to-do Jews who had lived in the better sections. Even some of the more intelligent Poles accepted this Jewish "gift" from the Nazis with a certain inner satisfaction, considering it an act of social and national justice.

It is impossible to describe the hellish scenes which took place in Warsaw's streets during those two terrible weeks. Everywhere there was wild panic, unashamed hysterical terror. People ran frantically through the streets, a deathly fear unmistakable in their grim, weary eyes. They searched desperately for any kind of conveyance to transport their belongings. The multitude filled the streets, a nation on the march. Long, long rows of little carts and all sorts of makeshift vehicles heaped with household possessions, wailing children, the old, the sick, the half-dead, moved from all directions toward the ghetto, pulled or led by the stronger and healthier, who plodded along, tearful, despairing, bewildered.

A father carried a small sick child, burning with fever and wrapped in rags. A dairyman from Peltzowisna led a cow, searching helplessly for living space for his means of support and for himself. A drayman from Praga led his skinny, pathetic-looking little horse, his only worldly possession.

Along the curbs sat little children and the exhausted aged, whimpering, "A little water, a piece of bread . . ."

In the ghetto the unfortunate hunted for living quarters— an apartment, a room, a corner of a room, anything. They searched the cellars, the hallways, the rubble of bombed-out buildings, for a place to lay their heads or shelter their children. They lay on the streets or roamed through the gutters, soaked by the rain, shivering from the cold, hungry, worn-out, helpless.

In this abyss of misery and suffering, the help provided by social organizations like the American Joint Distribution Committee, the Judenrat, and the various political parties was as a pebble thrown into a bottomless pit. At various points in the ghetto area offices were opened to supply assistance. They distributed small amounts of money for renting carts, located dwellings, and otherwise did their best to help the dispossessed. Thousands stood in line, often for days, waiting for help. Pain and despair were on every face.

We of the Bund mobilized all the members of the Zukunft youth group, the trade unions, the Yaff organization of women, and the Socialist Red Cross. We sent out groups to protect the homeless and uprooted who roamed the streets and courtyards. We had to guard their pitiful belongings, haphazardly strewn about, from almost inevitable theft. We had to arrange for provisioning, however meager and inadequate. On Smotcha Street we opened a refreshment hall especially for those who came from the more distant parts of the city. Our groups went about the streets with teakettles and bread, consoling, encouraging, comforting. We dispatched special brigades with a variety of conveyances to help our comrades move into the ghetto. Each brigade of ten or twelve was assigned a designated district in which to help the evacuation.

Since finding shelter was most difficult, there was a moral compulsion to share apartments. Everybody took someone into his small room or congested apartment. We were forced to break up families, separating man from wife, children from parents. There was no other way.

The transfer of the Jewish Hospital on Chista Street into the ghetto was a horrible experience. In return for a tremendous hospital, complete with modern facilities, we received two small buildings: the former branch of the State monopoly at 1 Leshno Street, and the public school at the corner of Leshno and Zhelasna. The entire school for nurses was moved to what had been the offices of the Sick Benefit Fund on Volinska Street.

There were about two thousand patients in the hospital, of whom hundreds were seriously ill, some recovering from dangerous operations. Many had to be discharged—sent to certain death. Hundreds were taken to the ghetto in little carts or carried on stretchers. Many could not survive such an expedition. The most elementary medical precautions, like isolating contagious cases, could not be taken.

The Nazis did not permit the removal of many of the most essential surgical instruments and hospital equipment. They forced the City Council, which had supported the Jewish Hospital before the war, to cut off all subsidies. The hospital had to be maintained by the Jews alone. The Judenrat instituted a special hospital tax,and collected linens, clothing, and instruments.

The epidemics, the starvation, and the general lowering of resistance constantly supplied the hospital with patients. In its new location, the sick lay on the corridor floors. Provisioning was solely through the ration cards of the ghetto inhabitants. These cards generally allowed a small amount of bread only. The doctors, the nurses, the untrained help often went hungry.

To add to all the troubles of the enforced migration, the boundaries of the ghetto were changed three times. Each time some streets were lopped off. Those who had already established themselves there had to move again, to find a new spot to rest their weary bodies.

Jews, Poles, and Germans haggled over every portion of every street, over every courtyard. No one could be sure that the corner acquired so painfully would remain his.

On October 31 the ghetto was definitely fixed and the gates shut. Under penalty of three months' to a year's imprisonment and heavy fines, Jews were forbidden to show themselves outside the ghetto without a special permit.

It is with a sense of pain and disgust that I recall the Jewish police, a disgrace to the half-million unfortunate Jews in the Warsaw ghetto.

66

Even before the formal establishment of the ghetto, the Germans had ordered the Judenrat to organize its own so-called *Ordnungs-Huter*. The Judenrat posted an announcement in the Jewish districts calling on men between the ages of thirty and thirty-five with at least a high-school education to register for service in this police force. At first it was limited to a thousand men, later it was increased to two thousand.

The recruiting office was swamped by the rush of eligibles to register. Being a policeman meant freedom from molestation by the roaming press-gangs. A policeman occupied a somewhat higher, more privileged position than the rest of the half-million, who were completely helpless in the hands of the Nazis. Many used bribery and influential connections to obtain a prized appointment to the force. People with college educations, professional men, former white-collar workers, idle and sheltered sons of the wealthy, rushed to get into the precious uniform—nothing more than a black cap with a blue Star of David.

The force was divided into precinct groups under the over-all command of Sherinsky, an apostate Jew who at one time had been a precinct captain in the Warsaw police.

He had been an anti-Semite before the war and an active member of the Narodova, a reactionary anti-Jewish political group. His infamous record as a Jew-hater had not saved him from being thrown into the ghetto with his "racial brothers." His appointment as police chief was logical—it gave even wider scope to his virulent anti-Semitism.

The police instructor was Prussac, also an apostate Jew. He too had a shady past, including service with the Polish Political and Criminal Secret Police. Other important personalities in the police force were the lawyer Laikin and Yussel Kapote, a precinct captain who before the war had been involved in extortion, intimidation, and other questionable transactions.

Originally the Jewish police worked closely with the Polish police. After the establishment of the ghetto the Polish gendarmes

67

were gradually withdrawn from the Jewish area. A few were left in Jewish precincts, however, so that the two police forces might serve as checks on each other.

When the rush to join the Jewish police started, we faced a crucial question. Should our comrades join in order to use it in whatever situation might arise? The Bund leaders were unanimous in their opinion: the police could only be tools, willing or unwilling, of Nazi policy toward the Jews. No member of the Bund was permitted to join.

Soon after the organization of the Jewish police, a new figure appeared in the ghetto, a man named Ganzweich, a journalist and one-time Zionist, originally from Lodz. He had arrived in Warsaw after the occupation of the city and had immediately organized a circle of artists, journalists, and would-be philanthropists for relief purposes.

After the Germans announced the formation of the ghetto, Ganzweich set up a bureau for distributing favors and concessions like jobs as house janitors or rent collectors. He seemed to have great influence with the authorities. People stood in line at his office, bribe in hand, hoping to enlist Ganzweich's aid to free an arrested member of the family, to get a better apartment, to procure a vital legal document. His carefully constructed network of connections and acquaintances kept his finger on every pulse of ghetto life, supplying him with information invaluable to the occupation authorities.

At first Ganzweich stepped forward as a Jewish public servant whose only interest was to defend the people from speculators, smugglers, and black marketeers. He called meetings of well-known public figures, sought contact with representatives of political parties—all to organize a fight against exorbitant prices.

He approached Loeser Clog, a well-known Bund leader and chairman of the Jewish Printing Trades Union. He used all the familiar tactics of flattery, referred to the handsome testimonial book issued on Clog's fiftieth birthday, complimented him on

68

his popularity among the Jewish printers, and so forth. Since all the Jewish printers were now unemployed, Ganzweich offered to get them jobs as janitors and house managers—on whose help and cooperation the police spy system of many European countries has often depended. But his suave eloquence fell on deaf ears.

Everyone knew that this creature was working for the Germans; that it was for them he was organizing this supposed campaign against exorbitant prices and smuggling. Nevertheless people joined his group for the same reason that others had joined the Jewish police. His "anti-profiteering" police numbered several hundred. Because their headquarters were at 13 Leshno Street, they soon became known as the "Thirteeners." They wore the same uniform as the other Jewish police.

The Thirteeners spread fear throughout the ghetto. They conducted raids, descending on entire blocks of houses, supposedly hunting for smuggled goods, speculators, and black marketeers. Actually they were on the scent of political material, illegal literature, and active workers in the underground. They fulfilled the function of the Gestapo in the ghetto. In time, Ganzweich and his Thirteeners became the authority on Jewish matters for the Gestapo and had its complete confidence. Before the rupture of the Stalin-Hitler pact, Ganzweich even enlisted Jews from the Warsaw ghetto to filter into the Russian zone to bring back information for the German authorities.

At first the Judenrat carried on a quiet fight against Ganzweich. It preferred to set up the organization of janitors and house managers and to tie it to the Judenrat and the "legitimate" Jewish police. But all efforts to eliminate Ganzweich as competition for police control in the ghetto failed. His connections with the Gestapo were too strong. His Thirteeners continued to function as a police unit, parallel to the Judenrat police but more closely identified with the specific features of Gestapo policy toward the Jews.

69

Aside from Ganzweich's Thirteeners, the Gestapo included some Jews in its own apparatus. One of them, Kokosoffsky, had been before the war a leader of the Maccabee, a Jewish sport organization, in Pabyanitza. Another agent, Andes by name, had previously been a boxer in the Zionist Maccabee. He now specialized in searching out illegal flour mills. Later he was sent by the Germans to the Oswiecim camp. Rumor had it that the millers paid substantial bribes to engineer this coup. At least one Jewish woman was on the Gestapo payroll—Madame Machno, a former Warsaw actress and dancer.

Through the hands of these creatures flowed tremendous sums as bribes for the Gestapo. They used to "arrange" passes for the ghetto gates, business licenses, exemptions from forced labor, and other privileges. A travel permit between Warsaw and Lodz cost thousands of zlotys; exemption from forced labor, tens of thousands. The scale of prices varied with the importance of the service.

These leeches attached themselves firmly and sucked, for themselves and the Gestapo, the last drop of blood from the Jewish population, spreading what they bred upon—complete demoralization and licentiousness without limit.

The Jewish police found their strongest and most capable opponent in Morizi Orzech. From the very beginning he fought them. He accused them of being the most important factor in keeping the Judenrat as an accomplice of Nazi policy. Unceasingly he tried to rouse the Jews to act against the Jewish police before it was too late. At one time the Judenrat formed a committee to purge the Jewish police of its worst elements. Orzech influenced Leon Berenson, once secretary to Poland's first embassy in the United States, to resign publicly from the committee and to issue a statement that any attempt to purge would be useless, that the police were rotten to the core, that they were an inseparable part of the Nazi apparatus for exterminating the Jews and must be treated like any other Nazi organ.

Orzech's hatred of the Jewish police once led him into serious difficulty. Encountering a police captain attempting to arrest an old Jewish woman for illegally selling vegetables in the street, he intervened. In the course of the argument, he struck the officer. Orzech was arrested to be handed over to the Germans. It took a lot of work and money to save him, particularly since he refused categorically to apologize.

Orzech could not be stilled. Later when the Gestapo began to hunt for him in the ghetto it was almost impossible to prevail upon him to remain hidden. He was not one to stay out of the thick of the fight. And the ghetto learned, all too soon, that Orzech's warnings about the Jewish police were well founded.

In the early days of the Ghetto there was danger that by squeezing and terrorizing the Jewish community the Germans would destroy it. Hysterical competition for a crust of bread and a place to sleep under the constant threat of death from starvation or a German bullet can destroy humanity in human beings. There were signs that we might become a mob in panic, each individual rushing for safety for himself, trampling anyone who stood in his way.

We had to find some means of restoring cohesion, of calming fears, of teaching people to help each other. We decided to revive the tenement committees, which had always been an important Bund instrument in election campaigns. After we had taken the initiative the idea caught on, and committees were organized on a large scale.

Each committee was elected by the residents of a group of tenement buildings facing on a single entrance court. The committees obtained relief for the needy, tried to prevent evictions for nonpayment of rent, helped the sick, tried to assure an adequate supply of food, organized kindergartens and communal kitchens. They set up little traveling lending libraries and arranged concerts and dramatic programs to lighten the hours after curfew. They took care of homeless children either by requiring the tenants to feed them in rotation each day, or by setting up feeding stations to which all tenants had to contribute. They even functioned as channels for distributing illegal literature.

Every courtyard became a little government in itself, leading its own closed existence, looking out for the welfare of its own citizens, their health, their nourishment, their cultural life, holding them back from the abyss of complete despair.

The tenement committees soon became quasi-official agencies for JDC and Judenrat relief work. Their activity grew to such proportions that the Bund set up a special commission to help systematize it and supply direction. The commission distributed money, provided entertainment talent, kindergarten instructors, and other essentials.

Later the tenement committees were organized into regions to coordinate the work more efficiently and to enable the richer tenements to share with the poorer. In time about a thousand tenement committees were operating in the Warsaw ghetto.

Even before the ghetto small epidemics of typhus, typhoid, and dysentery had broken out here and there. In Jewish districts signs of these sicknesses were handled with great brutality by Polish and German officials. Sanitation squads would descend on tenements in which illness had been reported, terrorize the inhabitants, "disinfect" the clothing in such fashion that it could never be used again, remove whatever valuables caught their eye, and then march the people to bathhouses, leaving them to wait naked in the street for their turns. In the bathhouses the unfortunates were further maltreated by the attendants, after which they got a slip of paper certifying that they had been through the regular preventive procedure.

Since these certificates were useful for avoiding a second round of brutal "preventive medicine," a brisk trade in forged sanitation certificates was soon developed. And the sanitation workers made it clear that a little bribery would avoid much unpleasantness.

The Jews appealed to the Judenrat to organize its own sanitation squads so that the danger of epidemics could be handled more humanely and intelligently. Shortly before the establishment of the ghetto the Judenrat received permission to do so, and it organized its own hygiene service. This made things somewhat better, although some Jewish sanitation workers also resorted to blackmail and bribery.

In the ghetto the terrible overcrowding soon had its epidemic effects. The Judenrat ruled that each room must house a minimum of four persons. Despite this crowding together, there were many, many homeless who took over institutional buildings like synagogues as living quarters. Though these had no proper facilities for food preparation or sanitation, they were packed with people. So completely was every available bit of space utilized that no synagogues were available for the pious Jews, and all religious ceremony took place in private apartments.

The first signs of disease appeared among the latecomers to the ghetto who were crowded like animals into the institutional buildings. So high was the death rate in these places that they were popularly known as "death points." It was not long before the first sparks of disease spread like a forest fire throughout the entire ghetto. The fierceness of the epidemic was beyond the powers of the small group of heroic doctors to control. The facilities for fighting disease were so inadequate that they often served only to spread it. Persons suspected of having typhus or other contagious illnesses were sent to the Jewish Hospital, where they were "quarantined" in the narrow corridors and were put under observation for three days before formal admission. There they lay side by side. Those who did not yet have typhus contracted it from those who did, so that when the three-day quarantine was over all had good reason to remain.

73

The Jewish Hospital did not even have sufficient linens to service the inadequate number of beds. This made proper sanitary measures impossible, and the hospital became a center of infection. People began to hide their symptoms for fear they would be sent there for diagnosis or treatment. The Germans did not permit the entry of serums or vaccines into the ghetto. Some small illicit traffic in serums went on, but this helped only a few of the richer ghetto inhabitants.

Among those who were untiring in their efforts to hold back the disease which was striking down people with such bewildering rapidity was Nobel Prize winner Professor Ludwig Hirschfeld, an apostate Jew. He had once been Director of the Bacteriological Institute of Warsaw University and was the author of many textbooks. With feverish energy he worked in the Jewish Hospital to produce typhoid and typhus serums. Since he lacked all facilities for such work, his efforts were hopeless. Though he poured his life into the vials and flasks of his primitive laboratory he could not even slow down the sweep of deadly infection.

By the early winter of 1941, shortly after the establishment of the ghetto, the death rate from typhoid, typhus, and dysentery had reached six to seven thousand every month. The wave of death swamped the doctors and undertakers. Even the bereaved were too overwhelmed by the magnitude of the calamity to express their sorrow. The dead were dumped naked—for clothes were valuable—into the streets. Every morning wagons drove through the ghetto to pick up the bodies and take them to the Jewish cemetery, where they were buried in mass graves.

The food situation was desperate. In independent Poland there had been a free flow of commodities. Polish merchants, peddlers, and peasants had been able to enter the Jewish districts to sell their products. Under the German occupation free exchange of commodities was restricted, and controls were tight; but even under those conditions a certain amount of legal and extralegal exchange had been possible.

Then the ghetto was instituted; a high brick wall and barbed wire separated the Jews from the Gentiles. There was no intermingling, no communication, no contact.

The amount of food assigned to the ghetto for filling its ration cards was pitifully small. Although his card entitled him to a great deal more, the ghetto Jew received about twenty grams of bread a day, a little kasha, and once in a very great while a little sugar—not even a subsistence diet.

At first it was at least possible to get along, because the ghetto Jews were permitted to receive food from the provinces by mail. Very soon, however, this was forbidden. Even food packages from foreign countries were seldom delivered. Later, in 1942, after the United States entered the war, there was general confiscation of these parcels. From time to time, trucks would drive up to the Jewish post office on Zamenhof Street to carry off the accumulated foreign food packages.

During the early months, Polish workers used to enter the ghetto to work in shops and factories in the ghetto area. They helped to smuggle in a small amount of food. Later all Christian workers were removed from the ghetto, and this food channel was shut off.

In the beginning the penalty for smuggling food into the ghetto was a fine of as high as a thousand zlotys, or from three to six months in jail. Later it was increased to ten thousand zlotys and one year. Then an order was issued making death the penalty for leaving the ghetto without authorization. Since most forms of smuggling required periodic visits to the Aryan side,[1] this was a severe blow. Many were shot for smuggling food.

But hunger broke through all barriers. Smuggling was organ-

[1] "The Aryan side" is a literal translation of the name the Warsaw Jews gave to the area outside the ghetto. They had inevitably picked up Nazi terms to express the realities of life under the occupation.

75

ized spontaneously on a large scale. It was carried on through various channels and by the most artful means. Along with the daring and cunning and the extraordinary improvisations operated one simple and powerful mechanism—bribery—which reached to the police of all varieties and the gendarmes of all ranks. So important were the operations of the smugglers that prices in the illegal ghetto market rose or fell depending on the results of the day's smuggling.

The streetcars played an important part. During the early days, Aryan as well as Jewish trolleys went through the ghetto. The car line went from Muranov Street through Zamenhof, Djelna, Karmelitzka, Leshno, Zhelasna, and Chlodna Streets to Twarda Street. The conductors and motormen would bring sacks of food with them and at previously arranged points hand them over to confederates in the ghetto. From the Jewish cars, this was done at the stopping points. From the others, which made no stops in the ghetto, the conductors or motormen would simply throw the sacks out of the cars to waiting smugglers. The guards and police were well paid and saw nothing.

A great volume of illicit commerce went through the janitors of Gentile buildings on streets bordering the ghetto. Particularly important were the janitors on Zlota, Tchepla, Prosta, and Walizov Streets; at 12, 14, 16 Krochmalna Street, which bordered the Mirovsky market; and those on Shwentoyerska, Franciskanska, and Rimarska Streets, near the former State Monopoly building now reduced to a pile of rubble one story high.

Near the huge DOK building, the former Polish military headquarters at Pzheyazd and Novolipya Streets, food was passed through holes gouged in the ghetto walls. The openings would be repaired, broken through again, and so on. The Jewish smugglers also contrived to throw ropes with hooks over the ghetto walls and haul in bundles of food. They would have torn at the ghetto walls with their teeth for a little food to satisfy the everlasting hunger.

The casualties in the battle for food were heavy, particularly heavy among the young. To scramble up a ghetto wall for a small package from the other side was much easier for children. As the youngsters worked, small groups of adults—expectant beneficiaries of a child's agility—would stand about, watching and waiting. The children would slink stealthily along the wall, listening intently for the familiar voice from the other side.

"*Srulek, yestesh?*" (Srulek, are you there?)

"*Yestem.*" (Here I am.)

Srulek would clamber up the wall, clawing frantically for a foothold. Breathless, he would make the top—I can see him standing on the top of the wall with outstretched arms, leaning forward to catch the precious sack. Suddenly—zing! Srulek falls to the ground on the Aryan side. The gendarme had an easy target.

A dull sigh rises from many broken hearts, perhaps the father and mother among them. Eyes full of tears stare at the bare spot on the wall. Then from the other side a sack comes flying over the wall, a sack with Srulek's bloody body. The Aryan soil doesn't want him—back to the ghetto!

Children used to steal over to the Aryan side by digging holes under the walls or by hiding near the ghetto gates and sneaking through when the guard momentarily turned his back. Then they would make their way to an apartment, cautiously and timidly knock on the door, and with eloquent eyes would beg for food. Occasionally they would get a crust of bread or a few potatoes. With their hard-earned treasure they would crawl back through breaks or chinks in the ghetto barrier. Parents would sit home all day nervously awaiting the return of their only breadwinner. In tears they would gulp the food brought at such great risk.

The large-scale, well-organized, gang-operated smuggling went on with the help of bribery. At the Transferstelle, for example, where the food allotment was delivered to the ghetto, the officials were heavily bribed to allow more than the allotted number of truckloads to enter. Here both German and Jewish officials lined their pockets. Secret warehouses received the smuggled goods. Because it was not obtainable on ration cards, meat had to be smuggled differently. Specially constructed mobile ramps were set against the walls on both sides to smuggle over live cows and oxen. Milk was ingeniously smuggled in on Kozla Street. From the window of a building on Franciskanska Street which overlooked the ghetto (half the street was outside the wall) a sheet metal pipe was lowered, and milk poured across the racial boundary.

Even death was made to serve life. Four undertaking establishments operating little hand carts tried constantly to keep pace with the death rate. The carts plied back and forth all day to and from the Jewish cemetery on Okopova Street outside the ghetto. Often the coffins would come back packed with food, transferred to the smuggler-undertakers through a Christian cemetery which bordered the Jewish.

Each branch of the smuggling operation developed its own technicians and specialists who constantly devised new methods and opened new channels as the old were shut off. They were a queer conglomeration. The big operators were for the most part former merchants or factory owners in the food industry—flour dealers, bakers, slaughterhouse operators. Around the great, the little fish would swarm—draymen and porters who had lost their professions, strong-arm men and thieves, the familiar petty crooks and underworld characters.

Smuggled grain was usually ground on primitive little hand mills, but there were also illegal flour mills operated by electric power. On Stavki and Leshno Streets such electric mills were operated deep underneath the ground. Their narrow entrances were well hidden, and only a very few people knew their location. The illicit operators feared not only the Germans but also Jewish extortionists who were constantly on the lookout for such a rich source of blackmail.

The entire population of the ghetto had a very real interest in the smuggling, especially of food, textiles, leather, and other necessities. In addition, there was a lively illegal trade in foreign exchange and jewelry.

The most important bourse for trade in foreign currencies was the new Court building, situated athwart the boundary of the ghetto. The Gentiles would enter through Biala or Ogrodova Streets on their side, the Jews from Leshno on the ghetto side. Here, on "neutral" soil, they carried on a brisk trade in various currencies, stocks and bonds, diamonds and other precious stones. The court clerks, Polish lawyers, and others who had obvious reason for passing in and out of the building, acted regularly as intermediaries for important Gentile principals.

In the ghetto, Jewish artisans were active in fabricating various gold ornaments for the Germans. They were a handy source of cheap but highly skilled labor. In most cases, Germans or other wealthy Gentiles would contract for this work through trustworthy Poles, many of whom took great risks to carry on this business. Some would become Jews for a day or two, sneaking into the ghetto with Stars of David on their arms—the business was worth while.

No artist can ever paint an all-embracing picture of the ghetto's streets. Certainly it is beyond the capacity of my pen. I strain at my faded memories to bring back those scenes, those experiences. I cannot really call them experiences, for that implies a series of transitory events. Actually it was not at all like that. It was one continuous experience which lasted for five years— a nightmare without interruption.

In 1941, when hunger and typhus were especially dominant in the ghetto cacophony, when the victims numbered six thousand, seven thousand, and more, each month, every dawn would find the sidewalks littered with naked corpses, their faces covered with

79

dirty newspapers. The bereaved did not have the money or the spiritual strength to go through a funeral with each death. The strictest religious laws were violated. The most beloved were stripped of their tattered but still serviceable clothing and laid out naked on the sidewalks to await the morning burial wagon. At the cemetery these nameless corpses, without family, without prayer, were gathered by tens into a common grave. So it went with thousands and tens of thousands in a monotonous rhythm of death.

Along the wall of the Catholic church on Leshno Street, I remember how sick children lay, half dead, almost naked, swollen from hunger, with open running sores, parchment-like skin, comatose eyes, breathing heavily with a rattle in their throats. The elders stood around them, yellow and gaunt, whimpering in their weakness, "A piece of bread . . . a piece of bread . . ."

The street was packed with people: death, death, and more death; yet there was no end to the overcrowding. People elbowed their way through the noisy throngs, fearing to touch each other, for they might be touching typhus.

An old man, barefoot, dressed in rags, the foam on his mouth emphasizing the insane look in his eyes, pushed a baby carriage with two children who cried out over and over again, "Bread . . . a piece of bread."

Suddenly there was a movement in the crowd. Someone shouted, "Catch him!" A barefoot, ragged boy, his legs blackened with dirt, splashed through the mud, tripped over a corpse, fell. In his hand was a small loaf of bread, gripped tightly with all his strength. The owner of the bread pounced on him and tried to tear the treasure out of his hands. That most valuable of all earthly possessions was now chewed and beslobbered, wet with the saliva of the little thief. Who could tell whether along with that saliva went the germs of typhus?

These young food-snatchers were a special category of criminal. Their hunger gave them the desperation and strength to break

80

the holy law of ownership over a piece of bread. They were savagely beaten by the people they robbed and by the police, but extirpating the snatchers was no more possible than extirpating the hunger.

Suddenly there was more running and shouting and whistling. A truck loaded with German gendarmes raced down the street at full speed, paying no attention to the crowds of pedestrians. It was just about noon and the guard at the Paviak prison was being relieved. The truck plowed right through the crowds. As it rolled by, the gendarmes leaned out to beat the people with lengths of pipe, rifle butts, or whatever they had in their hands, shouting, "Dirty Jews, scabby typhus-spreaders . . ."

At the corner of Chlodna and Zhelasna the ghetto was divided by a "Polish corridor" through Chlodna Street. The bridge on Zhelasna connected the two parts. Under the bridge, on the holy Aryan soil, were the Christians; and here at the ghetto gate the German guards would direct little scenes of hell. They continually seized passing Jews and sported with them. They stood small groups of tattered, abject Jews in rows, put bricks or heavy paving stones in their hands, and ordered them to lift them up and down, up and down, urging them on with blows and derisive laughter. They kept this up until even kicks could no longer revive their victims. Thus did the master race teach gymnastics to their inferiors.

I remember too the interruptions in the thick, noisy, clamorous ghetto sounds. The weeping and whining and the discordant shouts of the crowded multitude would suddenly be cut by the harmonious notes of music from a courtyard or a street corner. That would be a group of singers or musicians from a one-time chorus or from the Philharmonic, playing for their bread. A few groszys would drop into the outstretched hat or apologetic palm. With averted eyes the performers would silently nod their thanks and move on to another court.

The children—the orphaned or abandoned half-starved waifs who roamed barefoot through the ghetto streets, their tattered clothing revealing ugly running sores—the children were our most heartbreaking problem.

Although the death rate among these homeless vagabonds was fantastically high, their number seemed to grow constantly. There were child-beggars at every step. Singly and in packs they wandered through the courtyards and the streets, singing beggars' songs, crying out their unhappiness. Imploring fingers tugged at every passer-by. Sometimes, mingled with the new songs of wretchedness and protest, we would hear the familiar strains of an old revolutionary anthem or of a folk melody which had been popular in the prewar Jewish schools. These had once been our future, these broken little bodies, these cracked voices begging for bread.

We used our press in a campaign to organize help for these abandoned children. We demanded that the official agencies of the community take them under their protection and provide homes and proper care. Not much was or could be done. Centos set up several orphanages. Some Jewish businessmen—bakers, brush factory owners, merchants—contributed to a relief fund. The efforts of the tenement committees helped. The Bund established a home which housed about two hundred children. The Yaff, the Red Cross, and our teachers' organization directed its activities.

Our young comrades gathered the children from the streets, by force if necessary. They were washed, fed, and clothed and given medical attention under the supervision of Dr. Anna Broide Heller. We set up a little workshop in the building in which volunteers worked through the evening to remodel cast-off clothes to fit the little bodies. Mrs. Etkin, Manya Wasser, Sonya Novogrodsky, and many others gave all their spare time to this project.

In April 1941, six months after the formal institution of the ghetto, the Nazis relaxed the restrictions to permit education of

Jewish children through the fourth grade of elementary school. Instruction was permitted only in Hebrew or Yiddish, the Polish language was strictly prohibited.

Although classes were operated in two shifts, the classrooms allotted to the new legal schools were totally inadequate even for the number of pupils in the first four grades. Many of the younger children had still to be served by the illegal schools.

As a reaction to the campaign of hatred and discrimination against the Jews, educational and cultural activity took on new importance. The ghetto days were marked by a compulsion to build spiritual and moral defenses—compensation for our utter physical helplessness. With great sacrifice we managed to perform pathetic wonders.

In a ghetto population of more than half a million, our educational system, by far the greater part illegal, served about twenty or thirty thousand students. The demand was far greater, and there was constant conflict among the parents over the right to send their children. The tenement committees helped regulate the selection of pupils to make it equitable and to minimize recrimination.

There were almost no textbooks. Some textbooks were laboriously typewritten, and these served as syllabi for the teachers.

Each school had a group of adult patrons who helped to assemble teaching materials, to provide a daily bowl of soup for the pupils, to collect money to pay teachers, and so forth. The effort required was tremendous. During the winter, finding enough fuel each day to keep the classroom warm was a major undertaking. The fight for spiritual nourishment was carried on with the same intensity as the fight for material nourishment.

During the hot summer months the schools were supplemented by day camps. Since there was hardly a blade of grass in the entire ghetto, the camps were organized on the ruins of bombed-out buildings. Here, under the guidance of their teachers, the children played games, sang, and danced. It was better than the stifling apartments and classrooms, but, since the garbage collection system was inadequate for the crowded ghetto, people burned their refuse in what open spaces were available, enveloping the children's day camps in a foul fog from the smoldering heaps of garbage.

Parents were concerned that, even with some teaching and private tutoring, their children would be at a disadvantage when they re-entered Polish schools after the war. Our secondary schools therefore did everything possible to fulfill the formal requirements. This was doubly illegal, since instruction was in Polish, a language now strictly forbidden to the Jews.

Some of the secondary schools held final examinations, for which Polish inspectors were smuggled into the ghetto to "legalize" the diplomas. These were then carefully hidden away against the day when the parents would present their children for admission into Polish institutions of higher learning.

The ORT offered trade courses—in tailoring, hatmaking, corsetry, and so forth. It also received permission to open a technical school.

Medical courses were all organized illegally. One of the instructors was the same Ludwig Hirschfeld who worked so heroically to combat the typhus epidemics. He later escaped to the Aryan side during the deportations and is today the director of the university in Wroclav.

Through the efforts of Michel Klepfish and Zalman Friedrych our old physical education organization, Morgenstern, was re-created. It assembled groups for mass gymnastics, eurythmics, and competitive sport—on the ruins alongside the day camps.

We organized a program of adult education. Instruction in Yiddish had to be offered to those who had gotten along without it all their lives but found it indispensable under the ghetto conditions. We involved larger numbers of people in cultural programs to celebrate the anniversaries of Sholem Aleichem, Peretz, and other famous Jewish writers.

Indeed, to defend ourselves against the feeling of helplessness that engulfed us, we tried to rebuild and strengthen all the pre-war institutions, to create at least the illusion of a life that used to be.

In the crowded ghetto every bit of space was occupied. People were packed into apartments, and life spilled out into the hallways, the courtyards, and the streets in drab confusion.

The courtyard was a community center. It was often strewn with odds and ends of old furniture and other household possessions for which no room could be found in the apartments or the garrets. In one corner bedding was hung to air; in another someone worked patiently to fix an old broken table. Women with pale, drawn, lifeless faces sat on the stone steps and sewed; others washed clothes, leaning over their wooden tubs; some held yellow-faced infants to their breasts.

Somewhere in the courtyard a group of children danced in a circle, clapping their hands, singing a simple melody. Their attention was concentrated completely on a girl of fourteen or fifteen who led them in their play. Their eyes eagerly followed her every movement; they were alert to every new command. This was a kindergarten led by a young member of our Skiff.

I can remember the children with their blanched faces and shining eyes, caught up in their rhythmic game, dancing and singing in unison. For a while they forgot the gnawing hunger, the sorrowful faces of their parents, the inescapable woe and unhappiness. This was their moment of holiday. Childish joy lighted their faces.

Almost every courtyard had such "kindergartens"—though they had, in reality, only a name to recall a happier past. How far away that past was from the gruesome present! Only a year separated them, but it seemed an eternity. Once clean, neat, well-fed children had frolicked on the green grass and danced among the trees, the dawn of their life shining with happiness. In the ghetto courtyards an ersatz experience was created by our Skiff youngsters, who remembered that far-away yet recent past and tried to bring a little of it into the dismal present.

The Skiff took the initiative in organizing the kindergartens. It was their expression of a desire to make a responsible contribution to ghetto life. Many of the members were graduates of our secular Jewish school system and were able to teach the children folk songs and some reading and writing in addition to the games. The idea caught on quickly, and such groups were soon functioning all over the ghetto.

Number Twelve Novolipya was well within the ghetto boundaries, so it was unnecessary for me to move during the great population shift which marked the establishment of the Warsaw ghetto. Our menage became somewhat larger. Jacob, the son of my brother Hershel who had been killed in the First World War, moved in with his two younger sisters from Praga. Jacob was a leather worker and had worked in the factory owned by a brother of Sholem Asch. An intelligent tall blond Aryan-looking boy of twenty-eight, quiet and shy, Jacob was also a member of the Bund.

During the early ghetto days our lives became easier and our organizational work less difficult than they had been at first under the occupation. The shortage of food and living space was terribly severe and engendered a brutalizing and degrading competition for a place to sleep or a crust of bread. But, most important of all, during the first ghetto days the Germans left us, as individuals, pretty much to our own devices. There was an almost palpable feeling of relief. The people began again to learn how to go to sleep without the dread of being awakened by the sound of the hobnailed boots.

On the other hand, of course, the Bund's contact with the Aryan side of Warsaw and with the rest of the country became

86

a great deal more difficult. We expanded our underground organization and distributed our illegal newspapers and circulars more widely. Then the Gestapo began to pay closer attention to us. More and more comrades had to become "illegal" and go into complete hiding. Some who were hunted in the provinces came to Warsaw hoping that the crowded ghetto and our Warsaw organization would protect them. The number of "illegals" in the provinces continued to grow. Our Red Cross was taxed to the limit to care for them, to find hiding places, to obtain documents, apartments, and money.

My responsibility was to maintain contact between the various parts of our illegal organization. As the Gestapo noose tightened around us the work became more specialized, more difficult, and more important. Before the war we had been a legal and extremely active organization. My functions, as I have said, had made me a familiar figure to every policeman in the city of Warsaw, most of whom were now in the service of the Germans. Every stone in Warsaw's streets knew the tread of my foot.

My new conspiratorial role was not easy to play. I had to maintain the strictest secrecy, to move only in the shadows. My apartment was known to only a few chosen comrades. I was supposed to disappear completely so that I would not even be remembered or mentioned. I used two apartments, mine at 12 Novolipya and Perenson's at 24 Leshno. In both, the steady stream of visitors made complete secrecy impossible. Couriers from the provincial organizations, representatives of the Warsaw underground, members of our underground committee, were constantly arriving. But within the limits permitted by our work I tried to remain isolated, venturing outdoors as rarely as possible.

With the increased pressure from the Gestapo, we tried to take greater precautions and to cover our tracks more carefully. We instructed our active comrades wherever possible not to spend nights in their own apartments. We changed the name of *The Bulletin*, which the Gestapo now recognized as a publication of

87

the Bund, to *The Call*, to try to throw the Gestapo off the scent.

Our intelligence groups discovered that the Gestapo was hard on the trail of our printing plant, located in the apartment of Comrade Barenbaum at 30 Novolipya. The central committee assigned to Marek Edelman and Welvel Rosovsky the task of saving the plant from the hands of the Nazis. They mobilized additional comrades and in a single day of feverish work they moved everything, including the precious store of paper. The owners of the apartment, who worked in the plant, moved with it. The following day the Gestapo carried out its anticipated raid—on an empty apartment.

Abrasha, Berek, and I issued a warning to all members of the militia to recruit new members only with the greatest care Above all we asked our people to use every possible means to acquire weapons. Every passing day convinced us that life in the ghetto would soon enter a more terrible and bloody phase. We were obsessed with the fear that it would find us unarmed and helpless.

Morizi Orzech was sent to the Aryan side with one mission: to get arms at any cost. We approached the directors of the Joint Distribution Committee—Guzik, Guiterman, and Neustadt—for an arms fund. They promised to do everything they could. Our finance committee undertook a special campaign to raise money for this purpose We also approached all the Polish underground organizations for help.

The acquisition of arms became the one goal toward which we strained every sinew of our organization. It was clear that we would have to fight. How much time we had we did not know, but we knew it would not be enough.

The Germans integrated the ghetto into their tremendous war machine as a productive unit. Tebbens, a German industrialist, established huge factories on Prosta Street in the building of the Commercial High School and on Leshno Street in the building of the former Trades School. Here clothing was manufactured from the best and most expensive fabrics confiscated by the Germans in Poland. Schultz, a German from Danzig, who before the war had dealt extensively with Polish Jews, opened several factories on Novolipya Street for the manufacture of leather, felt, and fur products. The Pole Lestchinsky established large clothing factories on Ogrodova Street. A group of Germans, Volksdeutsche,[1] Poles, and Jews in partnership operated several brush factories. There were also shops for the fabrication of barrack components, such as doors, windows, and roof sections. In addition there were factories devoted to the production of haberdashery, shoes, mattresses, metal work, furniture, and textiles.

The raw materials for these enterprises were supplied by the German authorities, and the greater part of the output went to the military machine, particularly for the Eastern Front, where warm clothing was in great demand. Germans with influence in military circles diverted some of this production to private channels. By bribery and trickery a very small portion was kept in the ghetto.

The workers were exclusively ghetto Jews. They numbered tens of thousands. At Tebbens', for example, some fifteen thousand were employed at the beginning of 1943. The wages were extremely low, but in addition the worker was given an opportunity to buy two liters of soup daily for about sixty or seventy groszy.

Fear of the labor camps, the danger of being seized on the street for forced labor or worse, hung like a nightmare over the ghetto. Those who were able to get into the factory of a Tebbens, a Lestchinsky, or a Schultz were considered lucky. The working card they held was a precious talisman. With it they could walk the streets more safely, sleep more securely at home. Besides, they got a piece of bread or a bowl of soup to still the perpetual hunger.

[1] "Volksdeutsche" was the name applied to all citizens of occupied countries who could establish some proof of German ancestry.

Some three or four thousand Jews worked outside the ghetto on the railroads and in military or other shops. They too worked for starvation wages—anything to get the life-saving work card. Every morning at dawn they would assemble at various points near the ghetto gates, be marched off to work under a heavy armed guard, and be escorted back to the ghetto at night.

Through these workers, who enjoyed a breath of Aryan air each day, there went a trickle of illegal trade. The more cunning would smuggle out of the ghetto various things to be sold or bartered on the Aryan side and bring back products which were unobtainable in the ghetto. In the evenings around the ghetto gates relatives, friends, merchants, and peddlers would await their return and then would begin a buying and selling and bartering that recalled the busy hubbub of the one-time marketplace.

The horse as a means of locomotion disappeared almost entirely from the ghetto. Some horses were requisitioned by the Nazis, some were eaten. The drayman had no food to give his horse to enable it to help him. Oats were used to make soup for human consumption. No one would think of giving such a delicacy to a horse. So the drayman liquidated his horse—and put himself into harness.

On the streets there began to appear all kinds of carts drawn by men. The Chinese word "ricksha" became part of the Jewish language in the ghetto. There were rickshas for carrying passengers and for carrying freight. Some were cleverly contrived so that the human motor could operate the wheels in bicycle fashion. About a thousand such rickshas were operated in the ghetto, mainly by former professional men, chauffeurs, or students—generally by those whose physical condition enabled them to sustain the burden of the extinct horse.

The sword of the Nazi extermination policy hung over all Jews equally. But a social differentiation arose in the ghetto, setting apart substantial groups who had the means even under those infernal conditions to lead a comparatively full, well-fed life and enjoy some kinds of pleasures. On the same streets where daily you could see scenes of horror, amid the swarms of tubercular children dying like flies, alongside the corpses waiting for the scavenger wagons, you would come upon stores full of fine foods, restaurants and cafés which served the most expensive dishes and drinks. At 2 Leshno Street, where Gertner's Restaurant had been, there was a café called Sztuka, complete with floor show. There was another at 13 Tlomatzka Street, once the Metropole Restaurant. These establishments were run in partnership with members of the Gestapo by outcast Jews, the most important of whom was the dancer Madame Machno. There were also the well-known Schultz Restaurant at Karmelitzka and Novolipky Streets, A La Fourchette at 18 Leshno Street, Britannia at 20 Novolipya Street.

The clientele of these places consisted principally of Jewish Gestapo agents, Jewish police officials, rich merchants who did business with the Germans, smugglers, dealers in foreign exchange, and similar kinds of people. The worst nest of drunkenness and vice was the Britannia. The curfew did not apply to the habitués of this establishment. They made merry all night. Feasting, drinking, and carousing went on to the rhythm of a jazz band. At dawn, when the revelers left, the streets were already strewn with naked paper-covered corpses. The drunkards paid little attention, tripping unsteadily over the obstacles in their path. Around the restaurants and cafés hovered human shadows, swollen from hunger, who trailed after the well-fed drunks, begging for scraps; they were usually angrily pushed aside for disturbing the mirage of luxury and well-being.

The Nazis made moving pictures of such festive orgies to show the "world" how well the Jews lived in the ghetto. They also arranged appropriate film material to fill the gaps in their propaganda program. They led hungry, ragged Jews into Schultz's restaurant, seated them on soft couches at well-laid tables, and ordered them to demand food and drink from the waiters. In the newsreels this was billed as a demonstration by the hungry Jews against the rich and well-fed.

Another film was supposed to show Cherniakov, the head of the Judenrat, living in luxury. Elegantly made-up ladies dressed in expensive finery were brought to his apartment on Elektoralna Street. At lavishly set tables laden with rare wines and fine foods sat the well-dressed guests with Cherniakov at their head. The film was titled, *An Orgy in the Home of the Chairman of the Judenrat*.

At a *mikvah* (Jewish ritual bath) the Nazis drove naked Jewish men and women in together and filmed them, to show the wantonness and demoralization of the ghetto Jews.

The Nazi camera was carefully aimed—both when it took actual scenes and when it recorded dismal play-acting—to tell a story. The corpses scattered in the streets, the starved human skeletons, the half-naked abandoned children who begged for bread—these were never caught by the camera.

At the time the Germans established the Warsaw ghetto, we were watching with anxious interest the course of the presidential elections in the United States. It was clear to us that only some force in the distant world could possibly break the Germans' iron grip on Europe. We analyzed every item of foreign news for signs of hope.

Although we watched the election through a fog of German press releases, it was almost as if we were active participants. Each day's news sent our spirits up or down. When Roosevelt was elected, the Jews almost danced in the ghetto streets.

But we could not count the election of Roosevelt as a victory; it was only the avoidance of a crushing defeat. American aid was still remote and problematical. The fall of one country after another, the constant increase in fascist strength, weighed heavily on the ghetto's morale. Broken by hunger and typhus, feeling the whip of Nazi terror, and waiting for even more frightful terror to be unleashed, we watched with agonized helplessness as the Nazi juggernaut rolled over the Balkans, Jugoslavia, Greece.

When the Germans invaded Russia in June 1941, our hopes revived. The mighty neighbor who had forsaken us was at last pitting her strength on our side against the powerful German Army. But the Russians suffered defeat after defeat, and our elation ebbed, as it seemed that we would once again see a German victory.

When Japan began to rattle the saber in the Far East, our hopes turned once more to the United States. We followed and argued over every step in the Japanese-American crisis. Each report of the negotiations was scanned for hidden hints of what was to come. Every news item was picked to pieces. Some of us felt that Germany was pushing Japan toward a showdown with the United States. Such a step would inevitably involve America in the European war. Others could not believe that German strategists would be so blind to the consequences and thought that Germany would force Japan to back down at the last moment.

When the crisis erupted at Pearl Harbor, and Germany declared war against the United States, we felt that an immense load had been lifted from our minds. At last the forces which would bring an end to our ordeal had entered the field. At last the Germans had made the fatal mistake.

We refused to be discouraged when the German press poked fun at the "gum-chewing Yankees" who loved their life of ease too much to undertake a war, or boasted that the German U-boats would finish off the American Navy in a few days. In the derisive comments with which the German newspapers greeted President Roosevelt's program for thousands of airplanes and hundreds of ships, we could detect a faint undercurrent of anxiety. It was good to see the Germans even slightly worried. It was good at last to have a powerful friend. We did not realize that for us it had come too late.

One morning the janitor of 12 Novolipya burst in to tell me that he had just been visited by two Gestapo agents, apparently Jews, who had gone through his registry book. They had paid particular attention to the G's. He was sure they were after me.

Abrasha Blum happened to be with me at the time. We decided that I must get out immediately.

I glanced through the window and saw several people loitering at the courtyard gate. I decided to avoid the street. I hurried through a break in the courtyard wall which led into a schoolyard, and from there I climbed the wall into the courtyard of 14 Novolipya, where I took shelter in a friend's apartment.

Ten minutes later a Gestapo car pulled up in front of 12 Novolipya, and agents swarmed into the building. They ransacked my apartment, questioned my family and neighbors. They left a written order that I must report the following morning at the headquarters of the Gestapo at Allee Shucha.

The following day they returned to find out why I had not appeared. My brother was not at home, so they took young Jacob as a hostage.

This was an unexpected turn. My escape had placed my nephew in the hands of the Gestapo. My own decision was to give myself up in the hope that the Gestapo would keep its promise to free Jacob, but the party comrades forbade me to surrender under any circumstances. Judging by past experience, there was little reason to believe that the Gestapo would have freed him in any case. But that argument could not still my tormented conscience. I was haunted by a feeling of guilt and shame. It was because of me that he lay in a Gestapo cellar. No rationalization could change that.

94

Jacob was a Bundist and, living in my apartment, had seen comrades come and go on underground business. The Gestapo tortured him in an attempt to get information, but they were finally defeated when death brought an end to his agonies.

I could not stay at 14 Novolipya very long. After a few days my comrades dressed me in a long black coat and a rabbi's hat. Mrs. Etkin led me through the streets to her apartment at 36 Leshno. Accompanying us was an armed guard commanded by Berek. He alone knew the purpose of the mission, the others knew that they were to stay close to Berek and to carry out his orders. They did not know that the venerable rabbi whose footsteps Berek Snaidmil dogged was Comrade Bernard.

At Mrs. Etkin's I was given the room of Manya Ziegelboim, Artur's wife, who was away. The room was kept locked and the explanation to curious visitors was that Manya had asked that it be left undisturbed.

My sentry was Mrs. Etkin's ten-year-old nephew. He did not understand why, but he knew that no one must discover that a stranger was living in the locked room. Every time the doorbell rang, he would wait for me to gather up my things and race into my room. He would look around carefully to see that I had left no trace before he went to the door. He played his role perfectly.

To discourage pursuit we spread a rumor among the comrades that I had left Warsaw. My family was told the same story. But the legend that I was out of the city soon began to crack. Though I tried to exercise great care, I once made the mistake of raising the window shade. I was spotted by a comrade, a tailor, who lived across the court. The following day he let it slip to some of his fellow workers in the factory. I was seen a second time in the apartment itself. The Etkins tried to keep postponing their turn for the meeting of their tenement committee, which met in the members' apartments in rotation. They were not always successful. To avoid undue suspicion they occasionally had to agree to hold a meeting in their apartment. One evening after the close of such a meeting, the actor Sanberg was describing a role he had once played on the Polish stage. He reached a great dramatic moment and in the excitement of his re-enactment he smashed against my door with enough force to snap the lock. I was framed in the light streaming from the other room. He recognized me immediately. With only a moment's hesitation he continued his declamation as if nothing had happened, shutting the door behind him.

But the secret was now out, and it was decided that I should move again.

After two months with the Etkins, therefore, I moved to 13 Gensha Street, to Mrs. Manya Wasser's apartment. Registered at the house under the name of Malinovsky, I tried again to pick up the threads of my work. In so far as was possible, the few comrades whom I was required to see were given the impression that the apartment was a rendezvous and that my hiding place was elsewhere.

The apartment was a very busy place. With Manya, whose husband was already in America, were her daughter Anusia, her brother-in-law, his family, and her sister and niece. Although there were ten of us in all, we were relatively comfortable in the five rooms. Everyone who lived in the apartment gave his solemn oath to Abrasha Blum that he would not mention my presence, would never invite friends to visit, and would discourage any casual guest from loitering. I had the room at the end of the long apartment hall, away from the center of activity, but my presence hung over everyone.

With the Wassers lived a pretty seventeen-year-old girl, a member of our youth movement, who was active in organizing kindergartens, distributing handbills, and other underground work. One day she walked timidly into my room. Sitting on the edge of a chair, her eyes averted, she told me she needed my advice. There was a boy, Kostek, whom she loved very much, and he loved her.

They were sure that the end was near for all of us. Before it came they wanted to experience the fulfillment of love. Did I think it was right that they should do this? Would it be immoral?

I had known Kostek for many years. He was a handsome, lively, open-faced boy, very active in our youth movement.

"Under these circumstances you are breaking no law," I told her. "Take your sweetheart without shame and be happy."

But I could not understand why she had come to me with her problem. There were others within her reach better suited to receive her confidences. Then, as she sat waiting for me to say more, I suddenly realized that she wanted me to arrange the opportunity for a lovers' tryst. In the crowded ghetto there was no place where the sweethearts could have a moment alone. And he could not visit her here.

"Do not be concerned because of your promise to Abrasha," I said. "I relieve you of that promise. Send Kostek to me." She gave me a warm, grateful look and ran from the room.

The following day when Kostek appeared I told him that I wanted regular personal reports from him on his literature-smuggling activities and invited him to visit me to make them. Gravely he agreed to do so. The lovers thus found a few brief private moments in the apartment. During the deportations, Kostek and his sweetheart both perished.

Orzech, Abrasha, and I soon arranged a meeting in the apartment with Runge, the leader of the International Transport Workers' Union, a former member of the Polish Socialist party, and before the war a member of the central committee of the Polish Federation of Labor. He was now a member of the Left Socialist group which was later headed by Poland's Premier, Osubka-Morawska.

Runge was smuggled into the ghetto with great care. We even had to arrange for passwords to enable Anusia Wasser, who did

97

not know Runge by sight, to meet him and escort him to the apartment. Being a non-Jew, he was able to travel around the country with some freedom. We enlisted his aid in establishing contact with our comrades in provincial ghettos and in exchanging publications between the Jewish and the Polish underground. Most important of all, we wanted his aid in obtaining arms.

We were also able to arrange a meeting with our own Leon Feiner, who had recently managed to make his way to Warsaw from Soviet territory. He arrived on the Aryan side completely exhausted, showing the effects of months in a Soviet prison in Lida, near Vilna.

When he finally reached Warsaw he was lucky enough to make contact with an old friend, Stopnitzky, a Polish lawyer. Both had been active members of the Socialist Association of Jurists. Stopnitzky obtained forged Aryan papers for Leon and settled him in an apartment. Stopnitzky was in touch with Orzech, and through him we learned of Feiner's arrival in Warsaw. As a member of the Bund's central committee before the war, Leon automatically became a member of the underground central committee, and we were most anxious to get in touch with him. We took immediate steps to bring him into the ghetto for a plenary meeting of the central committee, but it was a long time before we succeeded.

One of the details which caused delay was the fur collar on Leon's coat. In the ghetto a Jew was not permitted to wear any fur. All of it had presumably been collected a long time ago for the German Army. Leon needed an untrimmed coat or a tailor who could refinish his so that it would not attract attention on the Aryan side. This took time to arrange.

Finally all the annoying difficulties were overcome. Leon's trip into the ghetto was managed by David Klin, who had obtained permission to accompany a sick man to Otvotsk. On the way back, the ambulance picked up Leon and, since the pass also covered one sick passenger, brought Leon through the ghetto gate to my apartment.

98

When finally we stood face to face, neither could control his tears. And I could hardly believe my eyes. I remembered Feiner as a tall aristocratic man, whose graying hair was the only hint of his fifty-eight years. Though he was a busy, prosperous lawyer, he had always managed to find time for skiing and mountain climbing to keep him in the best physical condition. The man with sunken cheeks who stood before me was old and starved. What had happened to his healthy elegance?

He smiled wryly at me. "I have 'recovered' during the last few weeks on the Aryan side. You should have seen me when I arrived from the Soviet zone."

In his quiet, deliberate way he told me the story of his experiences during the long months in the Soviet prison at Lida.

"I was in the Polish Punishment Camp of Kartuz Bereza a long time, but that cannot even be compared to what I lived through under our 'comrades' They cross-examined me for nights on end. They insulted me as a 'spy.' I told them I was a lawyer and had a long record of defending Communists in Polish courts. They laughed and called me a counterrevolutionary and a fascist.

"We received hardly any food. Often in our hunger we sucked our fingers. We got thin as sticks, dirty, and lousy. It is hard for me to say it, but what saved us is that the Nazis drew close to Lida. The Soviet guards did not even do us the kindness of unlocking the cell doors before they ran away. We had to break out ourselves, before the Nazis took the town. It took weeks for Fishgrund and me to reach Warsaw on foot. We arrived in terrible shape, barefoot, bloody, and starved, looking too far gone even to pass as beggars."

Leon Feiner remained in the ghetto only a few days. Our preparations for a meeting of the central committee and of the party leadership were interrupted by the events of the night of April 17. Everything had to be postponed. A few days later, when things had quieted a bit, we smuggled Leon back to the Aryan side.

99

Night was dark in the ghetto. Even the stars in the cool blue sky looked forbidding. The moon only emphasized the lonely blackness which filled our souls and spirits. Bed was a rack of mental agony after a day of fear, of suffering, of horrifying, unbelievable experience. Nothing could drive the nightmares from the mind or the low, penetrating sounds of endless misery from the ear.

Dark as usual was the spring night of April 17, 1942. In Manya Wasser's apartment at 13 Gensha Street I slept fitfully—again as usual—often starting out of my sleep in a cold sweat.

Suddenly I was awakened by the unmistakable sound of a shot close by. I sprang to the window. The darkness was cut by a small searchlight directed at the wall of the military prison opposite. Another shot sounded, and then another. I saw two people fall. The searchlight went out, and I heard heavy footsteps on the stone pavement fading into the distance. Again all was quiet and pitch-black. It was two o'clock.

I could no longer sleep. Until dawn I lay with my face pressed against the windowpane. My eyes searched the darkness vainly, waiting to see a repetition of this startling act or something that would explain what had happened on the street below.

I must have dozed. I awoke to see Jews with brushes and rags scrubbing a bloody patch of sidewalk beside the prison wall.

During that night, the Gestapo had visited scores of houses in various parts of the ghetto, had dragged people out and shot them on the spot. The bodies were left where they fell. Jewish police had accompanied the SS and Gestapo men, carrying a list of names and addresses, and leading the murderers directly to their victims.

In the morning, under orders from the police, the bodies were cleaned off the streets by wagons of the Chesed Shel Emmeth Burial Society and by other undertakers. The police drove the neighbors of the murdered men into the streets and forced them to wash away the blood.

That night we lost, among others, the following comrades:

Joseph Leruch was a bookbinder by trade, member of the executive board of his union, and well known for devotion and activity. In the ghetto, he had held the post of janitor at 4 Volinska Street. From this house he was taken that night, with his son, an active member of the Zukunft. They were shot at the entrance to the building.

Moishe Goldberg from Kalushin was president of the Barbers' Union, an active leader in the illegal Warsaw organization of the Bund. When the Gestapo called at his home to lead him to his death, his wife asked, "Where are you taking him?"

"It will just be a short while. He will return soon," she was told.

"May I come along?" she asked.

"*Bitte schon*," was the reply.

She took along their three-year-old child. On the street all three were immediately shot.

Paysach Zuckerman was a typesetter for the newspaper *Moment* and a member of the Bund. He was shot on the street.

Menachem Linder was a young worker in the Jewish Scientific Institute, active in the cultural life of the ghetto. He was shot in front of his home at 50 Leshno.

Bleiman was president of the Master Bakers' Association and well known in Warsaw. He was told to take along cigarettes and anything else he thought he might need. His wife was permitted to come along. Both were shot on Zamenhof Street near their home.

Schoen was a printer on the newspaper *Nash Psheglond*. His son saw the approaching police, jumped out of the window, and managed to escape. Schoen was taken to the square at Karmelitzka and Novolipya Streets and shot. He fell, severely wounded, and was left for dead. He recovered—to perish later in Treblinka.

Especially tragic was the death of our comrade, Moishe Sklar, a typesetter. He had been a member of the executive committee of the Printers' Union, and continued his Bund activity in the ghetto. He was arrested that night but not shot immediately as were the others. For two weeks he was held in the Paviak prison and horribly tortured. He was asked for the names of those active in printing illegal literature. He knew them all, but he endured the terrible pain and said nothing. At five o'clock in the morning, two weeks after his arrest, he was taken to the corner of Djelna and Smotcha, where he was shot.

Neighbors heard the shots and ran out. They saw a man lying in a pool of blood and a Jewish policeman leaning over the corpse, removing its shoes. When they recognized the body, they notified his wife, Esther, and his two sons. (The older son later died of tuberculosis in the ghetto, the younger perished in Maidanek.)

We buried him in an individual grave. On his body we saw the evidence of torture. The whole body was covered with black bruises and wounds. His fingers and his sexual organs were flattened and mashed, holes were burned into the soles of his feet. Later we identified the Jewish policeman who had done the ghoulish looting. He was dealt with appropriately.

Two of our comrades, Loeser Clog and Sonya Novogrodsky, cheated death that dreadful night. Late in the evening, Sonya received an anonymous note warning that mass arrests were about to take place. It was already after the eight o'clock curfew. Nevertheless, she left her home at 7 Novolipya to inform Loeser Clog, who also lived on Novolipya. Both found places to sleep elsewhere. The police came to call for them and left empty-handed. Sonya and Loeser thus won a few more months of life.

Sonya, the only woman member of the underground central committee, was an indefatigable worker. She was already fifty years old, thin, of medium height, with graying hair. As a girl she had worked in a hat factory and later as a teacher in the Jewish school system. In the First World War she had been imprisoned by the Germans for political activity. She was an earnest, intelligent, and quick-witted woman with a nervous temperament that drove her to ever greater efforts.

Several months before Hitler marched into Poland her husband had been sent to the United States as a delegate from the Jewish labor movement to raise money for cultural and political activities in Poland. He was stranded there by the war. Mark, their only son, then nineteen years old, tall and slim like his father, had escaped from Warsaw at the time I left the city. He made his way through Russia and Japan to America where he joined the Army and reached the rank of sergeant.

Sonya was a leader in the underground from the very beginning. She set up illegal schools, with the help of the JDC, she organized relief and soup kitchens for needy children. She did what she could to gather up the wandering waifs from the ghetto streets into orphan homes. She helped to furnish aid for arrested comrades through our Socialist Red Cross and to provide homes for fugitives. She even found time for cultural activities, particularly among children; she organized theaters, choruses, and group games.

Loeser Clog was a native of Vilna and still spoke with a marked Lithuanian accent. A printer by trade, he had joined the Bund at the age of fifteen. He was now fifty years old and the father of eight children. Dark, broad-shouldered, good-natured, he was always a source of encouragement for those around him. Underground political activity was nothing new to him. In the time of the Czar, he had operated an illegal printing plant.

The mass executions of the night of April 17 created a sense of panic in the ghetto. It was rumored that the Gestapo's purpose was to liquidate the illegal printing plants and all those associated with distributing underground literature. This was evidenced by the large number of printers among the victims.

The president of the Judenrat, Adam Cherniakov, summoned Morizi Orzech, and told him that he knew positively from

Gestapo circles that the executions would not cease as long as the
clandestine press continued to operate. He therefore asked the
Bund, through Orzech, to stop circulating illegal literature, and
not to cause further mass punishment.

Orzech tried to persuade Cherniakov that the Nazis were not
concerned simply with illicit propaganda—that this was the first
step in a mass liquidation of the Jews; that we already knew of
the burning of Jews in Chelmno and Belzhitz; that we could not
hope to satisfy the Nazi beast by compromise or appeasement.

Orzech then reported his conversation with Cherniakov to our
central leadership. Cherniakov's suggestion was rejected.

Now the terror in the ghetto entered a new and bloodier phase.
Almost every night the Nazis would break into a tenement, drag
scores of people into the street, and shoot them. People were
brought into the ghetto from the Aryan side at night and shot.
We did not know who they were or why they were murdered.

The ghetto became a place of execution. The Jews had to clear
the streets of the corpses.

Shortly after, in July, the mass deportations began.

Even before the Black Night of April 17 we had begun to see
new faces in the ghetto—hundreds and hundreds of elegantly
dressed Czech and German Jews. Automobiles brought them with
their handsome expensive-looking luggage from the railroad station to the ghetto. They were moved into specially prepared
quarters in the Tlomatzky Synagogue, the Jewish Library, and
the former school building at 84 Leshno Street.

Around them was created a distinctive atmosphere: these were
special Jews with special privileges. A separate division of the
Jewish post office and a well-staffed medical clinic were set up
by the Germans for their exclusive use.

The new arrivals would have nothing to do with the "Ghetto-
Jews." They looked upon their residence in the ghetto as some-

thing transient. They explained that they had left their possessions in Germany in the safekeeping of German friends. After the war they would go home and get everything back In the meantime, though some of them worked in the factories alongside the "Ghetto-Jews," they kept aloof. Many of them received food parcels from friends in Germany. Some had sons serving in the German Army.

A few of them were completely Aryan except for some compromising Jewish blood due to the incautious marriage of a grandparent or great-grandparent. They brought along their own pastor to conduct Christian services for them. When their pastor died, the Germans forced the Judenrat, in violation of Jewish religious law, to bury him in the Jewish cemetery.

The Czech Jews for the most part were not as optimistic as the German. They were troubled by the fact that at home the Nazis had burned their synagogues, while here in the ghetto they had been provided with a synagogue for themselves. They were more inclined to fear, like the Jews of the ghetto, that the Nazis were planning a bloody end for all of us.

At about the same time, shortly after the night of April 17, many gypsies were brought into the ghetto from Russia, Germany, Rumania, Poland, Hungary, and other countries. Some of them were locked in the ghetto jail.

It appeared to us that the Germans were making the ghetto an assembly point for all the "inferior races" whom they had decided to exterminate. This feeling was by no means shared by everyone in the ghetto. Many wanted to read into the fact that Jews from many countries were being collected in the ghetto a German plan to create a sort of reservation for Europe's Jews. After all, the new arrivals could have been killed in their native lands. If the Germans intended to kill them, why all the trouble and expense of transporting them to the Warsaw ghetto?

All this was material for the rumors which served the ghetto— cut off completely from the world—as a substitute for news.

The feeling of expectancy, of nervous waiting for an unknown but certain catastrophe, grew when the Germans began a new campaign of terror. From time to time in the past they had seized people on the streets and shipped them away into forced labor. After April 17, such abductions took place much more often and with much greater ferocity. The Jewish police, led by SS men and gendarmes, would descend on a ghetto area like a band of wild animals, grabbing every adult man and throwing him into a circle of armed guards in the center of the street. Ringed by the police, numbed by fear and bewilderment, the condemned would huddle there, waiting to be escorted to the nearest police commissariat and then to the freight cars for forced labor. Where? According to the German officials, they were being sent to Smolensk on the Eastern Front, where many men were needed to build fortifications, bridges, and roads. "Let the damned Jews stop milling around in the overcrowded ghetto! Let them be put to work!"

During such raids the streets would fill with dreadful sounds—the shrieking of women, the crying of children, the cursing and shouting of the police.

From the window of my hiding place at 13 Gensha I once witnessed a horrifying scene. A Jewish policeman held a thin young man, hatless, with matted black hair, who fought with insane fury to break loose from his captor's grasp. There was a mad look in the victim's eyes as he punched and kicked and pulled. With a rubber truncheon the policeman beat his hands, his legs, his entire body and then half pushed, half dragged him toward the square where the armed ring was waiting.

The ghetto police commissariats were besieged day and night by relatives of the wretches collected there. The commissioner of the ghetto, Herr Auerswald, finally announced that he would allow relatives to be out as late as midnight to bring food packages to the forced laborers.

This was the only time that the curfew was set aside in the

ghetto. Nevertheless, people were afraid to venture out after hours. Only those who had to bring food to an abducted loved one dared to go into the dark streets.

During this short campaign thousands upon thousands were brutally torn from their homes. Throughout the ghetto the air vibrated day and night with the wailing of broken families. There was hardly a home that did not weep over the loss of a dear one.

Apart from the seizures, the ghetto was kept at a fever pitch of terror by repeated, almost constant, indiscriminate massacres in the open streets in broad daylight. The sound of gunfire, now from one section, now from another, but especially near the bridge connecting the small and greater ghettos, became commonplace. SS men would stroll down the main streets shooting at Jews for the fun of it and leaving their targets where they fell.

At night the shooting would continue. The morning would reveal scores of bodies from which all identifying documents had been removed. In the case of women it was even difficult to determine whether the corpses were Jewish.

The terror was particularly severe in the districts near the ghetto walls where smuggling activities were concentrated. Approaching too close to the wall often meant immediate death on suspicion of smuggling.

The Germans seemed intent on destroying among the Jews any hope of maintaining contact with the outside world. They wanted to demonstrate that we were buried alive in a ghetto-grave from which no escape was possible.

It was rumored that Himmler had arrived in Warsaw with the Aussiedelung Brigades, whose work was liquidating Jewish communities and deporting the inhabitants. Crazy stories circulated through the ghetto about these brigades, composed of Germans, Ukrainians, and Letts, specially trained for their contemptible role, and about how they had done their work in other ghettos. The Jews called them *Vernichtung* (extermination) brigades.

Then it was rumored that the Aussiedelung Brigades had been

APRIL TO JULY 1942

sent away, thanks to liberal bribes distributed among Gestapo officials.

Wild tales, born in a miasma of stark terror, continued to circulate, each day's crop contradicting that of the day before. All of them underlined the inescapable feeling produced by the terror: that events were rapidly building toward a terrible climax, that the new catastrophe would dwarf everything that had gone before, that we were approaching the end of the ghetto—and beyond lay only chaos and annihilation.

In this steadily worsening situation we faced the life-and-death question, what are we to do?

We of the Bund knew what we *should* do. Immediately after the terrible night of April 17, 1942, we had set before us the slogan, "Resistance to the Death—Arm!" But even though we were in close contact with the Polish underground, we had not been able to obtain weapons anywhere. Meanwhile every hour of every day increased the terror.

During the night of July 18 the Nazis arrested more than a hundred prominent Jewish leaders, including many doctors and several members of the Judenrat. Among those seized was Jashunski, vice-chairman of the Judenrat, a prominent scientist, a writer for the *Volkszeitung* (the prewar daily of the Bund), director of the ORT, and one of the most inspiring personalities among the Jews.

On July 20 a gang of high Gestapo officials marched into the offices of the Judenrat with revolvers and riding crops in their hands. They assembled the Judenrat and announced that labor was needed on the Eastern front. The Gestapo had decided to send the ghetto's nonproductive inhabitants to fill this need. The Judenrat must cooperate in the *aussiedelung* of these nonproductive people, whom they estimated at sixty thousand.

The deportation was to be carried out in the next few days at the rate of ten thousand a day. The Judenrat was to post a notice announcing the *aussiedelung* and to order all those who fell within the nonproductive classification to report voluntarily at the Umschlagplatz at the corner of Stavki and Djika Streets, right near the railroad siding and the waiting freight cars. Any interference with the expulsion operation would be promptly punished by the death of all the hostages arrested on the night of July 18.

The Umschlagplatz, the transfer point, was where the final "selection" would take place. The Nazis would determine who would be deported and who would remain.

Umschlagplatz—the name and the place were to burn themselves deep into the soul of every Jew in the Warsaw ghetto.

The next day, as the Gestapo had demanded, the Judenrat posted the notice, signed by Adam Cherniakov. The proclamation threw the ghetto into a turmoil of excited debate. We of the Bund were sure that this was a disguise for extermination. We urged resistance by any and every means. Others were willing to accept the official version: that all that was intended was the removal of the sixty thousand nonproductive ghetto Jews to places where their work would be useful to the Germans, and that those who remained in the ghetto would be able to continue their miserable existence in peace. But although the official version was accepted, it was not really believed. It was the mirage that everyone tried hard to see; the truth was too horrible.

We had plenty of evidence on which to base our pessimism: the reports from Chelmno and Belzhitz, the stories of the death-cars tightly packed with Jews and hermetically sealed, the mass shootings in the towns and villages.

There was one more ominous sign. The Judenrat had suggested that its own labor department could organize and supply the necessary contingent of workers. The Nazis refused to consider such a solution. They declared that once and for all they were going to clear the ghetto of the nonproductive elements who were a heavy burden on the population in these times of hunger and scarcity. But why was it necessary to bypass the Judenrat in carrying out the deportation? It could only frighten the ghetto and stimulate the wildest rumors. It was clear to us that the deportation plan was only a pretext and that in reality the Nazi intentions were much more horrible.

Our arguments had little effect. The will to live was so strong that it created the illusions necessary to sustain it. People tried to convince themselves that all that was intended was a deportation of sixty thousand and then set about to avoid being among the sixty thousand.

In panic everyone hunted for a working card to prove that he was employed somewhere, was productive, and did not come within the deportable classification. Without some such document even a skilled worker was lost. Great sums of money, diamonds, gold jewelry, whatever one could lay hands on, were used to buy a working card, a permit to enter a factory. People paid Germans and Volksdeutsche tremendous sums for their influence in obtaining licenses to become partners in shops and factories. Some bought machinery from the Germans and opened up various kinds of small manufacturing establishments.

False-working-card mills sprang up. We ourselves established a counterfeiting plant to forge working cards. Since the employees of Zhitos, the Judenrat, and similar institutions were exempt from deportation, we duplicated their credentials and distributed them among comrades who had no papers. A working card became a talisman against death.

Within a few days after the proclamation the ghetto was sharply and visibly divided into two categories: the productive, the fortunate, the reprieved; and the unproductive, the unfortunate, the condemned.

We could see no obvious line of action. For three or four months our comrades in the militia had been in a state of partial mobilization, preparing for active resistance. At any hour we expected to hear that the long-awaited shipment of arms had arrived. But we knew that armed resistance would doom the whole ghetto instead of only sixty thousand. And who, no matter how convinced that the whole ghetto was doomed in any case, could take upon himself the responsibility for precipitating such a catastrophe?

On July 23, the day after the beginning of the deportations, representatives of the Bund and of organizations close to it met to consider the problem. A general conference of all Jewish groups was scheduled to meet that afternoon to consider a course of action for the ghetto. We assembled in Etkin's apartment on Leshno Street to instruct our delegates. All of us felt that active resistance and obstruction of the deportations was the only possible course. The ghetto had no right to sacrifice sixty thousand human beings so that the survivors might continue their slave existence a little longer. Whether we could obtain weapons or not, we owed it to ourselves to resist, with bare hands if necessary. We could do at least some damage to the Germans by setting fire to the factories and warehouses inside the ghetto. Would it not be better to die in the flames than to wait our inevitable turn to follow the unfortunate sixty thousand?

But how would the hundreds of thousands who were not immediately threatened with deportation react to such a proposal? Would they consent to mass suicide? Had we not ourselves conspired to obtain, and even forged, work cards for many people? After we had showed them this tiny ray of hope, would they permit us to snuff it out?

We saw no other choice. We finally resolved unanimously that we must ask the ghetto conference not to permit the deportations, to organize an unremitting resistance to the death, to ask the ghetto Jews to die now, honorably, as heroes, and not to permit themselves to be led sheeplike to slaughter at the convenience of their murderers. In this spirit we instructed Orzech and Blum to represent us.

Until close to the hour of curfew we waited for our delegates to return. When, finally, they came back, they reported that they had presented and defended our viewpoint at the conference but only the delegates of Hechalutz and Hashomer Hatzair had supported us. The overwhelming majority had given way to the general feeling of panic. They had persisted in clinging to the illusion that nothing more was intended than the deportation of sixty thousand to labor battalions In view of the temper of the great majority, it was impossible for us, on our own responsibility, to call for general active resistance.

We decided to urge the sixty thousand to do what little they could: not to report voluntarily at the Umschlagplatz, to go into hiding, to fight the police at every step. Morizi Orzech wrote our proclamation, which was printed in a new illegal bulletin, *Storm*. It said in part.

Jews, you are being deceived. Do not believe that you are being sent to work and nothing else. Actually you are being led to your deaths. This is the devilish continuation of the campaign of extermination which has already been carried out in the provinces. Do not let them take you to death voluntarily. Resist! Fight tooth and nail. Do not report to the Umschlagplatz. Fight for your lives!

Storm was widely distributed and posted on the streets. In three or four days it was necessary to turn out three additional printings.

FOUR

IN FRONT of the jail on Gensha Street stood rows of Jewish police; behind them were armed Germans, Ukrainians, and Letts. The street soon filled with a ragged mob whose starved yellow faces bobbed up and down as they strained to get a better view.

The jail was being emptied—liquidated. All the prisoners, among them many already sentenced to death for smuggling or other offenses, were being deported. The mob crowded closer. Everyone wanted to see who would be led from the jail, what condition they would be in, where they would be taken.

Suddenly there was shooting. The Nazis dispersed the crowd, shouting, "*Raus! Weg!*" The street was cleared quickly, but not for long. Again the people collected, against the walls, at the courtyard gates, on the streetcorners, warily edging closer.

The prisoners were led into the street between two rows of police with outstretched rifles. Bedlam broke loose. Shouts, screams, questions, hysterical farewells were thrown across the police barrier. As the prisoners were marched down the street, the crowd—mostly women and children and old people—followed along, held off on both sides by the police. There was more shooting. A few dead and wounded fell as the crowd melted away.

For a few moments the street was empty. Then it filled again.

From time to time one of the prisoners would break from the ranks and try to lose himself in the crowd. The police would seize him, beat him with their rifle butts, and push him, bloodied as he was, back into the procession. If he no longer had the strength to walk he was tossed into a cart. The column continued on its way to the waiting freight cars at the Umschlagplatz.

At the same time, the police were busy at the places where the homeless congregated—those who had not been able to find lodgings, the refugees from the provinces who were too late to find a corner in the overcrowded ghetto. Like madmen, the Jewish police, the SS men, the gendarmes, dragged them into the line of march. Sick and aged, women and children, were pursued like dogs and thrown into the wagons, receiving a thorough beating in the process. Here and there shooting cleared the streets of spectators.

In the confusion many bystanders found themselves on the wrong side of the police cordons.

A woman ran after a wagon, screaming hysterically. Her child had been taken. Her more prudent friends tried to restrain her, but she broke away. She followed the wagon, weeping bitterly. Finally a German, with the air of one whose patience has been overtaxed, walked up to her, beat her, and threw her into the wagon.

The legend that work was waiting at the end of the railway journey lost any validity during the next few days, when the orphanages and boarding institutions for children were liquidated. The beggars, the sick and weak who lay about the streets, were also taken. These were nonproductive elements, no doubt, but what sort of labor could be waiting for such deportees?

The panic grew from hour to hour.

And then Adam Cherniakov made his final gesture as president of the Judenrat. He was one of those who had clung strongly to the illusion that the deportation would end with the sixty thousand nonproductive. After the first few days, when even the sick and weak had been dragged from the jails, when orphanages had been emptied, the homeless taken, he began to understand that the Germans had bigger things in mind. He saw that they were only pretending to deal through the Judenrat; that the request for ten thousand a day was a mere formality. Actually the Germans were taking people without regard to the agreed plan. There was no longer any talk of sixty thousand. Who could tell whether the Germans themselves were bothering to keep count? He saw that the Germans were making him responsible for their acts in the eyes of the ghetto, making it appear that the Judenrat was expelling the nonproductive, liquidating the orphans and the feeble. Cherniakov finally understood. He took poison.

In his place the Germans appointed Lichtenbaum, an engineer. Over Lichtenbaum's signature a proclamation was posted asking people to report voluntarily for labor deportation, with their families, so that no household need be split up. As an added inducement each "voluntary" family would receive three kilograms of bread and one kilogram of marmalade per person. These were to be provided by the Judenrat at its own expense.

It was rumored, with the encouragement of the Jewish and German officials, that letters had been received from those already deported saying that they were working and well-fed. Such letters had come to Warsaw, so they said, from Brest-Litovsk, Kobrin, and even from Minsk.

The hunger, the despair, the miserable uncertain ghetto existence drove many to put their faith in the official rumors and the promises of the Judenrat. They would not listen to any accounts of the slaughter in the provinces. Munching bread and marmalade on the way to labor and a better life was too appealing. Hundreds, even thousands, presented themselves willingly at the Umschlagplatz with their bundles and valises. They took whatever they could carry from the poverty of their homes. The religious brought their prayer shawls and phylacteries; the artisans their tools. The German beasts were not even so kind as to limit the amount of baggage. Everything was done to bolster the fantasy that the Jews were being taken out of the overcrowded ghetto, away from hunger and epidemics, to work under happier conditions.

The German and Czech Jews were evacuated in a body. They were ordered to report with all their property at the Umschlagplatz. All the rickshas were commandeered to help them move. The procession started from the Tlomatzky Synagogue and from 84 Leshno Street. It was a strange sight, even for the ghetto. Long rows of rickshas, piled high with fine leather suitcases, beautiful bedding, and expensive household effects rolled down the street. Sitting in them or walking alongside were the self-assured, respectable, well-dressed German and Czech Jews. All of them, without exception, allowed themselves to be evacuated. They had consistently remained aloof, refusing to mingle with the other Jews, although they lived within the confines of the ghetto. They had considered themselves a superior society, not to be compared to the "Eastern Jews," and they knew little or nothing of the rumors, discussions, wrangling, and doubts aroused by the deportations.

The Nazis practiced a similar deception on the *Ausländer*, the Jews who held passports of neutral countries. (These were frequently obtained through Gestapo officials for tremendous bribes.) The Nazis ordered all people holding foreign passports to report to the Paviak jail with all their belongings. Among them were Neustadt, one of the directors of the Joint Distribution Committee, and the well-known Jewish actress, Clara Segalowitz. All the *Ausländer* were taken by special train to an unknown destination, which we later discovered to be precisely the same as that of the other deportees.

While calling for volunteers and deceiving the *Ausländer*, the Nazis directed a terrifying human hunt in the ghetto. The Jewish police would block off entire sections and break into the houses, searching, rummaging, seeking out hiding places, and dragging thousands of victims to the Umschlagplatz. The hunt would start at seven in the morning and end at six in the evening.

It was horrible to watch. Children hung on to their fathers, wives to their husbands. They grabbed at pieces of furniture, door-jambs, anything to keep from being dragged away by the police. They clawed at their captors, fighting against death with hopeless desperation. All day, somewhere, one could hear the sounds of the gruesome chase. The cries and weeping of the unfortunates were mixed with the violent abuse and the wild shouts of the police.

Some, who had money, were able to bribe the police, to buy some time, while the hunt went on, perhaps to reach them again tomorrow.

At the Umschlagplatz, in the early days of the deportations, the so-called selections took place. The Nazis, whips in hand, would walk along the rows of cringing candidates, selecting with practiced eyes the aged, the weak, the obviously sick.

The crippled were separated and, we learned later, sent directly to the Jewish Cemetery on Okopova Street. There they were shot and thrown into a mass grave without even the formality of registering their identity.

A second small category was selected for work near Warsaw at Rembertov and other near-by points. The existence of this group tended to bolster the illusion that the deportations were actually for work.

A third category, the great majority of those who "volunteered" or were captured, was put into freight cars at the Umschlagplatz. Two trains manned by German crews and guarded by German and Ukrainian soldiers left the railroad siding each day and traveled in the direction of Malkina and Sokolov.

We were certain that these trainloads of unfortunates were going to their death. We had sufficient evidence to believe that this was the real truth behind the deportations, and we did not cease our warnings to the ghetto. But where were they being taken? Where were these people being killed? How was this grisly work being done?

For the difficult task of getting more exact information, we appointed Zalman Friedrych, one of the most daring and tireless individuals in the underground. He was a strong, well-built, athletic, handsome young man who looked like a German propagandist's dream of the blond Aryan.

A Polish Socialist, a railroad worker, who often traveled the line and knew the direction taken by the deportation trains, advised Friedrych which route to investigate. With great difficulty Friedrych finally reached Sokolov. There he learned that the Germans had constructed a small branch railroad to the village of Treblinka. Each day trains packed with Jews were switched onto the new spur. At Treblinka there was a large camp divided into two sections, one for Jews, one for Poles. The residents of Sokolov had heard that terrible things were happening in Treblinka, but they had no precise information.

In Sokolov Friedrych stumbled upon our comrade, Azriel Wallach, Maxim Litvinov's nephew, who had just escaped from Treblinka. He was in terrible shape, badly bruised, bleeding, his clothes in shreds. From Wallach, Friedrych learned that all the Jews brought to Treblinka were immediately put to death. They were unloaded from the trains and told they were to be bathed and cleaned before being taken to their quarters and assigned to work. Then they were led into large hermetically sealed chambers and gassed. Wallach had been picked up in Warsaw. He had been shipped to Treblinka but had been spared from immediate death to work at cleaning up the freight cars, and had managed to escape.

With this information, Friedrych returned to Warsaw. We immediately published the gruesome report in a special edition of *Storm*. We were thus able to give the ghetto an eyewitness account of what actually happened to the daily trainloads of deportees.

Once again *Storm* warned: "Do not be deceived. Throw off your illusions! You are being taken to death and extermination.

Do not let them destroy you! Do not give yourselves voluntarily into the hands of your executioners."

It was the end of July. I still lived at 13 Gensha Street in Manya Wasser's apartment.

The terror generated by the deportations paralyzed the will, and the frightful sounds of the merciless hunt corroded the mind. The unnatural noises were always with us—the shouting, whistling, and shooting of the pursuers, the screams of struggling victims or the shrieking protests of their families, the whimpering and moaning of the bereaved after the cyclone had destroyed their little world and passed on to the next house or the next street.

The same scenes occurred day after day. From seven in the morning until six in the evening there were raids, blockades, shootings in the street, death marches to the Umschlagplatz. Some bit and clawed and fought back at their captors. Some went meekly, stupidly, their insane eyes glazed in merciful incomprehension.

Our tenement was blockaded several times. Because they worked in a clothing factory and each had that indispensable license to live, a working card, Mrs. Wasser and her daughter Anusia were secure for the time being. Her brother-in-law, who had lived with us, had already fallen into the dragnet. I had managed to save myself several times by hiding, not daring to rely upon the forged Zhitos working card in my pocket.

At eight o'clock one morning we heard the wild rush of heavy boots, accompanied by shooting, shouts, and screaming: pandemonium again. Our house was blockaded. Through all the entrances, over all the stairways, poured the Jewish police. The building resounded with the sounds of smashing doors and shattering windows.

They were at my door. I was caught off guard with no place to hide.

Before I had time to think, a Jewish policeman burst through the door. I showed him my card from Zhitos. He told me to go downstairs. My papers would be examined there. If everything was in order I would be set free.

I went down into the jammed courtyard and elbowed my way toward the gate. It was blocked by police. I showed my card, stuffed a hundred zlotys into a policeman's hand, and a moment later I was "free," on the other side of the gate. I was soaked with perspiration. My breath came in gasps.

I hurried toward the central office of Zhitos at 25 Novolipky Street. Abrasha Blum spotted me from the window and ran out of the Zhitos building to scold me for daring to leave the house. I told him what had happened. My hiding place was now useless; I must find a new place to live.

I was taken directly to Comrade Etkin's apartment on Leshno, where I had lived before. In the morning Sonya Novogrodsky was also brought there. Since she and I were man and wife on a foreign passport, it was simpler for us to be together. Perhaps that foreign passport would come in handy at the last moment.

For four or five days we lay hidden in Etkin's apartment. Every morning from our window which looked out on Ogrodova we watched the Jewish police assemble in front of their headquarters. Armed with clubs, they were divided into two groups. One marched out of the police yard through a gate into Leshno in the greater ghetto. The second went through Ogrodova in the direction of the Zhelasna bridge to the small ghetto. So began each day's bloody chase.

It was painful to watch them. My heart sank and my eyes filled with tears when I saw among these Jewish hunting dogs, employees of the Judenrat wearing armbands with the legend "*Aussiedelungs Hilfe.*"

The Germans had demanded that all employees of the social institutions who were exempt from deportation assist the Jewish police in carrying out their grim assignments. Whoever failed to do so would face deportation himself. Delegates from all social institutions, such as Zhitos, Centos, and Tos had met to determine their course. After long and painful debate, they had voted against any participation in the selection. The employees of the Judenrat, however, had accepted the shameful job. Now I watched them run with the pack—hounds pursuing their own brothers, even their own parents.

Another blockade—and again I was caught off guard. A drunken Ukrainian, his eyes bloodshot, broke in, seized Sonya and me, and pulled us down the stairs toward the Leshno exit where the police cordon stood. When we reached the first floor the drunk broke into another apartment for no apparent reason, leaving us on the landing. Sonya and I made a break for the courtyard, toward a small door in the fence.

We sneaked through into a court on Ogrodova. There I met an acquaintance, once a member of the Transport Workers, who was now the janitor of the building. He agreed to run the risk of hiding us. We lay hidden for several hours until the neighborhood became quiet.

In the evening we left and headed toward Smotcha, not knowing where to go. One thought drove us faster and faster from Ogrodova: to get as far away as possible from the headquarters of the Jewish police, to reach Smotcha and the more crowded part of the ghetto before curfew.

At Smotcha we ran into more shooting. We made a dash for the near-by apartment of Mrs. Buks, a manager of one of our soup kitchens and one of the finest women in the ghetto. Her apartment was already overcrowded and it was evident that we could not stay. Before curfew we managed to make our way to the apartment of Laible Kersh and his wife, in the tremendous Jewish Post Office Building which extended from Gensha and Zamenhof to Volinska Street.

Kersh was a member of the praesidium of the executive committee of the ghetto trade unions and had formerly been secretary of the Socialist Artisans' Union. Now he was working in the Tebbens factory in the small ghetto and was very active in the Bund underground.

The Kersh apartment seemed to be an excellent refuge, so Loeser Clog was also brought there. That day he had lost his wife and his little granddaughter to the selection gangs.

We settled down for what we hoped would be a long stay. At night we all slept in the apartment, but during the day, when Laible and his wife were at work, Sonya, Loeser and I would generally crawl up to the garret. It extended under the roof of the entire building and was generously supplied with nooks and corners in which to hide. It was cluttered with old trunks, cast-off furniture, and miscellaneous junk covered with dust and cobwebs. It was ideal. Besides, from the attic we had an excellent view of everything that took place in the street, particularly on the Volinska side, where there was a large shrapnel hole in the wall.

We would lie for hours at our little observation points, unable to tear our eyes from the streets below. Groups of Germans, Ukrainians, and Jewish police, armed with axes and crowbars, roamed about, smashing doors and windows, hunting for human loot. Wherever they went, they stole whatever was valuable enough to carry away. The near-by streets were deserted. Only the dull blows of the axes and crowbars broke the fearful silence. Now and then we would see dead or badly wounded bodies lying unattended in the street.

Once our attention was drawn by horrible screams from the roof of a building across Gensha Street. They came from a smoking chimney. "Help! Save me! I am burning!"

Some poor devil had dashed to the roof to escape the hounds and, fearing that his hiding place was too exposed, had let himself down into the chimney. Unfortunately someone had started a fire. The smoke was suffocating. He was unable to climb out, and to drop was certain death in the flames.

Firemen made their way to the roof and with great difficulty extricated the half-burned wretch from the chimney.

During those days Sonya was terribly depressed and agitated. She would have attacks of nerves, screaming that we must give ourselves up, that we must not make exceptions of ourselves. From time to time we received word of close friends and comrades who had fallen victims to the selection gangs. All this deepened her depression. To occupy her thoughts and divert her from the terrible things around us, we got her to play solitaire. It was at least something to do.

About ten days after we had moved into the Kersh apartment, we were sitting around the table drinking tea. Sonya was dutifully laying out her game of solitaire. Suddenly we heard the unmistakable sounds of a raid. The clatter of boots, the gunfire and wild shouting drew closer. We rushed for the attic, crawled into dark corners, pulled some junk around us, and waited. Now we could hear sounds from our apartment. The pursuers were close.

Suddenly a horrible fact dawned on me, and my heart sank. We had left our glasses of hot tea and Sonya's card game on the table. The devils could not be so stupid as to overlook such evidence.

They weren't. Someone was climbing the attic stairs. The door creaked open. A Jewish policeman stuck his head in, looked cautiously around, and walked in, moving carefully and flashing his light around him.

He was moving directly toward me, but I was well hidden. When he was close enough, I leaped at him and seized him by the throat. He went completely limp in my hands, paralyzed with fear.

Sonya ran from her hiding place and shouted hysterically, "Don't kill him! Don't kill him!"

I loosened my grip. He began to sob and plead for his life. He would do nothing to us if only we would let him go. A second Jewish policeman entered. I released the first. I told them we would not allow ourselves to be taken alive. If they tried to take us it would be our lives or theirs. The second bloodhound hesitated a moment. Then almost apologetically, he said that they could go back without us only if they took something of value to share with the Ukrainians waiting below. Sonya handed him five hundred zlotys, and they left.

Our hiding place was now exposed. We would have had to leave soon in any case. In mid-August the Germans ordered all Jews to clear out of the small ghetto. The inhabitants had two days to move into the greater ghetto. Whoever remained after that time without a special permit would be shot out of hand. The Judenrat was preparing to move all of its offices in the small ghetto into the Jewish Post Office building in the greater ghetto. All tenants, including our host Laible Kersh, were being dispossessed.

We debated where to go. It was finally agreed that Comrades Kersh and Mirmelstein, both of whom worked in the small ghetto at the Tebbens factory, would arrange to procure work cards from the factory for Sonya, Loeser Clog, and me. These would give us the right to live in the small ghetto in the neighborhood of the factory.

Comrade Gepner from Lodz was manager of the Tebbens storehouse. His son, Avrahm, a blond handsome youth who looked German, was a member of the Werkschutz—the uniformed factory guards. We arranged for Avrahm to escort us to the new hiding place prepared in the small ghetto.

It was a journey through hell. This was the second and last

day of the heartbreaking migration. The streets were scenes of horrible tragedy; they reminded us of those days long, long ago when the Germans had established the Warsaw ghetto.

Over all the streets and alleys which led into the greater ghetto, over the bridge at Chlodna and Zhelasna which tied the two ghettos together, moved thick masses of people. Their clothes were in tatters; their sallow faces were drawn and emaciated; their eyes stared stupidly and dully. They bent under packs of household odds and ends. They tugged at carts loaded with their possessions. Some carried children, little bundles of skin and bones, in their arms. Old people, crying and whimpering, struggled to keep up with the young. Here and there someone led a cow.

From time to time the steadily moving mass was startled by the sound of gunfire. Most of the shooting took place at the bridge, where the crowding was particularly great. The fear of death hung over all like a whiplash, driving them faster and faster over the bridge into the greater ghetto. Would they now have peace? Would this migration be the last? No one even thought about such things. Everyone was stupefied, indifferent, bewildered, helpless. There was no more strength to endure and no more hope for deliverance. Who would have believed, a short time before, that such things could happen to anyone, anywhere?

There was one difference between the earlier establishment of the ghetto and the present liquidation of the small ghetto. Then everyone had hunted frantically for a place to live, for any corner to make a home amid the terrible congestion. Now that was no problem. Space in the greater ghetto was plentiful. Hundreds and thousands of its inhabitants had moved, through the Umschlagplatz, to the gas chambers. Their apartments were empty, their belongings abandoned. The remaining candidates for extermination were free to take possession of the empty dwellings.

Avrahm led us against the stream of humanity pouring out of

the small ghetto. We made our way from Zamenhof through Novolipky, Karmelitzka, Leshno, Zhelasna, Grzibovska, Twarda, Tchepla, to Walizov Street. We worked our way through the crowd, between pushcarts and rickshas, among the dead and wounded who littered the street.

We finally made it over the bridge with the Tebbens work cards in our pockets. But one thought kept returning to us: Was all this worth it? A feeling of despair pressed on our hearts. What we had built with so much labor and blood was finished. A people, with all its works, all its traditions, all its hopes, was being destroyed. Only instinct kept us going, struggling against the inevitable. Each of us was driven only by a physiological will to live—we knew it was hopeless.

Our forged work cards were intended only to get us into the factory area. It was unthinkable that we could go into the factory to work. We dared not be seen by any of the few thousand workers, many of whom knew us well, or by the German officials and police. Again we had to bury ourselves alive in a hiding place.

We were taken to the three-room apartment of Comrade Gallant, who worked as a tailor in the factory. Here eleven of us, including Laible Kersh and his wife, Loeser Clog, Sonya Novogrodsky, and myself, made our home.

Loeser, Sonya, and I lay hidden day and night, never daring to leave the house. Those who went to work got two bowls of soup and a piece of bread each day. They would still our hunger with whatever they could bring back for us. Rushka Berkman, Laible's sister, worked in the factory kitchen and managed to sneak out an occasional potato or a crust of bread. Everyone did his best to share every morsel with us.

During the days when the inhabitants of the small ghetto were being driven into the greater ghetto there was an air of uneasy peace; there were no deportations. For a few days we did not see the repulsive faces of the Aussiedelung squads; apparently we were rid of them, and of their street-hunts and blockades. The deportations appeared to have finally ended. The nightmarish fog began to lift.

But the meaning of the short respite became clear in a few days. We received word of a new extermination campaign in the Otvotsk resort district outside of Warsaw. The summer resort towns were dotted with small improvised ghettos surrounded by barbed wire. In this area were many rest homes and sanatoriums, among them the Centos Orphanage. A hospital for the mentally sick, the Yusefuffka, had been located there until the inmates were slaughtered by the Germans and the institution transformed into a rest home for tubercular cases. There, too, was our own Medem Sanatorium for children. All of these institutions were supported by the Jewish welfare organizations of the Warsaw ghetto.

During their short absence from Warsaw, the brigades of murderers deported from the Otvotsk district every Jew and the inmates of every Jewish institution—orphanages, sanatoriums, and children's homes, with their entire personnel. All were taken in sealed freight cars in the same direction as the Warsaw deportees —to Treblinka.

Hardened though we were by this time to tales of horror, we listened incredulously to the fragmentary story of the destruction of our most beloved institution, the Medem Sanatorium in Myedzeshyn. At the sanatorium there were more than a hundred children, as well as teachers and a medical and technical staff. Early on a beautiful mid-August morning, as the children still lay in their beds, the buildings were surrounded by the fully armed Aussiedelung Brigades.

The youngsters were awakened by the command, "Everyone in the sanatorium must assemble in the yard immediately."

They began to cry. They refused to go willingly; they held on to their beds, to windows, doors, tables, anything that offered

127

an anchor. They bit the hands of their murderers, kicked, scratched, fought back.

Trucks jammed with weeping children and sobbing teachers and nurses were driven to the railroad line at Myedzeshyn. From there they were taken to Treblinka.

A few comrades managed to escape by hiding in the cellar. Among them were Manya Ziegelboim, Artur's wife, and her son, both of whom were to die later in the ghetto uprising. Chaim, Anja, and Perele Ellenbogen, now all alive in Sweden, also escaped at Myedzeshyn.

Friedman, a teacher, escaped into the woods and wandered about for several days, half-crazed, hungry, and exhausted. Mrs. Friedman, who looked like a typical village Christian and could have saved herself, refused to leave her husband, though he had been driven insane by the experience. Finally both fell into the hands of the Germans and were shot.

Several others managed to escape, but most of the teachers and technicians shared the fate of the children and went with them to death. Especially courageous among those who perished was Rose Eichner. She comforted the children and quieted them. She gathered a group of them around her and climbed into the truck with them. With her went her daughter, who was a nurse, and her younger son.

The destruction of the Medem Sanatorium was a hard blow to bear. Great effort and sacrifice had gone into building and maintaining that little oasis in the bleak lives of our children. To us it had been the only ray of hope that something would remain out of this holocaust, some seed that held the promise of a new life for our people.

The dreadful news of what had happened at the sanitorium was confirmed by word from Morizi Orzech. Only two steps ahead of the Gestapo, he had just escaped to the Aryan side to carry out his mission of informing the world of the events in the Warsaw ghetto.

128

Now the blockades and raids began all over again with even greater ferocity. To speed the bloody business, the Germans worked out a plan which would not have occurred to the devil himself. They issued an order directing every member of the Jewish police to bring seven people for deportation each day. Failure to do so would result in the deportation of the policeman himself.

The ghetto became a bloody bedlam. Each day, to save his own skin, every Jewish policeman brought seven sacrificial lives to the extermination altar. He brought whomever he could catch—friends, relatives, even members of his immediate family. There were policemen who offered their own aged parents, with the excuse that they would die soon anyhow.

I have no words with which to picture the life of the ghetto during those days. All of us looked upon ourselves as living corpses, as ghosts who no longer belonged to this world. Our every thought and every word was about death. Death seemed to be the only way to escape from the indescribable hell in which we lived.

Sonya and I spent hours in morbid conversation about death. Our thoughts turned to our sons and to our desire to say good-by to them before the end came. Sonya's son, Mark, was in the United States; mine was somewhere en route, in Japan or China.

Both Sonya and I had leather wallets, presents from people who were very dear to us. Hers had come from her sister in Mexico; I had received mine from Shloime Mendelsohn, who had brought it from New York some years before. We exchanged them, and we promised that if either lived he would give the memento to the other's son: I would give Sonya's to Mark; she would give mine to Jan.

One evening we learned that a "selection" in the factory proper and in the surrounding tenements was being prepared for the following morning. We had to act quickly. Our comrade Neumark, who was a gateman at the factory, made preparations to smuggle us into the factory and hide us there.

We sat up tensely all night, preparing for the ordeal. We resolved that we would not allow ourselves to be taken alive. We would resist by any means—better to be killed that way.

All night Sonya debated whether to accompany us. She kept playing with the idea that she ought to stay in the apartment, relying on her foreign passport and a forged document stating that she worked in the factory and was the wife of one of the managers. Perhaps, if worst came to worst, these papers would save her.

At dawn we made ready to leave for the factory. Neumark arrived. At the last moment Sonya made her decision—to remain in the apartment. Wordlessly Loeser and I bade her good-by and left.

We were taken through the factory gates and into the basement of one of the buildings. We found ourselves in a small room filled with cast-off machines and factory supplies. Neumark locked the door from the outside with a large padlock. Through a little crevice in the basement wall we could see a small portion of the factory yard.

At seven o'clock the whole area of the factory district was surrounded by SS, Ukrainians, and police. The night-shift workers, preparing to go home, were not permitted to leave. The day-shift workers were stopped at the gate and not permitted to enter. We could hear the wailing of women and children and the rough shouting of the murderers.

Through the narrow crack in the wall we watched the selection in the yard. SS men, headed by a leader in a uniform decorated with red braid, stood in rows. Past them shuffled the workers, worn-out and bleary-eyed after their night of heavy labor. We saw them walk to the right or to the left in response to the motion of a stick held in someone's hand. Those picked for the death camp were immediately seized and taken out to the street. Those who were to remain were led to one side of the yard

We lay in our little hole and watched. Our hearts beat wildly. The blood hammered in our temples. Our eyes were popping.

From the surrounding streets a tumult arose. Everyone was being driven out of the houses. The selection we had witnessed in the factory yard was being continued in the streets. The condemned were immediately surrounded by soldiers and police and marched off to the freight cars at the Umschlagplatz. Everywhere there was crying and shouting. Husbands tried to reach their wives, wives their husbands; they had been separated forever by the chance motion of a stick.

The inferno lasted until about two o'clock in the afternoon. About five hundred people were led away, among them many of our comrades. A sixty-six-year-old woman who lived with us crawled into a closet under the stairs and was overlooked. Our comrade Tzizik, a member of the Needle Trades Committee, later a partisan, now living in Warsaw, managed to sneak out of line when the group was led to the Umschlagplatz. Sonya was among the missing.

The news was sent immediately to the greater ghetto. Our comrades in the hospital near the Umschlagplatz made some attempts to save Sonya and the others But it was hopeless. Everyone had been shoved into the freight cars directly and taken away.

Loeser and I lay in our hole until four in the afternoon, when things became relatively quiet. Neumark unlocked the door and escorted us back to the apartment. From all the windows came sounds of weeping. In their grief people pounded their heads against the walls.

The comrades who remained were completely broken in spirit.

My nerves were at the snapping point. I had had all I could stand.

The executioner had destroyed the final illusion. The last charm, the last hope of life, the working card, was now worthless. The end was not far off.

Abrasha and Berek sent me a note from the greater ghetto telling me to come to them. Before leaving the factory I called together our closest comrades to discuss the new situation and the possibility of further activity. Everyone agreed that the tragedy was close to its bloody finale. How should we behave in these last terrible moments?

We resolved to prepare. We must maintain contact with every part of the factory, know it thoroughly and exactly. We must know where the supplies were kept—particularly the easily inflammable materials. In the event of another selection, we must not allow ourselves to be taken. The factory must be set afire. If we were to die, we must die leaving heaps of ruins. We must die in battle and not allow ourselves to be led to the slaughter like sheep. The comrades must stay together as much as possible; they must be constantly alert. The workers in the factory must be prepared to expect the worst and to act with us. All this would have to be done quietly and by each comrade individually as he saw fit, but the workers must be made to realize that no rescue was possible. That was the opinion of our meeting.

I said good-by to my comrades. In the morning I was to be taken to the greater ghetto.

That night Russian planes raided the city. Bombs hit 3 Djelna Street (formerly the Scala Theater) and 7 Djelna. The night shift at Tebbens stopped work and ran to the shelters. Even the Germans were panicked. The guard at the Umschlagplatz ran away and hid. Some deportees managed to escape.

The air raid raised our spirits and our hopes—but how much longer could we hold out?

Mirmelstein's son, who worked in the factory office, prepared an official letter for me, saying that I was a clerk at Tebbens' and was being sent to the greater ghetto to attend to various matters at the Tebbens factory there. Early the next morning young Kostek, a clerk at the factory, whose duties required periodic trips into the greater ghetto, came to take me with him. We passed the guards at the bridge with no difficulty and met Berek Snaidmil, who was waiting at the corner of Gensha and Zamenhof as arranged.

The atmosphere on the streets was taut with fear. Workers with bundles under their arms hurried to work, looking about them nervously and tensely, listening for any murmur, any sound. At this early hour it was somewhat safer to be on the street. The raids usually began after everyone was at work.

Berek took me to 31 Gensha Street, the temporary location of the Jewish Hospital's Nursing School, which was headed by Abrasha Blum's wife, Luba Byelitska. They locked me in the pantry, but only overnight. It was too dangerous to be there during the day. Every morning at dawn I climbed to the second story of a badly bombed building in the same courtyard, pulled the ladder up after me and settled down to wait for the day to end. I spent three days in this hiding place.

Abrasha Blum came to talk things over. He told me the decision of our comrades: I must leave the ghetto and go over to the Aryan side immediately. Our contacts with people outside the ghetto, on which we based all our hopes of getting weapons, had been badly disrupted by the intensified raids and deportations. My wide acquaintance among the Polish workers might enable me to make proper connections and solve the problem of procuring arms. In the ghetto I was only a burden. The comrades were devoting considerable effort to hiding me and running great risks to protect me.

Abrasha told me he had been at the Umschlagplatz twice during the few weeks of the deportations. Once he was able to steal out of line with the aid of the Jewish policeman Merenholtz, a member of the PPS, who often used to help us. This same Merenholtz later quit the police and escaped to the other side, where I met him.

The second time Abrasha had joined the deportees of his own accord. The entire personnel of the nursing school, including Luba Byelitska and their two children, had been seized. Hearing the news, Abrasha raced to the school. Under no circumstances would he leave his wife and children alone in the murderers' clutches. Fortunately, somebody, somehow, had managed to get the Germans to call off the deportation, and all were saved.

We returned to the problem of what I was to do. We weighed, we measured, we evaluated every factor involved in my staying or leaving. We finally concluded that I must get to the other side. Abrasha gave me a hundred dollars, which was all that could be spared from our badly depleted treasury, and left to arrange the details of my journey.

At seven the next morning Comrades Solnick and Schmuel Bankart the shoemaker took me to Schmuel's house on Stavki near Okopova, close to the ghetto gate. There I spent the day. That night we learned that a new selection had been announced for the following morning.

It was now September 5. Only about 120,000 to 130,000 Jews remained. The rest had already been exterminated.

The new selection was to be on a grand scale: it was not to take place in one section or one factory, but throughout the entire ghetto. It was to continue until every surviving ghetto Jew had been examined and his fate determined.

The orders were that all inhabitants, without exception, must be on the streets at six in the morning. They must gather at designated places, all of them close to the Umschlagplatz. Anyone found at home would be shot immediately. At dawn the entire district was occupied by SS men, Ukrainians, and Letts.

SEPTEMBER 1942

In the early morning my friends took me from Schmuel Bankart's apartment to the old Vronsky Tannery at 73 Stavki, which had become a German metalwork shop. A small door in the factory wall opened on a closed court, which was empty except for a large shack used as a storehouse for rags. From this courtyard a gate led to another courtyard bordering Okopova Street—on the Aryan side. This gate had played an important part in the food-smuggling economy of the ghetto. Through it smugglers had brought cows, oxen, horses, and other heavy contraband. Through it we, and the factory owner, Vronsky, hoped to reach the other side.

Our plans did not work out as we had expected. As Vronsky unlocked the factory door to the closed court, many of the workers surged along with us. No one wanted to be trapped in the selection. About eighty people broke into the courtyard, scared, excited, bewildered. The frightened janitor of the building on Okopova slammed the gate shut, increasing the panic on our side. Everyone rushed for a place to hide. The SS was expected to arrive at any moment to clear the factory.

The Nazis on the Okopova side heard the tumult in the factory yard and realized that Jews were trying to break out. They opened fire immediately and killed sixty people in the yard.

The Vronsky family, Simcha Solnick, Schmuel Bankart, and I managed to climb through a small window into the shack which stood in the yard. We burrowed into the rags and waited. We heard the shooting in the courtyard and, later, the noise of the factory being emptied as people were driven into the streets for the selection.

After dark we crawled out of the rags. We depended on Vronsky, who knew every nook and cranny of the factory, to direct us. We did not dare go back through the factory yard and the factory.

One end of the shack was alongside a court which led to Niska Street, still in the ghetto. Vronsky led us to that end of the shack and showed us, sunk in the floor under a pile of debris, an old tub which long ago had been used for soaking hides. Using whatever we could find, we began to dig it out. We spent many hours of hard digging before we managed to drag the tub from the ground. The deep hole it left gave us a good head start for a tunnel to the Niska court. We spent the better part of the night on our task. Finally we tunneled through, stuck our heads into the courtyard, found it empty, crawled out, and sank exhausted in the mud.

At dawn we entered the house on Niska, which we found completely abandoned. We washed ourselves and cleaned our clothes as well as we could. As soon as it was broad daylight we separated.

I walked the ghetto streets in a daze, not knowing where or to whom to go. I wandered among the people who were sitting out on the streets for the second day. They had assembled as they were ordered. Those who had friends living in the small prescribed area had spent the night with them. The great majority, however, had spent the night outdoors. Here and there someone boiled a kettle of water over an open fire or chewed a crust of dry bread. Most lay on the street, limply, with an air of resignation, waiting, waiting . . .

This last selection was being carried out with a refinement of the usual sadistic bestiality. The Nazis had found a new way to make Jews the murderers of their own brothers: to have them make a selection among themselves.

Every factory, every shop, every social institution—including the Jewish police—received a quota from the Nazi authorities. A specified number, considered by the Nazis necessary for the continued functioning of the organization, were to receive special tokens. The director of each organization had to decide, within the limit set by the Nazis, which of his subordinates should receive the talisman of life, and which should be condemned as "excess," "unnecessary." The holder of a token was to present it at the selection. It was not a guarantee that he would not be taken, but it would weigh in his favor. The final selection would be made by the Germans. The holders of tokens had some reason to hope; the others had no hope at all.

No one, perhaps, can imagine the torment of those whose task was to sift the lists and decide who was to be sacrificed.

At the selection area those without tokens who still had the strength of desperation ran wildly from one person to another, pleading, begging, hoping against hope that somehow they could still get the precious little slip of paper.

I wandered about aimlessly.

I met Anka Wolkowitz from Wlotslavek. She told me that some of our comrades were in an apartment at 51 Mila Street, waiting for the selection to get under way. She took me there. I found a small group, sitting with heads bowed on their bony hands. There was Leon Michelson with his wife and daughter, Damazer with his wife and daughter, and Victor Mendelsohn. For a long time nobody looked up. They just sat in absolute resignation.

Mrs. Damazer was the first to see me. "Comrade Bernard," she said, half questioning, "after all, one *can* have another child." She kept staring at me, as if waiting for an answer. I realized what she contemplated doing. To walk up to the selection with her daughter at her side was certain death for her and the child. Otherwise, perhaps only the child . . .

I returned her stare. I could find no words, no thought.

"No! No!" Damazer hammered his head with his fists. He was convulsed with sobbing. "No! No! I am going with my child."

Anka Wolkowitz spoke quietly through her tears, "I wish I had gone with mine." Her child had perished in the Medem Sanatorium.

Victor Mendelsohn drew me aside and whispered that he knew of a good place to hide right in this courtyard. I told him I would be back later and rushed out of the apartment. In the street the queues were forming.

On Ostrovska Street the workers of the brush factories from Shwentoyerska were gathered. People sat on the sidewalks or stood waiting with their bundles on their backs. I noticed an extraordinary thing. Men were shaving, washing, cleaning up. Women were applying powder and lipstick, looking into hand mirrors, combing their hair, adjusting their clothing. They were busy making themselves attractive to the devils. Up ahead the selection had started. The lines were beginning to move. One must look healthy, neat, able to work, useful.

My God, how far had we sunk?

I saw Comrade Woyland, a poet and musician, with his three-month-old baby in his arms. He rocked it gently, standing and waiting for his turn.

There was Abramek Borkenstein, the most active member of our youth movement. On his back was strapped a large valise with holes punched in it at the top and bottom. Inside he had hidden his child. He, too, stood and waited in torment. Would he get through? Would he pass safely with his treasure?

Ruta Perenson stood with her son, Nicko. "You must not be afraid," she was saying. "Terrible things are going to happen soon. They want to kill us all, but we won't let them. We will hit them as hard as they hit us . . ."

Near her were her niece and her sister; and Liebeskind with his wife; Comrade Kotsholek from Lodz; the massive Comrade Gobid, talented journalist of the *Volkszeitung*, whom we had brought to Warsaw only three months before from the small village in Galicia where he had been hidden. Yankel Grushka greeted me with his sparkling dark eyes; near him stood Grilak and his wife. All waited silently.

It was a beautiful summer day. A bright sun beamed down on

138

the ruins of houses and the ruins of people, on a multitude re-
signed, beaten, staring death dumbly in the face.

The yellow dust from the rubble penetrated my throat and
nostrils. My body burned from thirst and hunger. . . .

I took my place in the lines among the brush workers. The
comrades gave me the identity card of a factory worker who
had already been taken to the Umschlagplatz. He, too, had had
a beard, and there was some resemblance. I had no doubt that
I would soon find myself with my double. A Jew with a beard
is not a very useful worker, and besides I had no token.

I saw Abrasha Blum. I still had the hundred dollars he had
given me a few days before. I handed him the money. I was
certainly headed for the Umschlagplatz. He looked younger,
and he had a token. Perhaps he would get through.

We kept moving along steadily. In the distance I could already see the uniforms of the SS. Near me a mother pushed
her child away; it was safer to face them alone. She primped,
fixed her make-up, put on a sweet smile.

I could hear the shouted commands. "Right! . . . Left'" After
each shout of "Right!" a crescendo of weeping and screaming
arose, mingled with the sound of swinging whips and ropes;
the wretch was shoved into the waiting hands of the Ukrainians and Letts who threw him into the mass of the condemned.
After a sufficient number had been assembled on the right they
were marched toward the Umschlagplatz a few blocks away,
while another group was being collected.

A woman walked up leading a child. They tried to tear the
child from her. She was being sent to the left, to work, to life,
but she refused to give up the child. After a short struggle she
was given an impatient shove to the right. She could keep the
child—and die with it.

Berek Snaidmil rushed past me, red-faced and agitated. I
watched him having a heated argument with one of the factory
managers who still held a few tokens. Berek demanded them

139

for close comrades. Perhaps some could still be saved. But the factory manager had his own to look after, and there were only a few tokens.

It was a gruesome lottery of life and death in which even the holders of the lucky tokens could not be sure they would collect their winnings.

I was already at the corner of Smotcha, where the selection squad stood. I kept moving closer. Around me stood comrades who held tokens. They tried to surround me, to keep me deep in their midst. Perhaps they might manage to smuggle me through.

"To the right!" I felt a sharp pain in my head and then realized I had been struck with a whip. A few strong shoves and I was in the group on Smotcha Street—about two hundred people—with a cordon of armed beasts on both sides of the street.

Around me were none of my comrades. I was alone in the abyss of wretchedness and despair. Dully, I looked at the uniformed beasts with human faces. They sniggered mockingly. One of them walked up to a frightened Jew, ripped his watch from his hand, took his ring, then smacked him again and again. No one even paid attention. We had lost the power to react to such things.

My mind began to function again. From the chaotic welter of my thoughts came a decision, a command, an imperative: I must save myself! I must! Everything was lost. There was nothing more to risk. I could gamble everything because there was nothing left to lose.

The crowd began to move. There was some scuffling, angry imprecations from the guards. "Halt! Halt! *Halt!*" The shouting and shoving increased. I dashed out of the mob and sprang like a cat into a courtyard opposite the Aronowitz Metal Works. I raced up the stairs and into an apartment. It was empty—not a living soul.

I tried to calm myself, to catch my breath. I tiptoed along a wall to the window, peeked through a tear in the curtains. The guards were still struggling with their victims. How could they have missed seeing me? I moved back and listened. No sounds of pursuit. I was "free."

I waited until the guards below got their charges moving again toward the Umschlagplatz and the street became quiet. I had gambled on getting through the selection and lost. The very best I could hope for now if I were found wandering about the streets was to be forced to go through the selection a second time with no hope of faring any better. I needed shelter from the dragnets which were picking up the stragglers and dumping them into the queues.

I recalled that earlier that morning Victor Mendelsohn had mentioned a hiding place at 51 Mila Street. I knew of no other place to go, so I headed back to find Victor.

On the streets people were still numbly waiting their turns to go through the selection. I stopped here and there to exchange a word of greeting with comrades and friends.

At 51 Mila the courtyard gates were locked. In the street were soldiers and police. People who had tried to hide in the houses were being dragged out and thrown behind the cordon.

Anka Wolkowitz, Michelson and his wife and daughter, Damazer with his wife and child, all of whom I had seen at the apartment that morning, stood glumly with hundreds of others behind the police lines. Victor Mendelsohn did not seem to be among them. Perhaps, after all, he had managed to hide as he had planned.

I walked back through the waiting crowds. Workers from factories or trades stood in groups under identifying banners, as though waiting to parade. I saw a familiar group of bakers, spick-and-span in their white caps and aprons, with the name of their bakery on a sign above them.

Everyone was ready. Everyone was looking his best for the fateful choosing.

At the corner of Lubetska Street I met Comrades Gobid, Liebeskind, and Dorata Kotsholek. They told me they too had escaped from the ranks of the condemned and were wandering through the streets with no place to go. All of us were hungry and parched.

I decided to join them in a hunt for bread. After all, I knew all the bakery workers, and they all knew me. With some luck . . . Whether we found a place to hide or not, we had to have something to eat.

We started toward a bakery in an old synagogue on Mila. As we walked into the courtyard we heard shots close by. I dashed up the steps and into the building. There was more shooting, and then silence. I walked back into the street, but there was no sign of my friends. I learned later that this time they had not escaped Treblinka.

I trudged on alone. I was dead-tired and feeling my hunger more keenly with every moment. I was stopped by Nuchem and Sholem Chmelnitsky, two brothers who had graduated from our school on Krochmalna. Nuchem was a close friend of my son and of Mark Novogrodsky. They looked extremely tired, but they were not dispirited.

"Bernard," they said quietly, "we have learned something of great importance. The entire personnel of the Oxako factory on Sochatchevska has already gone through the selection, and the factory has resumed operation. It is full of workers. We think the guards can be bribed. Once inside the factory we are safe."

The factory occupied a considerable area, including parts of Niska, Okopova, and Mila Streets, and bordered the one-time Feiffer Tannery near the Aryan side.

I did not have much money.

"We have money," they assured me, "and a gold watch. Let's go."

We started along Mila toward the factory gate at Sochatchevska. We found a large crowd in front of the gate. The news had traveled fast.

Suddenly the guards began firing over the heads of the crowd, shouting that everyone was to lie down on the ground and remain still. Fortunately we were still near the edge of the throng. I lay prone with the others. We could hear the crying of the wounded.

I began to crawl on my stomach back along the way we had come. When I had put enough distance between me and the factory guards, I stood up and ran along Mila and around the corner at Lubetska.

At Niska and Lubetska I stopped running. I leaned against the building to catch my breath. I felt completely beaten. It was hopeless. Neither my body nor my nerves could stand any more of this.

A horse-drawn wagon, piled high with boxes, crates, and odds and ends, was moving slowly down the street toward me. The wagon bore the sign "Oxako"; two men were sitting in the front seat. Absently I noticed that a Jewish policeman was sitting beside the driver, and the driver—the driver was Welvel der Grober. Welvel was a transport worker; we had known each other for a long time. He would help me.

My reactions were so slow that the wagon was past me before my mind put things together. I ran after it, shouting to Welvel.

He stopped the wagon and leaned down to get a good look at me. "Who are you? What do you want?"

The voice was not friendly; he did not recognize me. My beard was more of a disguise than I had dared to hope. He was curious to know who had been shouting his name.

"Welvel," I said, "I am Bernard."

"Bernard? Bernard?" He leaned closer, screwing up his eyes; they suddenly filled with tears. He began to whisper, "Bernard, Bernard . . ."

Then he said abruptly, "Get on the wagon."

The policeman had been watching this scene quietly but with great interest. This was too much for him. "Hey, you, how much are you collecting for this head?" he growled roughly to Welvel.

"You bastard, you no-good son-of-a-bitch!" Welvel's voice rose. "Do you know who this is? This is Bernard!"

The policeman's manner changed completely. He silently offered me his hand and helped me mount to the seat. He did not know me but he had heard my name.

We drove on. At the factory gate, both Welvel and the policeman leaned down for a quiet conversation with the guard. We drove into the factory yard.

Welvel brought the horse to a halt, and we all got down. We stood silently for a while. Now that we had gotten this far it was plain that neither of them knew what to do. They were as frightened as I was.

Welvel began to wring his hands nervously. "Bernard, I have no place to hide you here. What will happen? What will we do? What will we do?"

The policeman ended the uncertainty. He put his arm on my shoulder. "Come on. I will find you a place."

He led me about half a block further into the factory compound to the door of a bakery at 74 Niska Street. I recognized the shop. It had been a cooperative bakery before the war, I knew all of the workers well.

The policeman led me in and announced, "I have brought you Comrade Bernard."

I was immediately surrounded by a group of curious workmen. At first there was no recognition in their eyes, but soon I was being treated with a friendliness that warmed my heart. They brought me a glass of tea and a piece of bread, and someone handed me a white apron. They suggested that for the present I walk around the bakery, pretending to be at work.

I wandered about, listening in on conversations which made my hair stand on end. A hateful trade in Jewish lives had been going on in the factory area. Jews from the bakery, in partnership with German guards, had been collecting large sums for admitting fugitives from the selection. In most cases, after stripping their victims of everything they had, they turned them back into the street to shift for themselves.

It was late at night. I lay huddled in a corner somewhere, dreaming. Somebody shook me.

"Comrade Bernard. It's a raid. The entire place is surrounded. If they find you we are all lost. They will shoot all of us. Hide! Hurry!"

I ran into the courtyard, trying hard to clear my brain, to orient myself. From the street beyond the gate came the familiar sounds of the killers, loud wild shouting and the clatter of hobnailed boots. Searchlights swept the yard. I dashed into an open doorway and up a flight of steps. Below me a searchlight caught the doorway, then the stairs, and paused. I scrambled higher. Hobnailed boots were already on the steps.

I reached the attic and felt my way in the dark. The headboard of a broken bed leaned against the wall. I crawled behind it and stumbled into a human body. It was warm and trembling. Whoever it was, he was alive and as frightened as I.

The space was not big enough for two of us, but it was too late to turn back and look elsewhere. I could not have if I had wanted to, for my companion clutched me in convulsive fear. It was a woman. She was breathing heavily and trying hard to stifle her gasps. We pressed against the wall. She twisted close to me and her chin dug into my shoulder. Her heart was pounding heavily. She did not say a word; I heard only her muffled breathing.

Several times they came into the attic and flashed their lights about. We crouched, trembling, expecting that at any moment the light would pick us out. Each time we heard the hobnails on the steps she tightened her grip on me. Each time her heart beat more wildly. Both of us shivered spasmodically.

145

Through my mind raced the fear that she would have a heart attack at any moment, and that she would die here with her arms clutched tightly around me.

Again the damned boots came. *"Hier ist niemand. Wir waren schon hier."*

The clatter faded into the distance. A deathly stillness descended around us. For a moment, at least, we were safe. Suddenly I realized that every muscle in my body ached.

My companion could no longer control her sobbing. She pressed her face into my shoulder, and her whole body twitched. She did not loosen her grip. I tried to calm her.

Finally a little sunlight came through a hole in the roof. Our hiding place was brighter, I could begin to make out shapes around me. She relaxed her hold a little; but she was still trembling and sobbing.

I could see her face. She was a young, attractive, intelligent-looking girl in her twenties. Through her sobs she poured out her story. Her parents, her brothers and sisters had all been killed. She had friends somewhere in the factory. For a great sum of money she had bribed her way in, hoping to find them, but had been unsuccessful. She had eluded all efforts to drive her back into the street and had managed to find this hiding place. Since noon she had been crouching behind the headboard.

She had gold, jewels, and money. She would give me anything if I would help her. Another paroxysm of sobbing interrupted her pleas.

I spoke to her soothingly, telling her that I did not need her jewels or her gold; I myself was trying to find safety. Perhaps with a little luck we would both survive.

The tenseness over, both of us began to feel the pangs of hunger. It was twenty-four hours since I had had anything to eat or drink. She was sufficiently at ease to let me go in search of food. The steps were still very dark, but it was broad daylight in the factory yard. There was a long queue in front of the bakery door. The bakery operated officially only for the Oxako factory, and the workers were waiting in line for their rations. I joined them. Since the bakers knew me, I was able to buy a loaf of bread and get a bottle of water.

Walking back, I noticed a friend in the line—a former slaughterhouse worker. He obviously did not recognize me. When I identified myself he was amazed but protested unhappily that he could not help me. He was hiding in a crowded bunker on the factory grounds, but if he brought me back with him, the others might throw him out.

He looked away in shamefaced helplessness. We stood silently for a moment.

Suddenly he nudged me and directed my eyes across the yard with a nod of his head. "There are your old friends, Itzhock Meisner and Moishe Furman. They are now factory guards. They should be able to help you."

Before approaching them, I returned to the attic to give my unfortunate comrade the bread and water. I told her that the next half-hour, while the shifts were changing, would be the best time for her to venture out to look for her friends. If I did not succeed in finding a better hiding place, I would come back. She thanked me tearfully.

Itzhock and Moishe were still standing where I had seen them before. With them I went through the now familiar routine. At first, they did not recognize the miserable, bearded Jew, and after I had identified myself they tearfully lamented their inability to help me. "Comrade Bernard, we have no place to hide you. What are we going to do? What are we going to do? . . . We cannot masquerade you as a worker in the factory. Everybody knows you. Somebody is certain to betray you, and then many will suffer."

As we talked, a uniformed factory guard walked by. My friends stopped him, took him aside, and began conversing earnestly.

After a few moments the strange guard walked up to me and said without expression, "Come, Comrade Bernard."

I asked no questions and followed.

We crossed Niska, past a barbed-wire barrier which ran down the middle of the street. Now we were in a sort of no man's land, separated from the factory area. It was a "neutral" section between the ghetto and the Aryan side. The guard led me to a small one-story wooden house. The shutters were locked, and the building looked abandoned, but the door was open. He took me inside, indicating with a gesture that this was to be my home.

I followed him outside again. Behind the house was a small yard, surrounded by a high wooden fence. He lifted one board of the fence, revealing, between the fence and the wall of the next house, a cavity large enough for one person to stand erect. He told me to step inside and let down the board. There was not even enough room for me to shrug my shoulders; I was held perfectly straight and tense. He lifted the board and let me out.

"That is one hiding place," he said. "Follow me. I'll show you another."

We went back into the house. He set up a small ladder, and I followed him into the attic through a small trap door in the ceiling. The attic was thick with dust and cobwebs, cluttered with rags and odds and ends of worthless junk. He carefully lifted a dusty board out of the floor revealing a narrow coffin-like opening.

"This is your second place," he said, inviting me to lie down.

With the floor-board over me I felt as if I had been buried alive. After he had let me out he explained that the board must be handled carefully to preserve the thick layer of dust which camouflaged the hiding place.

This strange guide, who kept calling me "Comrade Bernard," gave me further instructions. I must remain on guard all day, watching the streets through a crack in the shutters. I could turn on the electric lights during the day, if necessary, but under no

148

circumstances at night. If I noticed any signs of an impending raid, I was to run to the hiding place in the courtyard fence immediately. That was the safest. If it was too late to leave the house, I was to use the attic, but I must remember to pull the ladder into the attic after me. Several times he told me to practice getting in and out of both places. When he was satisfied that I understood his instructions perfectly, he left.

He returned in the evening with a pot of soup, a piece of bread, and news. The raids were still in full swing. Things were steadily getting more desperate, and the toll of victims was mounting. He added one important instruction. I was not to go to sleep at night. I was to be on guard constantly, for even at night there might be a raid. He told me that my comrades had arranged for him to bring food to me and to relay messages. But none of them could come to see me. It was much too dangerous.

Alone, I remained in the dark, straining tensely to hear and interpret every suspicion of sound. All my nerves were on edge.

Suddenly I detected a movement in a corner of the room. I broke out in a cold sweat. There was no mistake about it; it was not a hallucination. Something was moving. Then I relaxed and smiled at myself. These were friends—rats. In my loneliness their presence was comforting. After all, we were not so far apart. I, too, lying hidden in my own burrow, was a hateful and hunted animal, cowering in the face of death.

I spent a long night in the company of my rats. My overstrained nerves marked their every movement. Time and again they roused me from a brief doze and brought me back to painful wakefulness.

In the morning I glued my eyes to the crack in the shutters. I watched as workers from the houses on the other side of Niska walked sleepily to their work. Long after they had gone I maintained my vigil, hoping to see across the barbed wire barrier the approach of my strange friend.

He arrived about noon, bringing food and water and cigarettes to calm my overwrought nerves. My curiosity about him was now thoroughly aroused. I offered him money and asked him his name.

"I can give *you* money if you need any," he said. "All that I bring you is sent by your comrades. As for my name, it means nothing to you."

He changed the subject and began discussing the latest news about the deportations, which continued unabated. The great selection was not yet over. Long lines still filed past the dreaded baton—"Right! Left!" Crowded freight cars continued to move from the Umschlagplatz.

Again he called me "Comrade Bernard," but when I asked him his identity he lowered his eyes and refused to answer.

That night he came again with food, including a piece of salami, a delicacy I had not even seen for months. For several days he continued his twice daily visits to bring me food and news, but he still parried every question about himself. Finally I told him categorically that I would not accept another morsel unless he told me who he was and how he knew me.

His eyes still fixed on the floor in front of him, he said, "I know you because my brother was a member of your party. My name is Kalman, of the Wolkenbrot family. My brother, Shimen, knew you well. My father was called Fishel Manyes. He used to sell oats on Lubetzka Street.

I remembered Fishel Manyes. He had had a somewhat shady reputation in that section. Shimen, a fur worker, had been a member of the militia under my command.

I recalled, too, an extraordinary meeting with Shimen's brother. It had taken place about five or six years before the war, when a sick comrade, Joseph Leshtchinsky, a member of the central committee, was preparing to go to Otvotsk for a much-needed rest. He had packed all his things and piled them into a wagon in front of his home at 15 Karmelitzka. Somebody had stolen his trunk which contained every stitch of clothing he possessed.

150

Since my duties had made me familiar with the near-underworld of Warsaw, I was asked to try to recover the stolen goods. From the Jewish transport workers who frequented the corner of Karmelitzka and Novolipya I learned that Fishel Manyes' son, a well-known petty thief, had been seen loitering in front of the building that morning. I found him and demanded that he return the loot. After a long and heated argument he admitted that the trunk had been given to a fence for safekeeping. In exchange for the storage fee he would have to pay the fence, he returned the trunk intact.

That, in short, had been my only meeting with Shimen's brother, who now stood before me, unable to look me in the eye. He spoke again, with a little more spirit and self-assurance. "Later, I became an entirely different person. I was abroad, even rich for a while. Just before the war, I returned to Warsaw. Now—now I am here."

After I had spent six days under Kalman's friendly patronage, the ghetto became calmer. On the sixth day he brought with him Itzhock Meisner and Moishe Furman.

"Comrade Bernard, you are free!" they told me cheerfully, hugging and kissing me. "The bandits of the extermination brigade have left the ghetto. You are free to go."

We said good-by warmly. I left with a grateful backward glance at the little frame house. It was a sunny day, hard on eyes so long accustomed to the dark. I was a little dizzy and walked unsteadily. But I felt a lifting of the spirit. In this dismal, terror-ridden life, three men out of the gray, frightened, brutalized mass had shown humanity, tenderness, and friendly consideration. Under no greater compulsion than a decent feeling of compassion they had risked their lives for a fellow man.

Again I walked the ghetto streets. My nerves were somewhat calmer now that the long nightmare was over, but my body burned. I had not taken off my clothing for ten days, and I could not remember how long it was since I had changed my under-wear. I was covered with filth, matted with dirt and dust.

Everything looked strange. There was no trace of the tumul-tuous, pushing, spirited multitude which only six or seven weeks ago had been the ghetto. Stores gaped, open and empty. Houses were abandoned. In the courtyards, here and there, were scat-tered household effects, broken pieces of furniture and odd bits of clothing. Gloomy desolation hung over everything.

People had left everything in disorder. There was no further need for the things which had been so great a part of their lives. A tornado had swept the ghetto, smashing everything in its path, leaving behind only an empty wilderness.

Occasionally I saw people hurrying like frightened ghosts along the street. They would stop to peer at me closely with insane, frightened eyes, hoping to recognize in me a dear one who had somehow saved himself from hell's fire, somehow torn himself from the devil's grasp. Their quick, eager scrutiny dis-appointed, they would shrink from me and scurry away.

From time to time the few people on the streets would dash into doorways, spying an approaching uniform in the distance. Death might return at any moment, and they knew how to recog-nize his face.

I met the woman who had been my chance comrade during the frightful night in the attic of the Oxako factory. We greeted each other like old friends. For the first time I learned her name —Silberman. She came from a wealthy Warsaw family. She told me that she had once more bought a place in the Oxako factory, for a large sum of money. Now she was out searching for mem-bers of her family or for friends. Perhaps, perhaps . . . After all, one must not give up hope.

On Zamenhof I met Comrade Israel Wiener, a tailor, a leader of the militia in the garment union. He was distressed to find me in such miserable condition and took me home with him. With several other comrades, he lived and worked in the tailoring shops at 23 Karmelitzka.

I was able to wash and to change my clothes. Mrs. Wiener brewed tea and gave me something to eat. They put me to bed and sent word to the brush factory. In the evening Abrasha Blum, Marek Edelman, and Berek Snaidmil came over to see me. But at first we could not talk; words refused to come. They had given me up for dead.

The last six days had cost the ghetto a hundred thousand lives. Of the original five hundred thousand, only forty or fifty thousand now remained, most of them registered in the factories and social institutions. The chaos and confusion were still so great that not all the factories had resumed operation.

What curious chance had decreed that we should not be among the tens of thousands who had been dragged to their deaths? We looked at each other with misty eyes, thinking how wonderful it was to meet again, how precious we were to each other, how much we needed each other. Then, slowly, we began to talk about the last few days, and about our present situation.

A letter had just come from Orzech on the Aryan side. He wanted to know what had happened to me, why I had not arrived as planned. He told us that he had got word to the outside world about the recent events in the ghetto. He was working day and night to obtain arms. He had promises and hoped for early results.

I had to get to the Aryan side as quickly as possible to help organize and supply aid for the final ghetto battle. We surveyed our resources. Abrasha and I spent the night working out all possible avenues of action We compared reports on the attitude of the ghetto survivors. Even the most optimistic workers in the factories had cast aside all illusions. They realized now that this was only a pause in the methodical business of extermination. It would all begin again—and soon. Escape was impossible. The choice was either to submit willingly or to wage a death-struggle. All were determined that this time they would fight.

153

In the morning Abrasha left for the factory.

Everyone at 23 Karmelitzka was in a state of extreme anxiety. The Germans were fencing in each remaining factory as a separate ghetto. No movement from one factory to another was permitted. Workers who had permission to live outside the factories, employees of the Judenrat, the police, the hospital, and other institutions were limited to specified streets for living quarters. No one was allowed on the streets. The workers marched to and from their factories in groups under police guard. Even the sick were escorted to the hospital by police. All streets outside factory limits or not assigned to specific groups as living space were shut off. They were now forbidden territory.

All the ghetto gates were closed. The Germans had moved the boundary inward, past the few isolated boarded-in factories standing amid rows of empty, deserted tenements, past Leshno, Solna, Orla, Ogrodova, Karmelitzka, Pzheyazd, Novolipya, Novolipky, Pavia, Djelna, Smotcha. A new gate was set up at the corner of Gensha and Zamenhof. Only in the little island factories of this no man's land was there life—elsewhere, the heavy silence of death.

In the center of the former ghetto was a small area set aside for the few Jews of various categories who did not live in the factories. Mila Street was reserved for the *platzufkazhes*, the few thousand Jews who worked at various tasks on the Aryan side. At dawn each day they marched in military formation through the new Gensha-Zamenhof Gate, through the ghostly stillness of the deserted streets and out through the old Leshno-Zhelasna Gate. Every evening they returned the same way to their beds.

After removing every human being from the closed sections, the Germans, with typical Teutonic efficiency, began the salvage of every usable article. For this purpose they organized a *Wertverfassungstelle*, the task of which was to gather everything from the abandoned houses. They kept a thousand Jews busy collecting the material, sorting and packing it at the depots in the Tlomatzky Synagogue building and in the Catholic Cathedral on Novolipky, whence it was trucked out of the ghetto.

The *Wertverfassungstelle* had some competition. As the remaining Jews recovered from the ordeal of the deportations, the need for food revived the smuggling trade. The Gentiles no longer considered money acceptable, but they gladly took the goods which smugglers collected from the deserted homes, in exchange for bread. Daring smugglers crept into the forbidden districts to compete with the organized ghouls of the *Wertverfassungstelle*.

In the tailoring establishment at 23 Karmelitzka lived Benek Weitzman, a young tailor, member of the Warsaw committee of our youth movement, Zukunft. He was a devoted Socialist, an intelligent young man, even an accomplished speaker. He came to me and asked in troubled seriousness, "Comrade Bernard, is it permissible that we, party members, idealists, and Socialists, may also take something from the unoccupied buildings to exchange for something to eat?"

Benek had already lost everyone. His wife and two-year-old child had been taken. Now he waited, hungry and alone, for his turn. Still his conscience wrestled with the problem of whether the survivors had the moral right to benefit from the abandoned possessions of the murdered. Would this not make us ghouls? There were many like Benek who would rather have starved than trafficked in the possessions of the dead.

Except for Number 23, both sides of Karmelitzka were already completely emptied. It seemed unlikely that the Germans would continue to leave this little island untouched. Everyone expected momentarily to be taken to the Umschlagplatz. As their only hope for survival, the workers at 23 Karmelitzka were negotiating with Tebbens for admission into his factories, which were still operating full blast.

Since I could under no circumstances go to Tebbens, I moved

to 48 Gensha to live with the hospital personnel. There I spent a few hours for the last time with one of my most treasured friends, Anna Broide Heller. Although she came from a very wealthy family, she had given a lifetime of service. Before the First World War she had studied medicine in Switzerland, where, in the émigré Bundist colony, she had become acquainted with socialism. There also she met her future husband, Heller, an engineer. She returned to Poland in 1914 and in the chaos of the war organized a home for orphans and abandoned children.

Between the wars, she was active in children's aid. She was one of the moving spirits in organizing our Medem Sanatorium and served as an adviser on medical matters. She became medical director of the great Children's Hospital on Shliska Street. Anna was always to be found in the poorest sections of the city, doing what she could to make the lot of the children easier.

The outbreak of the new war was a signal for her to work even harder. She threw herself into the work of our illegal Red Cross. Through all of the selections and forced migrations, she refused to leave the hospital for a safer place. After each blow she would reorganize the hospital, find new people and new facilities, and carry on. When the deportations finally forced the Children's Hospital out of existence, she organized a new General Hospital. I arrived as the hospital was being set up in its new quarters.

In the evening, as we sat around talking over a cup of tea, I reopened the old question. I begged Anna to let us smuggle her out of the ghetto.

"This has been suggested before, Bernard," she said with a smile. Her voice was grim. "I am not going. I have agreed to send my son and his wife and child. As long as there are Jews in the ghetto I am needed here, and here I will stay."

Further attempts at persuasion were hopeless. We sat around the table with other doctors and nurses. Conversation turned to the old days, to the people we had known and loved and lost.

156

My stay at the hospital was short. It was much too busy a place, with people coming and going constantly. Besides, an inspection of the new premises by the Germans was expected any day. After three days I decided to move to the apartment of the Bartmans, both of whom had been leaders in our culture league. Short, blond Dr. Inka Schweiger put on her white coat and cap and led me through Nalefky to Franciskanska like a doctor leading a patient. Fortunately we were not stopped.

Comrade Bartman worked in the *Wertverfassungstelle*. His wife, Chava, who later escaped to Belgium, was employed in the Judenrat. Despite their jobs they were on the verge of starvation; yet they insisted on dividing their meager food with me.

In the same tenement lived Comrade Chaimovitch, formerly an official of our cooperative movement. Now he was liaison man between the Judenrat and the *Transferstelle*, which supplied the ghetto food allotment. He had the right to visit the Aryan side, wearing a uniform cap with a blue ribbon and a Star of David.

I went up to visit Chaimovitch and found him and his wife greatly agitated. He had just returned from smuggling their ten-year-old daughter out of the ghetto. A Christian friend had arranged for her admission to a children's home run by a convent somewhere in Poland—where, he was not permitted to know for fear that he might disclose the dangerous secret.

"The child did not want to go to the Christians," Chaimovitch told me, weeping. "She cried and pleaded to be allowed to stay with us. If our fate is to die, she wanted to die with us. It was only with great difficulty and against her will that we were able to get her across." He wrung his hands. "Where is my little child? Will I ever see her again?"

That day Comrade Grilac and his wife moved into the same tenement. Before the war he had worked in the Jewish section of the Polish Labor Federation. Now he was very active in the underground. He and his wife had been hiding in the brush factory on Shwentoyerska, but there were rumors that a new selection would soon take place in the factory. Since he did not have a token, he had to leave immediately. Although his wife did have the precious token, she insisted on facing an unknown fate with him. They got from Shwentoyerska to Franciskanska by crawling through the intervening attics and cellars and over courtyard walls.

Grilac reported that the fighting groups in the factory were ready. They awaited only the expected shipment of arms. At my request, Guzik, the finance director of the American Joint Distribution Committee, came to visit me at Bartman's. I begged him to do everything possible to obtain registration numbers for our most valuable comrades. We also discussed the problem of raising money to finance the supply of arms.

Guzik told me despairingly about the great difficulty of getting numbers. All his resources were exhausted. He realized the urgent need for money, and was attempting to arrange a new "transfer." If it worked out, he promised to give the money to Abrasha Blum.

Guzik had been the finance director of the JDC for many years and was liked. He had worked in a bank and had never lost the habit of measuring all organizational problems in terms of money, like a banker making an investment. He was short with blondish hair and had no markedly "Jewish" features, but he was extremely pious. Though he spoke no Yiddish he had a weakness for Orthodox Jews, and they seldom left his office without getting what they wanted if it was in his power to grant it. A long black coat, a gray beard, and sideburns always made him forget his banker's training. He was not very quick-witted, but his heart was in the right place. I had known him for a long time and liked him. We were to get to know each other better before the end.

For three or four days I remained with the Bartmans waiting for the opportunity to cross to the Aryan side.

FIVE

ACCORDING to a carefully worked out plan, I was to be smuggled out with a group of ghetto Jews who worked at the Okentche Airport. They lived in special barracks at the airfield, but every two weeks they were permitted to return to the ghetto for a day. This cost them plenty in bribes, but it also had its financial rewards. They brought food into the ghetto, and on the trip back they took out articles to sell to the Gentiles.

Comrade Henik Tuchmacher, a member of our sport organization, Morgenstern, was a foreman of the Okentche workers. He had arranged everything. I was to be added to the list of workers, and given a work card. If necessary, he was even prepared to bribe the guards or the SS. On the Aryan side, Zalman Friedrych was to meet me and take me to an apartment which had been prepared for me.

Marek Edelman escorted me to 15 Mila, the assembly point for the group. He carried a work card from the Jewish Hospital. We left the Bartmans and walked slowly toward 15 Mila. I was very weak, barely able to walk on my swollen feet. My beard added greatly to my aged, weakened appearance; I was hardly a suitable figure to have been selected from the remnants of the ghetto to work on the Aryan side. But it was too late to do anything about that now. I had to go through with it. Everything had been carefully prepared. Once again, everything hung by the thin hair which separated life from death.

159

Slowly we walked through the desolate streets. A dismal silence hung over the open doors and windows. Here had once pulsated a vibrant life—a miserable, oppressive, despairing life, but life nevertheless. Where were the throngs of tenants that had overflowed these empty houses and abandoned courts? Swallowed by the Umschlagplatz. Fed to the insatiable German death-machine.

Two and one-half months ago, when the Gestapo had demanded the deportation of the "nonproductive," we had been a crowded ghetto community of more than half a million people. Now we were nothing, not even a ghetto. The handful of forty thousand survivors, locked behind factory stockades or huddled into a few tenements, waiting for the Germans to finish their work, could not even be called a ghetto.

I looked up at the gaping windows of the familiar buildings. They seemed so strange and foreign and unreal. Yet all this had happened in a few short weeks; the most dreadful prophecies were now bitter, heartbreaking, unbelievable reality.

The first news of the early deportations, which we had sent to the outside world with such difficulty, had been met with indifference, with disbelief. The world was cynical and suspicious of "atrocity stories." The empty stillness mocked us. We were completely, utterly, unbelievably alone.

I looked into the dark eyes of the thin sickly twenty-year-old boy who was my escort. Marek was one of our own. He had been graduated from our elementary school with my own son and had joined our youth organization at the age of twelve. His father, also a Bundist, had died of tuberculosis when Marek was a child. His mother had been a leader of our women's organization, Yaff. She had also died shortly before the war, leaving the boy completely alone.

As usual, Marek was carelessly dressed. Neatness never seemed important to him. Life had made him outwardly unsentimental and hard, but behind that close-mouthed grimness were keen intelligence and warm generosity. And he was utterly without

160

fear. He led me by the arm. A young hospital worker was leading an old, weak man. My mind spun around the one frightening question: Would it work?

A year or two before, this same Marek had escorted me through the ghetto to illegal meetings. He would walk behind at a distance of ten or fifteen paces without taking his eyes from me for a moment. Then he would stand patiently in the street outside the building, guarding the meeting place. Today Marek was escorting me along another road. Today he led me by the arm. We were much closer now than we had been then, but how far, far apart we soon would be!

My feet protested every painful step. Past us dashed a cat, probably the only living creature left in the entire tenement block.

It was not yet noon. We must get to the meeting place on time, because the group would begin its march to Okentche promptly at two o'clock.

At 15 Mila I spotted familiar faces among the workers. They were amazed to see me. How would a walking corpse, an old man who could hardly stand on his feet, get past the guards? Some suggested that I shave my beard. I refused. I would be recognized immediately. Others insisted that under any circumstances it was too dangerous to take me along; my presence would jeopardize the whole group. But Henik Tuchmacher told them categorically that I was going along and that he would permit no grumbling.

Our group started along Mila toward Zamenhof, Marek following at a distance, just in case he should be needed. At the corner of Zamenhof we went past the new guard-post. Everything went well. They made no attempt to check the list of names. They simply counted the number in the group and waved us on. Past the guard-post, we met a German patrol.

"*Achtung!*"

Our entire group stiffened, walking past the German uniforms in straight military rows. The Germans scanned us closely as we walked by, their eyes showing their hatred. We marched rigidly erect, looking straight ahead.

We were already past Novolipky, Karmelitzka, Leshno. At the gate of the Tebbens factory stood a comrade, Carola Scher. She watched me silently. Her eyes, filled with tears, greeted me. Thus I said good-by for the last time to a dear friend. She later died in Treblinka.

During the entire march I stayed in the middle of the group, not to parade my beard too openly. Finally we arrived at the Zhelasna ghetto gate. Here we found an unpleasant surprise. The SS men who were to inspect the group at the gate and escort it to Okentche had not yet arrived. For an hour we waited at this favorite loitering place for extortionists, swindlers, smugglers, police and Gestapo agents. My beard and my sickly appearance, it seemed to me, were attracting all eyes. I was the center of everyone's attention.

Finally the SS arrived. The individual check against the list of names began. They called me. The SS man took one look at me and pushed me to one side. He would not let me pass, and continued with his list. I walked into the group of bystanders on the sidewalk and sidled over toward Marek to wait.

All this time I had been vainly scanning the area beyond the gate for a sign of Zalman Friedrych. Until I saw that familiar blond head I dared not risk trying to get through. Alone, I would not know where to turn and would surely fall into the hands of the police. My heart beat so wildly I could hardly breathe. My mind wrestled nervously with the problem of whether to try to steal through if the opportunity should present itself. Torn by indecision, I stood in the small knot of people, terribly conscious of my beard, my swollen feet, and my sickly face.

I turned toward Henik Tuchmacher, who was dashing about among the workers and SS men. From the distance he gave me an expressive wink. Friedrych was there, and Henik had already pressed the money into the SS man's hand.

162

I managed to squeeze Marek's hand in farewell and sprang onto the back of a small wagon piled with the suitcases and parcels of the workers I tried to look as if I had been assigned to guard the baggage with the three other workers already sitting there. In their fear that my presence would bring them disaster they tried to push me off the wagon as unobtrusively as possible, but I wedged myself in tightly.

The wagon moved through the gate.

In the distance I saw Friedrych sitting on the platform of a small open truck. As we passed the truck I dropped lightly from the wagon, and on Friedrych's signal I got into the cab of the truck alongside the driver. I ripped off my Star of David armband. The driver headed quickly into Ogrodova Street and turned into Chlodna and then Djelna. He stopped, and Friedrych went off with a valise that Pavel Orzech, Morizi's brother who worked at Tebbens', had sent for him. We waited a short time until Friedrych returned. Then the auto raced down Wola.

After the first realization that the plan had really worked, I experienced a psychic relapse. The sudden break in the mental and emotional tension threw me into a state of deep depression. Almost with indifference I looked out on another world.

It was a beautiful, bright November day. The golden rays of the autumn sun shone over the buildings and streets. Through the truck windows I watched the noisy movement in the streets. Streetcars clanged past. Thick masses of people hurried here and there. We passed busy stores, cafés, restaurants. There were military men in autos and on foot. From a dead city I had been thrown into a stream of rushing, boiling life.

The auto stopped on Ordonna Street. Friedrych stepped down. The chauffeur and I waited. In about twenty minutes he returned with an eighteen-year-old Polish boy.

The boy took me by the arm, saying, "Come along, uncle." He led me through narrow alleys toward the great Zbroyovnia armament factory, which now belonged to the Viennese Steyr com-

163

pany. Alongside the plant buildings was a tenement for factory workers and Germans. My guide took me to a small three-room apartment on the first floor. Mr. and Mrs. Chumatovsky, with whom I was to stay, worked in the factory. The boy was Mrs. Chumatovsky's brother.

In a tiny room in the apartment I found Zille, Friedrych's wife, and their five-year-old daughter, Elsa. Friedrych himself lived elsewhere. It was a melancholy reunion, a sad way to meet after so long a separation. Zille wept on seeing me. I held her at arm's length. She was the same prim, beautiful Zille. Her eyes, behind the glistening tears, had that same look of subtle understanding. It seemed as if she were reading in my face the words I could not speak.

The only furniture in the small room was a narrow bed standing near the tiny window overlooking the courtyard. I slept in another room, but all day the three of us remained locked in this room. Neighbors, from whom every hint of our existence had to be kept, often came to visit the Chumatovskys, especially in the evening to play cards or to exchange the latest rumors.

Five-year-old Elsa was a pretty, active blond child whose blue eyes radiated life and spirit. She could not understand why we had to remain constantly cooped up in our small room, not even going for a walk in the courtyard. In other ways, however, she sometimes frightened us by her awareness of the dangerous situation.

Sometimes I would forgetfully lapse into Yiddish. The child would become almost hysterical. "Stop speaking that language. Don't you realize it means our lives?" she would hiss sharply in Polish.

Elsa would sit at the window, watching other children at play in the yard. Often she would cry. Fearful of attracting attention, her mother would try to quiet the girl. Sometimes the only way was to stuff a handkerchief into the little mouth. The child's cry-

164

ing made our landlady very nervous. The neighbors knew that she had no children. She was afraid that we would be discovered. She had heard terrible tales of how the Germans stamped out the lives of little Jewish children with their boots, and then shot the mothers and their Gentile hosts as well.

Our landlord, Chumatovsky, was tall and friendly, with a quiet reserve that contrasted sharply with his wife's temperament. He had been a forester before the war. Now he worked in the armament factory and was an active member of the democratic underground movement. He frequently brought us information obtained from the illegal radio.

Mrs. Chumatovsky was a thin, blue-eyed, attractive woman with one shriveled hand. She was nervously energetic and very jumpy in tense situations. Hiding Jews was a terrible mental strain for her, but she could not bear to have us fall into the hands of the Germans. She had been born in Germany of a German mother who had died when Mrs. Chumatovsky was still a young girl. Her father, Shcherbinsky, had brought her back to Poland, but her two brothers remained in Germany and were now in the Nazi Army. She had had an unhappy childhood marked by frequent beatings from her father, until she finally ran away from home to marry Chumatovsky. She had since become reconciled with her father, who was also hiding some of our comrades, including Friedrych, but she still did not trust him and warned me against him.

She was torn by contradictory anxieties. She had refused to declare herself a Volksdeutsche. That had cost her a job in one factory, though she had managed to find new employment with her husband at Steyr. But desire to see Germany defeated was mixed with fear for the fate of her two brothers in the German Army.

Of all this she unburdened herself to me in long sessions. I was a good listener and we became close friends.

Chumatovsky was her senior by twelve years. His quietness irked her. He had helped her escape from Shcherbinsky, but the marriage was far from idyllic.

One of our neighbors was an engineer from upper Silesia, a bitter nationalist and a member of the underground of the National Democratic party, the Polish anti-Semitic reactionary party. He worked with Chumatovsky at the factory and often came to visit in the evening. When he was there, we sat huddled in our little room, holding our breaths, always watchful to see that the child did not betray us with a whisper or a cry. Those were the most painful hours of our clandestine existence.

One evening the engineer came to the Chumatovskys and asked them to let him sleep there that night. He was afraid to remain in his own apartment because the Germans were rounding up all former officers of the Polish Army who had failed to register as ordered. Our hosts were in despair, but they could not refuse him, no matter how much they feared that he might discover their secret.

It was a nightmare. Zille and I sat up all night, trembling for fear that the child might wake up and cry or talk too loudly, maybe ask for a drink of water, maybe—anything would have doomed us.

The nervous anxiety soon began to tell on our hosts. Our landlady was often in tears. Her hysteria multiplied our own fears. Together with our hosts we began to cast about for a way in which little Elsa might be removed to safety. Our landlord had a sister who was Mother Superior in a convent near Cracow. We decided to send the child to her.

Mrs. Chumatovsky went there first to discuss the project and to make the necessary arrangements. When she returned with a favorable answer, we prepared the girl for the trip. She was told that she was going to an aunt's where there were other children with whom she could play outdoors and have lots of fun. For several days our landlady taught the child how to say prayers in preparation for her new life and new name under the crucifix. The child slowly accustomed herself to the new role. Her intuitive understanding of the danger which hung over her and her

166

mother drove her to do her best. She seemed to know instinctively that all this was necessary to avert a terrible catastrophe.

With a heavy heart, her lips pressed tightly together to restrain her sobs, Zille packed Elsa's things and sent her away.

Mrs. Chumatovsky stayed with the child at the convent for several days. Elsa would not let her leave. She wept and pleaded not to be left alone. When the child was somewhat calmer Mrs. Chumatovsky was able to return.

Exactly where the convent was, the Chumatovskys, of course, refused to say. In case of arrest the parents might not be able to endure the torture and might give the information to the Gestapo, bringing tragedy to the convent and all its inmates. Besides, the parents, in their anxiety, might attempt to communicate with the child and unwittingly betray the secret. The Chumatovskys obtained a Catholic birth certificate in the girl's new name and assumed legal guardianship over her. Thus formally ended the connection of Zalman and Zille with their only child.

For twelve days I did not once leave the house. My hosts considered it too dangerous. Friedrych was permitted to visit us once a week.

I finally contrived to leave the house by telling the Chumatovskys that my money had run out and I had to get more. Friedrych, meanwhile, had arranged for me to meet Morizi Orzech and Leon Feiner, both of whom lived on Zholibosh Street. I was to find Morizi waiting at Wilson Square at the appointed hour.

I walked into the street like an actor making his debut. I was conscious of every motion of my body. My cane felt hot in my hand. I glanced out of the corner of my eye at every passer-by to see if he was looking at me. I felt a compelling urge to look behind me to see if I was being followed, but I was afraid that it would attract attention. I forced myself to look straight ahead and walk slowly, casually.

By the time I reached the trolley stop, I had a better grip on my nerves. As I entered the streetcar I stepped into the path of a man who was elbowing his way out. My heart sank. He was an officer of the Polish police who knew me very well from the old days. He used to be assigned regularly to Bund demonstrations and mass meetings. He looked straight into my eyes and stopped short. I returned his gaze. His mind seemed to be occupied with placing the familiar face. Slowly and deliberately he reached behind him to pull his coat free from between two passengers. Then, with an impatient shake of his head, he stepped past me

All this must have taken a fraction of a minute. I was wet with perspiration. My clothes stuck to my skin. My beard seemed to be dripping. The streetcar lurched forward.

I marveled at the sights in the streets. It was so different from the ghetto. The people were so well dressed. Here it seemed that nothing had changed.

I got off at Wilson Square. Some of the men loitering at the streetcar stop seemed to be looking at me suspiciously. However, I walked erect and with assurance—an old man with a cane, walking purposefully on his way. A short middle-aged man with a small well-trimmed mustache threw me a glance and walked off. It was Orzech. I followed. I was amazed at how badly he looked. It was two months since we had met in the ghetto. A cloud had descended over his face. He no longer seemed to have the old alertness, the sureness of motion, the impulsiveness of spirit.

When the Gestapo had begun to hunt for Orzech in the ghetto, we had had a great deal of difficulty with him. He absolutely refused to remain quietly in one place. During the deportation in July 1942, the Gestapo searched for him in earnest. In August we managed to get him over to the Aryan side, just in time for him to confirm the tragic story of the liquidation of the Medem Sanatorium. As I walked behind him now, I felt grateful that this dynamo of energy, this unbreakable spirit, though seemingly tired and worn, was still with us.

Immediately after we got to Orzech's apartment Leon Feiner arrived. He, too, had changed a great deal since April, when we had met in Manya Wasser's ghetto apartment. He looked old and extremely tired. He was neatly dressed, however, and his gray hair and long gray mustache gave him the appearance of a Polish country gentleman.

This was considered a formal meeting of half the members of the central committee of the underground Bund. The other half—Abrasha Blum, Loeser Clog, and Berek Snaidmil—were in the ghetto.

We tried to assess the situation, each contributing whatever information he had. They were better informed than I about recent events. We already knew that the entire Otvotsk region and Otvotsk itself had been cleared of Jews. The same had happened at Kalushin, Shedltze, Myendzyzhetz, Minsk-Mazovietsky. We already had a detailed report on the destruction of the Medem Sanatorium. There was also unmistakable evidence that the Gestapo was concentrating on finding Orzech on the Aryan side.

I was horrified to hear of what had happened to Manya Ziegelboim, Artur's wife, and their child. As I already knew, she had managed to hide in a cellar in the sanatorium. After the raid she escaped to a village near Myedzeshyn. For a time she lived in a peasant's hut. When she could no longer remain there, she came to Warsaw and managed to get to the home of Stopnitzky, the Socialist lawyer. She spent the night there, but it was too dangerous to remain. All of Stopnitzky's efforts to find a place for her came to naught. For several weeks she wandered about in the open fields near Zholibosh and then in desperation smuggled herself back into the ghetto.

I reported on the organized groups in the ghetto who were awaiting the arrival of arms. Orzech and Feiner assured me that arms would certainly be forthcoming from the Polish underground. We made plans for buying additional arms in preparation for the final moment.

169

We also made plans for establishing contact with the various labor camps to which workers from the ghetto had been sent. We took steps to buy more apartments on the Aryan side. The tragic example of Manya Ziegelboim was a clear warning to us.

Orzech reported on our contact with the outside world via the facilities of the London government. He had already sent several messages through the clandestine radio and through delegates of the London government, reporting the most recent wave of deportations and the new situation in the ghetto. So far, however, he had received no answer.

We arranged for future methods of keeping in touch with each other and of informing the other comrades of our decisions for action. I went back to the Chumatovskys, determined to find another apartment which would give me greater freedom of action.

All my efforts to find new quarters were in vain. The number of Poles who were willing to risk their lives on behalf of Jews was very small. After the latest deportations the number of fugitives on the Aryan side had increased. The search for apartments became more intense each day, and each day the Jew-hunt became greater. *Schmaltzovniks*—blackmailers who lived off Jews hiding on the Aryan side—were having their heyday. Hundreds of Jews were shot on the sacred Aryan soil during that period. It was dangerous to walk the street, no matter how well you were disguised and how well provided with documents.

We had to do the best we could with the apartments we already had. We took another boarder in with us, Pola Flinker, the wife of my friend Henik Tuchmacher, who had smuggled me out of the ghetto.

One day our landlady informed us in great agitation that she expected a visit from the sanitation commission. They would of course examine every room. We had no alternative but to leave for a day or two. We asked Mrs. Chumatovsky's father, Shcherbinsky, with whom Friedrych lived, to take us in for a few days. That was not so simple. He already had Friedrych, Fishgrund, David Klin (who, after the war, was put in a Polish jail), Gala Leshtchinska, and a few others, all very much wanted by the police. Moreover, Shcherbinsky's apartment also served as a rendezvous for various leaders of the underground, such as Berman of the Left Poale Zion (who became the postwar head of the Jewish Committee in Poland), Guzik of the Joint Distribution Committee, Kirshenbaum of the Zionists, Dr Ringelblum of the Poale Zion, and others. But we had no alternative.

I went alone and got there without incident. Pola and Zille went in the company of Mr. Chumatovsky. They carried small packages with their necessities. On the corner of Mlynarska a group of *schmaltzovniks* stopped them. Chumatovsky managed to get away. The scum took everything from Pola and Zille, leaving them practically naked and barefoot in the cold. They finally managed to get to Shcherbinsky's apartment.

After the visit of the sanitation commission, we returned to Chumatovsky's. A few weeks later Mrs. Chumatovsky told us that a second visit from the commission was expected. We went to Shcherbinsky's again but were not very much surprised when this time the Chumatovskys refused to take us back. We prevailed upon Shcherbinsky to allow us to remain until we could find another apartment, but this visit stretched into several weeks. During it, Berek Snaidmil made a flying visit from the ghetto to discuss the preparations for armed uprising. We sat up all night going over the plans down to every small detail, arranged to coordinate the work, and parted again.

I did not consider Shcherbinsky's apartment very safe, and our prolonged stay made me uneasy. Some of us suspected that he was playing both sides of the fence; that he had regular dealings with the Germans.

We soon had circumstantial evidence to support this belief. While we were there, Shcherbinsky took in a fugitive Jew and his daughter. The next day, the Germans came—to bargain with the Jew about ransom money. We learned later that the Germans left with fifteen thousand zlotys. The transaction lasted several hours, during which six of us—Pola, Zille, Gala, David Klin, Gottlieb, an official of the JDC, and I—were hidden in a dark room listening to the conversation with bated breath, expecting that at any moment the German-speaking strangers would break in on us.

Immediately after paying the ransom, the Jew left Shcherbinsky's house. We suspected that Shcherbinsky had arranged the trap with some German friends.

Finally we succeeded in buying an apartment at 11 Shwentoyerska, just outside the ghetto walls. Into it moved Pola Flinker, Ruta Perenson, and Zille Friedrych. We arranged also to bring Greenberg, a confectioner, to the apartment from the ghetto.

The idea of again moving into an apartment with such a large group did not appeal to me. I begged the Chumatovskys to take me back into the apartment where I had spent my first days on the Aryan side. They agreed—and thus saved me from sharing in an ill-fated enterprise.

While taking Greenberg over the ghetto wall on Shwentoyerska, Henik Tuchmacher and the Christian landlord of the apartment were arrested. Greenberg escaped back into the ghetto. The Germans searched the apartment, found the hidden Jews, and discovered a store of arms in the basement. The landlord admitted that the arms had been brought there by Tuchmacher. Henik and Esterson, a member of the Morgenstern who was discovered in the apartment, were taken to the Befehlstelle at 103 Zhelasna. There they were murderously beaten and finally shot. Henik's wife Pola and Zille Friedrych were sent to the women's camp at Lublin. We learned later that they were killed in Maidanek. We managed to buy the release of Ruta Perenson and her thirteen-year-old son Nicko and get them back into the ghetto.

Our intensive work of preparation, both inside and outside the ghetto, began to show results. We no longer had to convince anyone that the deportations meant death and annihilation. The hopeful illusion had been destroyed. From its ashes grew a determined spirit of resistance. Every section of the ghetto was now pervaded with the feeling that the end could come only in a battle to the death. Every one of the forty thousand who remained alive burned with impatience to come to grips with the enemy. They stood at their work in the ghetto factories, they dragged themselves under heavy guard to slave labor on the Aryan side, every thought, every hope working in only one direction, toward only one goal—a fight to the death. Everyone in the ghetto, whether enrolled in organized fighting groups or not, thought only about arms and weapons.

Our problems were now organization and supply. The Jewish fighting organization, Zhidowska Organizatzia Boyova, representing every Jewish ideological grouping, was already established. In every factory, every shop, every office in the ghetto, wherever there was a concentration of workers, the fighting groups organized, collected arms on the factory grounds despite the watchful eyes of the enemy, prepared fighting places, hiding places, communication tunnels, and worked out their strategic plans. The old conspiratorial groups of fives and tens were now broadened to include larger numbers. They became the battle preparation centers in the factories and the shops.

On the Aryan side the Council for Aid to Jews was organized, representing almost all the Polish parties. It was a subcommittee of the underground government. Its task was to supply Jews with documents and apartments, to help Jewish children, to raise money and arms. The Bund's representative on it was Leon Feiner. The Jewish National Committee, to which all Jewish political parties except the Bund belonged, was represented by Adolph Berman, a Poale Zionist.

At about the same time we set up in the ghetto a coordinating

committee of all Jewish parties. The Bund was represented by
Abrasha Blum and Berek Snaidmil. The Jewish fighting organization was directed by this coordinating committee.

Our center for arms procurement on the Aryan side was at 3
Gournoshlonska Street in the home of a Polish worker, Stefan
Macho. Michel Klepfish had worked with him in a metal factory
before the war. Stefan helped us buy and smuggle the weapons.
Similar groups to obtain weapons were set up by Hashomer,
Hechalutz, and others.

In the midst of this feverish work, young Michel Klepfish was
arrested on the street by a Polish police agent and held in prison
for about ten days. We tried everything within our means to free
him, without success. He was sent to Treblinka. On the way he
managed, miraculously, to remove the bars of the freight car window and jump off the train at night. He hurt one foot very badly,
but managed to drag himself back to Warsaw. He lay in excru-
ciating pain for about a week, impatient to be up and at work
again. After he had recovered he left Warsaw to take a course
given by the military division of the PPS. Being an engineer, he
quickly absorbed the instructions in the preparation of explosives,
especially in the making of grenades and bottle bombs filled with
incendiary and explosive material.

Buying arms was very difficult and dangerous. Nevertheless,
little by little, driven to take great risks by the desperate feeling
that we were working against time, we managed to achieve some
success. The usual place for carrying on the illicit transactions
was the great market at Kazimierz Square. People who knew
where weapons could be obtained brought us the information.
We bought stolen arms from guards at army dumps, from German soldiers, from Poles who worked in arms factories. With
restless hysteria, we explored every avenue, tracked down every
lead, knowing that the end was close and that we must be ready.

Then the morale of the Jewish workers in the ghetto received a heartbreaking blow. Through the Polish underground radio we learned that our comrades Henryk Erlich and Victor Alter had been murdered by the Soviet government.

Even now I can see before my eyes the faces of our people during the first days after we learned that our two most beloved comrades and leaders had been shot to death in Stalin's GPU dungeons. Heads were bowed in deep sorrow and bitter anger. Helpless rage glistened in their tear-stained eyes.

For us Henryk and Victor had typified unselfish idealism and devotion. They had risen among the Jewish masses of Poland as great popular leaders, teaching by word and deed the possibility of a fuller, better, more decent life. They had won a place in the heart of every Jewish worker, and everyone felt the loss deeply and personally.

We published a special memorial issue of *The Bulletin* which expressed our sorrow and bitter resentment. At memorial meetings we tried to analyze the motives which had led to such a hateful crime. We could not understand the twisted political thinking of a regime which could commit such murders.

The news also affected our non-Jewish comrades. The Polish illegal press carried articles reviewing the role of the murdered Socialist leaders in the Polish and in the international Socialist movement.

In the human jungle in which we lived, this crime struck at the only thing which gave us hope—our faith in ultimate human decency.

Since our dispatches about the events in the ghetto seemed to have made no impression on the outside world, we resolved to send a living witness out of the country to inform the Allied countries in person. It was becoming more and more evident that Morizi Orzech was in great danger and that the police might close in on him at any moment. Since he was in all respects admirably suited for this mission, we decided to send him.

He got as far as the small village of Kolomya in Galicia on his way to the Rumanian border. There he was arrested. With great effort and a resort to bribery we managed to have him returned to Warsaw, but all attempts to free him were unsuccessful. Later, in August 1943, he was murdered in the Paviak prison.

In 1944 his wife was arrested on the Aryan side and disappeared without a trace.

His only daughter lived through the Warsaw uprising, in which she served as a courier for the underground army, but after her evacuation to Prushkov with the army prisoners she was never heard from again.

During the early part of 1943 the terror throughout all of Poland entered a more severe and terrible phase. Armed German bands descended upon small towns and villages, indiscriminately dragging out inhabitants, men, women, and children, and shipping them away. The Germans did not even go through the formalities of preliminary warnings. All Poland became the scene of a wild human hunt. Day in and day out, hundreds of Poles were dragged away. People went outdoors only under the pressure of extreme necessity. A thick fog of fear hung over the entire country.

By contrast, the ghetto was somewhat more peaceful. It seemed almost as if the beasts had forgotten the tens of thousands of Jews who, like ghosts, haunted that empty wilderness.

Suddenly, on January 18, 1943, at six o'clock in the morning, the several ghetto streets which housed the slave laborers of the shops and factories were filled with wild shouts, volleys of shooting, and the sharp blasts of truck and motorcycle horns. German murderers raced into the courtyards and tenements and began to drive the people out. The laggards were beaten or shot. The rest

176

were marched toward the Umschlagplatz. Groups of workers on their way to work were also led away with shouts, blows, and shooting. Documents, work cards, tokens, were no help.

It all happened so quickly that even organized factory battle groups were cut off from their hidden weapons and were unable to offer resistance. Only four battle groups, Zamenhof, Mila, Muranovska, and Franciskanska, managed to get into action. They opened fire and threw several hand grenades, killing about twenty Germans.

The Nazis were amazed. Jews fighting with guns! Impossible! Nothing like this had happened in the ghetto before. After taking a few thousand victims they broke off the raid and retired from the ghetto.

In the fight that day we lost a great many people, among them Rubinstein, a faithful Bundist of Lodz, Chaimovitch, Cholodenko from Lodz, Abram Feiner, a tailor and member of the Zukunft. Itzhock Guiterman, a director of the American Joint Distribution Committee who had returned to Poland with Orzech from the German prisoner-of-war camp, was shot on the steps of his home as he ran to hide.

Among those taken to the Umschlagplatz were the vice-president of the Judenrat, Josef Jashunski, and his wife, together with their son Mischa, a doctor who was very active in our underground, and his wife. At the Umschlagplatz Jashunski was seen by a Gestapo officer. The two men knew each other from the sessions of the Judenrat. The officer walked up to the aged Jashunski and slapped his face as a special sign of recognition.

The debut of the ghetto fighters made a tremendous impression inside and outside the ghetto. The mere fact of an organized armed blow strengthened the will to further resistance and increased the tempo of preparation for future battles. The entire Polish underground press, regardless of political ideology, greeted the battle of January 18 with enthusiasm.

177

We received from the official underground army, Armia Kryova, a small transport of arms: fifty revolvers, fifty grenades, and some explosives.

Morale in the ghetto was rising. The Germans began to realize that a remarkable change had taken place, that an armed force was being created. In the evenings, Germans no longer walked alone in the ghetto streets.

In further preparation for the events ahead, the Jewish fighting organization took steps to clear the ghetto of all Jewish servants of the Gestapo. Special counterespionage groups tracked down every Jewish Gestapo agent and liquidated him. For example, there was Alfred Nossig, a Jewish intellectual from Galicia. He had been a contributor of articles in Jewish, Hebrew, and German to various journals. He had served as an informer on Jewish matters for the German government even before Hitler. His specialty was the Polish Jewry. After the First World War, when Poland became independent, he used to visit Warsaw from time to time. Now he appeared in the ghetto on special work for the Gestapo. One of our comrades discovered his apartment and searched it. An identity card showed that Nossig had served the Gestapo since 1933, the year Hitler came to power. The fighting organization passed sentence of death, and he was shot.

Fuerst, one-time director of the prewar Jewish Students' Home in Praga, and a Gestapo informer, was shot by order of the fighting organization. Lolek Kokosovsky, a Maccabee leader from Zgerzh, was a Gestapo agent whose specialty was political information about the ghetto and the members of the underground organizations. At first he escaped our agents with only a bad wound. His friends took him from the ghetto, and he recovered. Later, however, he was shot and killed on the Aryan side as he walked out of a restaurant.

Sherinsky, an apostate Jew, already has been mentioned as the commissioner of the Jewish police. Our attempted execution of him failed, though he was seriously wounded. Afterward he took his own life. Laikin, who had been a lawyer before the war, was Sherinsky's assistant. After Sherinsky's death he assumed the position of Jewish police commissioner. Greatly hated in the ghetto, he was sentenced to death and shot.

These executions further strengthened the morale of the fighting groups and increased the prestige of the Jewish fighting organization. It felt sufficiently powerful now to levy a tax on the entire ghetto to buy arms; it even taxed the Judenrat. Some of the wealthy who refused to pay the tax were arrested. The authority of the fighting organization began to be felt throughout the ghetto. Its influence and power grew with every passing day.

At the beginning of the deportations we had appealed in vain: "Refuse to go willingly to the slaughter! Fight back tooth and nail!" Now our words began to take on meaning. The forces of resistance continued to grow and become more aggressive. Once, as a group was being taken to the Umschlagplatz, the members of the fighting organization lay in wait along the route, fell upon the guards, and created enough diversion to disorient them. Scores were able to escape in the confusion.

In addition to the fighting groups in factories and shops included under the over-all plan of the underground, special battle units of young people were now organized and installed as garrisons in strategic houses. Food and supplies were provided for them, and they were maintained in a state of constant readiness, arms in hand. This reorganization was necessary after the bloody lesson of January 18, when the Germans had raided the ghetto so suddenly. At that time the resistance forces were scattered throughout the entire ghetto and could not even reach their arsenals. The small groups which did have arms lost very heavily. It had not been possible to broaden the battle and bring in reinforcements from other districts. The new arrangement set up various strong points in the ghetto, garrisoned by groups ready to fight at a given signal.

The Bund, under which almost all the factory fighting groups were organized, contributed only four groups to these special garrisons. We were fearful of unduly weakening our factory strongholds. In most cases, the workers were not in a position to leave the factories, where they received their food and where they sometimes were able to hide members of their families. Besides, since the organized groups constituted a small part of the ghetto population, it was imperative that they be concentrated in population centers, so that in the moment of battle they would be able to draw everyone into the fight. If they failed in this the German military machine would finish off the small organized groups in short order.

The Bund, being a workers' party, counted on the close comradeship of fellow-workers to spread the contagion of the spirit of the most daring and determined and to draw the others into the fight. Our goal was to broaden the resistance and give it a mass character; otherwise it would be only an irresponsible, desperate adventure. Our reliance on the people proved to be justified, for when the final battle was joined our factory groups were able to draw into it all the factory workers. Even the so-called "wild" people, the illegals without any credentials who lived wherever they could hide, joined the struggle.

Alongside the organized battle groups, individuals made ready for the final hour as well as they could. The entire ghetto seethed with preparation for conflict.

"Death is coming anyhow. Let us at least meet him with arms in hand. Let us take some small revenge upon our torturers. Let us not give up our lives so easily." Such was the feeling, without exception, of the entire ghetto, and of our little group on the Aryan side, preparing the weapons for the last battle.

Michel Klepfish, Zalman Friedrych, and I sat in one of our conspiratorial apartments on the Aryan side one evening, discussing the details of plans for smuggling more weapons and explosives into the ghetto. Michel's specialty was now explosive bottles. With the help of the PPS, he had already smuggled two thousand liters of benzine into the ghetto. He had also organized a factory for manufacturing the explosive bottles and had taught a group of comrades how to make and use them.

Michel was always unsatisfied. Too little was being done to get guns and dynamite. He demanded that more money be made available and more resources used. He was always agitated and impatient and always complaining. More must be done, and more, more!

He was especially absorbed that evening in his own thoughts, weighed down by his responsibilities. He burned with the desire for vengeance. Every once in a while he would rise from his reverie to contribute a fragment to the conversation; then he returned to his thoughts as if to a different and more mysterious world. "My father and mother have already been burned. . . . My sister is buried in a Christian cemetery. . . . My child is in a foundling home. . . . My wife is a servant in a Gentile home. . . . All I want now is to be consumed in the battle for vengeance."

His blue eyes burned with excitement, with courage, with despair. His thin lips were pressed tightly together in determined stubbornness. As I looked at him, I recalled the year 1920, when the new independent Poland was at war with the Soviet Union. The Bund had been outlawed and had had to go underground. At the home of Michel's parents at 30 Shwentoyerska we set up the illegal party secretariat. There I would often see Michel, a spirited little boy, dashing mischievously through the house. Years later he was a student at the Polytechnic, a member of the militia under my command. He was outstanding in the fight against the fascist students in their attempt to institute "ghetto benches" in the colleges. Now that little blond boy was himself a father and a hero in the most frightful and hopeless struggle the world has ever witnessed.

I looked at Zalman Friedrych. He, too, had grown up before my eyes, a product of our own schools. He had joined the Bund while still a student and had later assumed a leading position in our school system. He had been active as secretary and magazine editor of the sport organization, Morgenstern. Before the war he had served in our militia, where his healthy mountain-climbing physique had stood him in good stead. He had been captured by the Germans while serving with the Polish Army but had later been freed under the Nazi policy of weeding out all Jews from among the war prisoners.

He sat before me, a thirty-year-old handsome blond man, his narrow face white, his thick lips drawn hard, his head bowed. He too was living and reliving his recent personal tragedies: "Father, mother, sister, all burned . . . my Zille in Maidanek . . . my only child in a Catholic convent . . ." He clenched his fists over his blond head and said hoarsely, "Revenge! Revenge!"

The ghetto now became a center of intensive excavation and construction as we concentrated on the building of "bunkers." These were hiding places for men and supplies. The builders resorted to the most artful improvisations, revealing extraordinary inventiveness. Groups of inhabitants in a tenement or in neighboring tenements organized, collected money, and hired engineers and technicians to supervise the building. Any of the prewar Jewish engineers and specialists that were left in the ghetto found plenty to do.

The bunker took various forms, depending upon the physical layout of the building and the ingenuity and skill of the builders. Sometimes it was a double wall, parallel to the old one, with enough room between the two for several people to wait out a raid. Access to the double wall might be through an old wardrobe standing in a corner. It would look like any other wardrobe, but in a way known only to the initiated, its side might be lifted or swung aside to allow one person at a time to crawl into the corridor between the walls. If the double wall were in a kitchen, one might enter it by slithering through the oven and replacing the clutter of pots and pans from inside the hiding place to camouflage the entrance.

Sometimes a bunker was a double cellar, constructed by digging a tunnel under the old cellar and hollowing out a large cavern at the end of it. The entrance to the double cellar was camouflaged by covering it with the same dust, rags, and accumulation of debris as the rest of the basement. In some of the double cellars crude ventilation systems were installed, as well as connections for electricity and water.

In addition to the hiding places, tunnels were dug to connect one courtyard to another. Passages were constructed through the cellars and the attics—a communications system which proved to be of great strategic value during the ghetto uprising.

Some tunnels led to points on the Aryan side; some connected with the sewage and water-supply systems. Heating systems were built into some bunkers. Stocks of fuel and food, especially hard candy and cereals, were accumulated.

The entire ghetto worked with singleness of purpose. The preparations went on in the conviction that the final battle of annihilation was inevitable. There was no deliverance! Even on the Aryan side only a few could save themselves, and those only at the cost of tremendous sums of money. News constantly trickled back to the ghetto of Jews on the other side who had fallen victim to the *schmaltzovniks*. The fugitives were in constant danger of falling into the hands of the enemy, for it was almost impossible to obtain documents or a place to live. Each day the terror on the Aryan side increased. There were constant raids, arrests, and executions for the slightest hint of contact with Jews. Many Jews had to return to the ghetto-hell because the danger on the outside was too great. They could find no way to establish themselves.

There was no deliverance! This certainty embraced everyone in the ghetto. Almost everybody was trying to buy arms. They paid fantastic prices. Everyone was willing to give up whatever possessions he had for a gun. What use were money, jewelry, or clothes when the last hour was so close, and when they could be exchanged for a weapon to kill the enemy?

All eyes in the ghetto looked to the underground organizations, to the coordinating committee, and to the Jewish fighting organization. Their orders were carried out without question. They commanded complete confidence. The "all-powerful" Judenrat was now ignored. The new head, the engineer Marek Lichtenbaum, no longer had any power or influence. No one paid the slightest bit of attention to him. When the Germans asked him to help carry out the evacuation of the factories he answered that he had no influence in the ghetto, that power resided in other hands.

The Germans probably understood the new frame of mind in the ghetto and knew that the people were arming. That may be why they decided to carry out the last step in the liquidation of the ghetto quietly, slowly, without terror, without the bestial scenes of the selections and the seizures. They proposed an evacuation plan.

The forty thousand Jews who remained were almost all workers registered in the factories producing for the military battlefront. As evacuation commissioner the Germans picked Tebbens, one of the most important factory owners. He was given the task of moving all the workshops, including their human and material inventories, to Travniki and Poniatov, both well-known places near Lublin.

Tebbens had a large propaganda staff, members of which appeared before the assembled workers in each factory and described all the blessings of working peacefully in the lap of nature in the countryside, with fresh air and good food, so different from

184

the Warsaw ghetto, poisoned with epidemics, filth, and sickness. Tebbens himself attended such meetings and gave his word of honor that the factory workers and their families were being moved only to continue work. He begged them not to credit the "malicious" rumors which were spread in the ghetto that deported Jews were killed.

The Jewish coordinating committee and the Jewish fighting organization posted a proclamation stating that Travniki and Poniatov meant a new deportation, a new form of extermination and death, that no one should believe the sweet words of Tebbens' propagandists or accept his word of honor, that the Jews knew very well what the executioner's word of honor was worth, and that no one must present himself willingly at the evacuation points.

On the day of the evacuation, out of the thousands of workers in the factories, only a few presented themselves at the appointed places. From the brush factory on Shwentoyerska, in which several thousand people worked, not a single one volunteered. Tebbens tried to wage a polemic battle with the Jewish fighting organization through posters. Again he assured the ghetto that it was being emptied to give the workers better conditions to labor and to live. Indeed, the Jews now heard a new, sweet voice from him, different from the one that had thundered death and extermination for three years. But everyone understood the change in German tactics. Tebbens' propaganda, by its tacit respect for the strength of the resistance, served only to raise the ghetto's morale and strengthen the will to fight.

In the few weeks before the ghetto uprising the determination to come to grips with the enemy began to express itself. Where the Germans tried to carry out the evacuation by force, workers set fire to factory stores and buildings. That happened to the warehouse of Allmann's woodworking factory on Smotcha. At the brush factories, the wagons loaded with machines and materials were set ablaze. At the Umschlagplatz, a large group of workers who had been gathered to be shipped out refused to enter the freight cars. One of them, the Bundist youth leader Peltz, addressed the crowd and urged them not to go willingly. The guards opened fire, and about sixty men were killed.

Since January 18 the entire ghetto had been transforming itself into a battleground. Not for a single moment was there any relaxation in the intensive work of preparation, of digging bunkers and communications tunnels, of building fortifications, of stocking weapons and supplies. The atmosphere seethed with feverish preparations and eagerness for battle. Every Jew became a soldier. From the sufferings of hell he forged the weapons of resistance and battle.

Shortly before the uprising the Germans changed their tactics again. Suddenly there were rumors that the plans for evacuation had been abandoned and that, on the contrary, work in the Warsaw factories would be stepped up because production was badly needed for the battlefront. The Germans were supposed to be planning to add new cadres of workers to raise the output. This was certainly a trick to relax the vigilance of the ghetto, but it came too late to have any effect.

We on the Aryan side utilized every means of obtaining arms— private channels, professional smugglers, Armia Kryova (the "official" army of the government-in-exile), and the military organizations of the Polish government and the Polish Socialists. Arms from the various sources were dispatched to the ghetto as soon as we received them. Every channel of communication with the ghetto was guarded by comrades of the fighting organization, who were on the lookout day and night for our transports. The comrades on the Aryan side would escort shipments of arms into the ghetto, remain a few days, and then return for new shipments.

No one could tell when, on what day, at what hour, the beasts would break into the ghetto with their overwhelming armed might. We knew they would not wait much longer, that the hopeless Tebbens campaign would not continue. The Germans, recognizing the ineffectiveness of the sugar-coated propaganda, would return to their old and favorite methods of brutal force to liquidate the ghetto completely.

We were in a state of tense expectation. We strained every nerve to gather ammunition and arms quickly and yet more quickly, and to throw them over the ghetto walls, rushing feverishly to make the most of what might be the few remaining moments.

A few days before the uprising, Michel Klepfish and Zalman Friedrych brought the last shipment of arms into the ghetto.

SIX

WITH bated breath the ghetto waited for the battle—for the finale of the weird, nightmarish tragedy which had lasted three long years. Every night scouts stood at their posts listening for the faintest sound, the slightest murmur. Near the gates of the ghetto, observation points were established. Patrols watched for the slightest movement on the other side, ready to sound the alarm immediately if the enemy should come.

And he did come—at two o'clock in the morning on Sunday, April 19, to the First Feast of Passover.

On the Aryan side of the ghetto wall, which extended many kilometers, appeared military and police guards, SS men, Ukrainians, Letts, and Poles. They stood twenty paces apart. They did not intend to let anyone escape.

At five o'clock in the morning, when the normal trickle of people in and out of the ghetto began, the gates were barred. No one was permitted in or out.

At six o'clock, under the glowing rays of a bright spring sun, the black Nazi death-battalions marched into the ghetto in full battle array, with panzer cars, machine guns, tanks. Boldly they marched down Zamenhof in the direction of Kupyetska, Mila, Muranovska, Franciskanska, toward the so-called "wild ghetto." Here lived those people who worked in various institutions, and others who were not registered in factories. The Germans appeared to be isolating the "factory ghetto," giving the impression that the factories and their workers were not to be molested. Just the final roundup of the nonproductive elements . . .

The scouts signaled all battle stations. When the proud German column reached Mila Street it was met with fire from three sides—from the corner of Mila and Zamenhof, from 29 Zamenhof, and from 38 Zamenhof opposite. Grenades and incendiary bottles cascaded down on them. Many Germans fell dead. Two tanks burned with their crews. But our battle groups suffered no losses.

Such strong resistance apparently surprised the Germans. They quickly left the ghetto.

The next morning, after cutting off the electricity and the water supply, they were back. This time they did not parade down the center of the street. They came singly or in small groups, moving close to the walls, shooting machine guns into every window and every opening of every building from which they might expect a blow. This time they came from the Tlomatzka direction along Nalefky Street toward Mila, Zamenhof, and Shwentoyerska. Battle groups from the brush factories on Shwentoyerska, from Tebbens' and Shultz's, as well as groups from Leshno, Novolipya, Novolipky, and Smotcha Streets, were thrown into the fight. The Germans moved under a hail of hand grenades, dynamite bombs, and incendiary bottles thrown from windows, roofs, and attics A detachment of three hundred Germans penetrated past Valova Street deeper into Shwentoyerska. They were ripped to bits by an electrically activated mine which our fighters had planted with great care at 30-32 Shwentoyerska. Shreds of uniform and human flesh flew in all directions. Our fighters withdrew through attics and over roofs.

But the fighting had only begun. On Shwentoyerska Street it raged around the brush factories. A group under the command of Michel Klepfish took a heavy toll of Germans. They battled for every building and for every floor of every building. They fought along the stairways until they were forced to the top floors. Then the Germans usually set fire to the building. Our fighters would dash through prepared openings in the attic walls to begin the fight again in the adjoining building.

On the fifth day of the battle, in executing such a withdrawal, Michel's group found themselves caught in an attic with German soldiers. In the dark, the fighting was confused. A German machine gun held Michel's men at bay by sweeping their side of the attic from behind a chimney.

Two comrades managed to get close enough to the main body of Nazis to throw a hand grenade. At that precise moment, Michel hurled himself upon the machine gun. It stopped firing.

An hour later, when the Germans were cleared out, his comrades found Michel's body with two neat rows of bullet holes across the stomach.

The Nazis soon changed their tactics in the brush factory area. The house-to-house fighting was proving too costly. They withdrew their troops and surrounded the entire section. Then they set fire to the blocks of buildings from the outside and waited.

Five groups of Jewish fighters were trapped. Flames were everywhere. Every building was burning. The asphalt pavement melted into a black, sticky, flowing mass. Blazing rafters and broken glass showered the streets.

The only escape was into the central part of the ghetto through a break in one of the ghetto sub-walls. The fighters bound their feet in rags to deaden the sound of their footsteps and as protection against the hot cobblestones. They made their way through the flames to the breach in the wall. Single file, in a crouching run, three groups dashed through the opening. As the first member of the fourth group stepped out, a German searchlight illuminated the whole section of the wall.

A shot rang out—sharpshooter Romanovitch—and the light reddened into darkness. Before the Germans could collect themselves the last group, Marek Edelman's, was through and away.

Then the sea of flames engulfed the central ghetto. Artillery fire thundered above the crackle of burning buildings and the crash of collapsing walls. Safe from the small arms and home-made grenades of the ghetto fighters, the Germans placed artillery and machine guns at Krashinsky Square, Parisovsky Square, Zhitnya Street, and Bonifraterska Street. These points were outside the ghetto. From them a hail of shells and bullets poured into the burning streets.

There was no air to breathe, only black asphyxiating smoke, heavy with the stench of burning bodies. The flames drove the people from their hiding places in basements and attics. In the streets the cobblestones and walls radiated the heavy, unbearable heat. Stone stairs glowed in the flames. Charred corpses lay on balconies, at window recesses, sprawled on the staircases. Thousands staggered into the streets—easy marks for the German patrols. Hundreds jumped from the fourth and fifth floors of buildings to end the torture quickly. Mothers threw children from the rooftops to spare them the agony of the flames.

Berek Snaidmil's group and another fighters' detachment escorted several hundred people in broad daylight from their burned-out shelter at 37 Mila to new quarters at 7 Mila. They held off the Germans there for more than a week.

Through the fire and smoke, without water, our fighters moved from one burning block to another, from one bunker to another. The battle groups were isolated. Each fought alone, holding out in its bunkers, cellars, and attics, without knowing how other groups were faring. A coordinated general battle plan was no longer possible.

Into this inferno the enemy threw his mechanized might. Every battle station became an isolated, beleaguered stronghold, surrounded by fire, wrapped in clouds of smoke. With revolvers, grenades, and incendiary bottles in their hands, wet handkerchiefs over their mouths, our fighters fought back against the overpowering force of an enemy armed with the most modern and efficient murder tools. Every remaining inhabitant of the ghetto without exception was now drawn into the battle—literally everyone, young and old. The organized battle groups, in which only a limited number of Jews had been enrolled, suddenly found that everyone clamored to be used. People did whatever they could. Everyone who could fight, whether armed or not, did so. Others acted as couriers, running from building to building with food, water, and ammunition.

The ghetto fighters made several counterattacks. German uniforms which had been prepared for the occasion were useful in permitting small groups to draw close enough to the enemy to deal a blow with their puny weapons.

The unceasing hail of incendiary bombs and artillery continued. Wherever the Germans met resistance or noticed any signs of activity, they let loose these terrible weapons, against which the ghetto fighters were all but helpless. The ghetto became one huge bonfire. At night the artillery fire would halt, and it seemed as if the silence of death had descended. The surrounding area was lit up by the burning ghetto. Small groups of Germans leading bloodhounds would prowl through the courtyards and buildings seeking out the fighters in their hidden bunkers. Anyone they caught was tortured to reveal other hiding places, or the location of stores and arms.

The Germans strengthened the guard around the ghetto; no one was allowed near the walls. They suspended streetcar traffic through Bonifraterska Street from which passengers could see what was happening inside. On the streets near the ghetto small groups of the curious would gather, hoping to catch a glimpse of the fighting. The police would disperse them, but they would gather again. The heavy artillery fire shattered the windows of outside buildings. The Germans cleared all inhabitants out of houses close to the ghetto walls.

193

On all the streets placards were posted, reading: "Death to every Pole who hides a Jew!" There were incessant searches for escaped Jews. The Germans had tasted resistance in the ghetto and were afraid that the Poles might also be stimulated to violence. "Security measures" on the Polish side were strengthened to forestall incidents.

The German press reported briefly that the ghetto Jews were resisting the transfer to work. The illegal Polish press of all shades wrote of the uprising sympathetically. Some even compared it to the historic Barkokba uprising against the Romans. Almost every day they carried communiqués from the battlefield, reporting the number and character of the German units that had entered and left the ghetto, how many ambulances with wounded Germans had driven out of the ghetto gates, the progress of the artillery bombardment, and so forth.

The average Pole was not quite so friendly.

Among the knots of people who gathered at Shwentoyerska Street and Krashinsky Square to watch the progress of the Jews' fight, all sorts of opinions were heard. Many were sympathetic, but one would often hear a cynical "Thank heaven the Germans are doing this for us." The broad mass of the Polish people was completely disoriented. Most of them had no understanding of what the uprising meant for the Jews, or even for the Poles. The four years of Nazi terror, persecution, and anti-Semitic propaganda had poisoned their souls and completely destroyed in many of them any feeling that the Jews were human.

Even among the members of the organized underground, who expressed friendliness to the ghetto fighters, there was no stomach for a brush with the occupying power in order to help the Jews. "An open fight at this time," they said, "would mean complete extermination for all of us." They refused to organize street demonstrations and turned down our request for a protest strike as a gesture of sympathy.

In the first days of the uprising, the Jewish underground issued

194

a message to the Polish population and, through the radio, to the entire world. It said.

> Poles, citizens, soldiers of freedom. Through the thunder of artillery which is shelling our homes, our mothers, wives, and children; through the sound of machine guns, through clouds of smoke and fire; over the streams of blood which flow in the murdered ghetto of Warsaw; we, the prisoners of the ghetto, send you our heartfelt brotherly greeting.
>
> We know that you watch with heartbreak, with tears of sympathy, with horror and amazement, for the outcome of the struggle we have been carrying on for several days with the hateful occupier.
>
> Be assured that every threshold in the ghetto will remain, as it has been until now, a fortress; that though we may all perish in this struggle, we will not surrender; that we breathe as you do with a thirst for vengeance and punishment for the crimes of our common enemy.
>
> This is a fight for your freedom and ours, for your and our human, social, and national pride! We will avenge the crimes of Oswiecim, Treblinka, Belzhitz, and Maidanek! Long live the brotherhood of blood and arms of Fighting Poland! Long live Freedom! Death to the executioners! A fight unto death with the occupier!
>
> Jewish Fighting Organizations,
April 23, 1943.

A similar declaration was issued by the underground Bund. "At least let the world know that these are the last agonizing days," we thought. "Perhaps some day there will be vengeance. . . ."

To our appeals for help, the outside world sent its answer. Through the underground radio we received the news that brave and loyal Artur Ziegelboim, our representative with the Polish government-in-exile, had given us the only aid within his power. During the night of May 12 he committed suicide in London as a gesture of protest against the callousness and indifference of the world.

In his farewell letter he said:

I cannot be silent—I cannot live—while remnants of the Jewish people of Poland, of whom I am a representative, are perishing. My comrades in the Warsaw ghetto took weapons in their hands on that last heroic impulse. It was not my destiny to die there together with them, but I belong to them, and in their mass graves. By my death I wish to express my strongest protest against the inactivity with which the world is looking on and permitting the extermination of my people.

I know how little human life is worth today, but as I was unable to do anything during my life perhaps by my death I shall contribute to breaking down the indifference of those who may now—at the last moment—rescue the few Polish Jews still alive from certain annihilation. My life belongs to the Jewish people of Poland and I therefore give it to them. I wish that this remaining handful of the original several millions of Polish Jews could live to see the liberation of a new world of freedom, and the justice of true Socialism. I believe that such a Poland will arise and that such a world will come.

The meaning of Artur's suicide was bitterly clear to all of us. He was tendering us the balance sheet of all his efforts on our behalf. Through an edition of *The Bulletin* issued on the Aryan side, we let the underground know that another fighter, who had suffered and fought with his ghetto comrades until his last breath, had fallen in far-off London.

The mighty Allied armies were in action against the enemy on all fronts. Every day great military struggles were taking place. But the Warsaw ghetto front remained isolated and alone. Its heroic fighters burned in its rubble, their cries for help choked in the clouds of smoke, drowned out by the thunder of artillery.

We, the small group who remained on the Aryan side, were torn with grief, with anguished shame. We suffered from a jumble of emotions: the desire to strike a blow at the enemy, pride in our fighting comrades, helplessness, desperation. Every artillery shot hammered into our brains. Why were we not there? Why were we not dying with them?

I would lie in my hiding place at night. The burning ghetto turned the entire horizon red. The light was dazzling. The awful silence called, "We are burning, we are dying. Help!" I would lie there, bathed in my perspiration, hot tears pouring down my face, and I would bury my face in the pillow to stifle my helpless sobs.

On the tenth day of the uprising, April 30, two special messengers of the Jewish fighting organization managed to get out of the ghetto. They were our comrade Zalman Friedrych and a member of the Hechalutz, Simcha Roteiser. The command of the uprising had delegated to them the task of organizing the rescue of the few surviving fighters.

They came through an underground sewer on Muranowska Street, near the streetcar barn, late at night. They crawled into an empty building to wait for the lifting of curfew. The floors, they found, were piled high with corpses. In the morning, as they stepped out of the building, they met a streetcar worker on his way to the carbarn. They told him they were Poles who had smuggled themselves into the ghetto to buy things from Jews and had been trapped by the uprising. They had been waiting all this time for a chance to escape. The worker congratulated them on their good fortune and told them that the bodies in the building they had just left were those of Jews who had tried to escape and had been caught by the Germans.

With some difficulty the two delegates of the fighting ghetto made contact with the Jewish representatives on the Aryan side. They met with the representatives of the Jewish fighting organization, "Mikolai" (Leon Feiner of the Bund) and "Antek" (Zuckerman of the Hechalutz), to whom they communicated the purpose of their mission.

Bright fire continued to rage over the entire ghetto as the fight went on for every house, for every bunker. The Germans were using poison gas. Our comrades were fighting desperately, using every conceivable means to strike back at the enemy. When all hope was gone, they killed themselves rather than fall into the hands of the Germans. The ranks of the fighting organization were already decimated. Burned by fire, suffocated by smoke and gas, torn by cannon shell, the small remnant was beginning to look for ways to escape from the inferno.

The only way into or out of the ghetto was through the underground sewer system which carried the filth of the great city. The sewers extended in a complicated network under all of Warsaw. To crawl through the sewers without a very good idea of their geography meant certain death—suffocation or drowning in the vile stream. Many had already tried this method of escape and had met a horrible death in the treacherous labyrinth.

The Polish underground helped us. It provided several men who had worked in the sewer system. They mapped the routes through which it would be easiest and safest to reach a particular rendezvous in the ghetto. In addition, we made contact with several smugglers who had used the sewers as an avenue of commerce. Kazik went back into the ghetto with them on the rescue expedition.

On May Day, the ghetto fighters undertook a one-day "offensive." In the evening they held a roll call of their decimated ranks and sang the "Internationale."

On May 3 the German police dogs and sound detectors located the bunker of Berek Snaidmil's group at 30 Franciskanska. As the battle was joined, Berek was severely wounded in the stomach by a hand grenade.

As his group prepared to withdraw, his comrades tried to carry him with them. Berek drew his revolver and waved it at them. "Don't forget to take this," he shouted. "Keep fighting!"

198

Before anyone could stop him, he thrust the revolver into his mouth and pulled the trigger.

David Hochberg was so young that his mother had strictly forbidden him to join the fighting organization. But in the ghetto battle he was a group commander. His bunker sheltered several hundred people.

When the Germans approached one of the narrow entrances to the bunker it seemed that everyone was lost. David stripped himself of his weapons. He wedged himself into the narrow bunker opening and let the German bullets find him.

By the time the attackers had pried his body out of their path the bunker had been evacuated through other exits.

In a small bunker in the courtyard of the Jewish Hospital on Gensha, Jewish patrols found among a number of bodies that of Anna Broide Heller. She had died at her post.

Escape seemed impossible. Many committed suicide. On May 8, the very night that Kazik's rescue expedition reached the ghetto, the Germans surrounded the headquarters of the Jewish fighting organization at 18 Mila. After trying for two hours to take the bunker by storm, they threw in a gas bomb.

Many were gassed; many took their own lives, including Commander Anilevitch. Only a handful miraculously escaped to join the remnants of the brushmakers at 22 Franciskanska.

The wave of fire receded. There was little left to burn. Here and there small groups still held out without water, without food, without ammunition. All hope of striking back at the enemy was gone. There was nothing left to do but try to escape.

On May 10 a group of fighters led by Abrasha Blum, Marek Edelman, and Zivia Lubetkin made their way through the sewers to Prosta Street. With the help of guides they negotiated the barbed-wire obstructions and the booby traps.

It was miraculous that the plan did not meet with complete failure. They reached the Prosta Street sewer exit at night, but the two trucks which were to pick them up were delayed. They had to remain in the sewer until ten o'clock in the morning. For forty-eight hours they were in sewer pipes twenty-eight inches high. The water reached their lips. Every moment someone lost consciousness and had to be revived. In their thirst, some drank the slime.

By the time the trucks arrived the streets were alive with people. A large crowd watched incredulously as human skeletons with submachine guns strapped high around their necks crawled one by one out of the sewer. An armed group of the Polish underground who were supposed to cover the retreat in case of trouble never arrived—so the group protected themselves. Jurek Blones and a few other fighters stood at the trucks with their submachine guns directed at the crowd, standing guard until the last one had climbed aboard. They were exhausted, dog-tired, but the look in their leaden eyes assured the crowd that they would not hesitate to fire at anyone who took a step toward them.

The trucks took the fighters to prepared hiding places in the Lomyanki Forest near Warsaw. During the wild ride they held their guns ready to make their lives expensive to any Germans who might stop the truck.

A second group, which was to follow, never got out of the sewers. The Germans, hearing of the bold escape, surrounded the entire district and dropped gas bombs into the sewers. No one else managed to get through. All those trapped in the sewers were killed.

It was impossible to find hiding places in the city for all the rescued comrades, and they could not remain in the Lomyanki Forest more than a few days How we searched and conspired and pleaded and maneuvered to find them a safe place to live!

The renewed terror on the Aryan side had frightened many Poles whose attitude toward the Jews was friendly. The intensive activity of the Gestapo made hiding a Jew more dangerous each day. *Schmaltzovniks* were everywhere. Every decent instinct was choked off in the atmosphere of terror, executions, extortion, lawlessness, and complete human demoralization.

One group, including Loeser Clog's daughter and her two-year-old child, was taken to the village of Pludy. Friedrych also brought another group to this hiding place. Soon after the arrival of the second group, the German police and Gestapo drove up, a fight broke out, and all the comrades were killed, including the heroic Zalman Friedrych. The only survivor was the two-year-old granddaughter of Loeser Clog, who was saved by an old Christian woman of the village and hidden in her home. The child is alive today.

Another group left Lomyanki for the forests of Wishkov where they joined the partisans.

Abrasha Blum was killed several days after his escape through the sewer. This tall, slim, quiet intellectual with his glasses and thinning hair had been a tower of strength. Although physically weak, he had been one of the earliest to urge armed resistance. In his calm, quiet way he had fanned the determination of the youth. He had resisted every suggestion that he leave the ghetto before the battle. In moments of crisis it was to this unarmed intellectual that the fighters turned. In the heat of battle they drew strength from his quiet courage and sympathetic understanding.

Once the brushmakers' group was in a very tight spot. Their commander ordered, "Everyone to the attack!"

Abrasha asked if that included him. In the confusion of the moment, without stopping to consider, the commander said, "Yes." With bare hands, Abrasha rushed to the attack with his comrades.

He could not find a satisfactory hiding place outside the ghetto.

He was forced to wander about, spending a day here and a night there. His wife, Luba, was hidden in one place, his two children in a second. Death dogged his every move. One night, at 28 Dluga Street, the Gestapo caught up with him. He tried to make a rope of bedsheets to let himself down out of the window. He had to jump from the third story and broke one or both of his legs. We never did find out for certain . . .

The very day he emerged from the sewer, *schmaltzovniks* attached themselves to Welvel Rosovsky, one of the front commanders in the uprising. The leeches drained every penny he had and then wanted more. At great risk, he left his hiding place in Zholibosh and went to the city to raise money for the blackmailers. As he was hurrying to get back before curfew, he was stopped by a German railway official who shot him dead.

The ghetto was still burning. The few Jews on the Aryan side lived in constant fear of falling into Nazi hands. Then, suddenly, before them a ray of hope appeared.

During the month of May there were rumors that the Gestapo had received a large number of visas from foreign consulates for citizens of neutral countries. According to the stories which made the rounds, most of the people for whom the visas were intended were no longer alive. The Gestapo was prepared to sell these visas to other persons for large sums of money and to allow them to assume the names of the dead.

Jewish Gestapo agents, like Koenig, Adam, and others, were the "official" representatives of the Gestapo in these transactions. Those who obtained the visas were to be sent temporarily to special camps for foreign citizens near Witel and Hanover and would then be taken out of the country.

An office was set up in the Hotel Imperial on Chmelna for registering foreigners. The rush was so great that there was not enough room for all the applicants, so the office had to be transferred to Hotel Polski at 29 Dluga Street. From the hotel the registrants were transferred to Paviak jail where they were held in the women's section to await transportation to Witel and Hanover.

These "foreign citizens" were permitted to take baggage and valuables. Many who were afraid to carry large sums of money exchanged it for gold or jewels.

It was good business for the Gestapo. Entire families put their faith in salvation through this scheme. They gladly paid tens of thousands of zlotys for a single passport. I know of a family who paid 75,000 zlotys. From Witel, Hanover, and other places came letters describing the excellent treatment under the supervision of the Red Cross. The letters reinforced faith in this avenue to safety, and the eagerness to buy passports increased.

The Joint Distribution Committee contributed financially to obtain passports for a number of organizational leaders. The JDC director, Guzik, sat in the Hotel Polski, helping to register people for passports. Guzik believed so strongly in the scheme that he provided passports for his own brother and his family.

Then the Polish underground government issued a warning. According to information in its possession, all this was only a confidence trick of the Gestapo, a trap to gather in the remaining Jews and destroy them.

Our own underground had had serious doubts about the scheme from the start. But our warnings were of little use, especially since it was known that many Jewish Gestapo agents were sending their families out of the country on these passports. Adam, for example, sent his entire family during the first days of the registration, and then went himself. Ganzweich, the leader of the Thirteeners of unhappy memory, sent his own wife. The well-known dancer and Gestapo agent, Madame Machno went, and so did many other important and minor officials of the Jewish police.

One night the Gestapo raided the Hotel Polski. Scores who

were not yet registered were arrested and the following day were shot. Still the desperate refused to heed any warnings and stormed the Hotel Polski offering anything for a visa in the name of some dead soul. The holder of a visa considered himself lucky beyond belief. His friends regarded him as a resurrected corpse. In the Hotel Polski there was a continual round of gay parties to celebrate the newly acquired visas.

The Hotel Polski campaign lasted until November 1943. In February 1944 we received the tragic news that our warnings had been well founded. Everyone taken to Witel, Hanover, and the other camps for "foreign citizens" had been killed.

The ghetto still smoked and flickered like a dying candle. We could still hear the sound of explosions and occasional gunfire. We learned that a large group of Jews had been taken alive. Some were sent to labor in the Travniki and Poniatov camps and some to death in Treblinka and Maidanek.

In June the Germans recruited Polish workers to clean up the ruins, to tear down the tottering buildings, and to salvage whatever iron and other useful metals they could. They also formed a separate labor unit of Jews from Greece, France, Rumania, and Hungary who were brought from various labor camps. They wore prison dress of striped trousers and gray blouses and were quartered in the Genshuffka, the buildings on Gensha Street which had once housed the institutions of the Jewish community. The Poles and Jews worked in complete isolation from each other and were not permitted to communicate. The Jewish workers were prisoners from camps and were so treated. The Poles were volunteers and were permitted to pass in and out of the ruined ghetto.

The Polish workers took the job willingly. In the ruined bunkers they found stores of food, clothing, and hidden valuables. The corpses yielded gold teeth, rings, watches, earrings, and so forth. One Pole showed me a small silver Menorah which he had found in the ruins. Another found a stock of leather and a rich collection of foreign postage stamps. Once in a while they happened upon living Jews who would trade anything they had for a little food. One of the Polish workers told me that a friend of his had been shot by the Germans for maintaining contact with Jews hidden in a bunker. As late as July we received messages through Polish workers from Jews in the bunkers, begging us to provide food and other necessities.

Many months after the uprising, one could still hear the demolition explosions. Digging out and cleaning up the ghetto was a long job. The rotting corpses were burned. The Germans built two small railroads to bring the salvage out of the ruins. One went through the Jewish Cemetery on Okopova and the other through Bonifraterska Street.

When the Germans finished, nothing was left in the ghetto except a broad field of rubble, three stories deep.

SEVEN

THE GERMANS now feared that Jewish courage might find an echo among the Poles. They intensified the terror on the Aryan side. Several exceptionally bold blows by the Polish underground gave the Germans some cause for concern.

At the corner of Krashinsky Square and Dluga Street the underground carried out an armed attack on a police patrol wagon which was taking prisoners, some of them condemned to death, to the Paviak jail. The police guards were killed and the prisoners freed. The underground also cleverly ambushed an auto carrying money from Bank Polski. A handcart loaded with large empty crates was pushed into the path of the automobile. The street was blocked by the scattered crates, and the auto had to stop. After killing the occupants, the raiders escaped with the money.

Such bold acts, in broad daylight in the heart of Warsaw, nettled the Nazis and made them more vicious. In the fall of 1943 the German Labor Minister, Dr. Ley, visited the city. He spoke over the radio to the Warsaw population and threatened that the slightest armed manifestation would lead to the destruction of the entire city; not a single stone would be left standing.

As in the early days of the war, the Germans resorted to public executions to terrorize the population. They hanged five people from a balcony on Leshno and left the bodies dangling over the street for two days. On Senatorska Street, in retaliation for the murder of a German, they stood a score of people against the wall of the Agricultural Ministry building and shot them all.

Incidents multiplied. Kerzelak Square, which was always packed with peddlers and buyers, many of them black marketeers operating with the connivance of the Germans, was surrounded by soldiers and police. They dispersed the crowd, confiscated all the merchandise, and set the booths afire. The great square was left in havoc.

The wave of raids and kidnaping, the great manhunt in the city streets, began all over again. Entire blocks of houses were closed off. Bloodhounds sniffed and snooped everywhere. Nazi gangs dragged people from their homes, from attics and basements, beating and killing them. In the tense atmosphere that descended on the entire city, the few Jews who had escaped from the ghetto again experienced the most terrible fears.

I have already mentioned the activities of the *schmaltzovniks*, the blackmailers and extortionists. The name comes from the Polish word *schmaletz*, which means fat. These scum would approach their victims with the words, "Hand over your fat." They were a terrible plague upon the Jews who lived on the Aryan side. In addition to the Gestapo, SS men, and others who hunted them relentlessly, the Jews lived in constant danger from these dregs of Polish morality, who made a business of Jewish lives. Hundreds were engaged in this hateful occupation—searching out the unfortunates who now lived on Aryan documents, or who hid under the protection of Gentiles.

They entered the business in various ways. Students recognized former fellow-students; neighbors recognized Jews who had lived with them on the same street or in the same building; storekeepers, peddlers, or tradesmen recognized former customers or competitors; police officials recognized former residents of their precincts. All of them fattened on the desperate fugitives, holding over them the threat of exposure and death. Jews who had nothing and were not profitable were handed over to the

208

Nazis. Others had to pay monthly blackmail. When they finally had nothing left for the blood tax, they were handed over to their fate.

Many *schmaltzovniks* operated in gangs. They formed a far-reaching organization, dividing the city into districts. Each group watched for victims in its district, studying every unknown person on the streets, every stranger in the streetcars or trains, following his every step, poisoning and embittering the life of everyone they suspected of being a source of revenue. Once in their grasp, the victim did not find it easy to extricate himself. After he had paid off one, another would approach him with the same threats, then a third and a fourth, without end. Throughout the length and breadth of the city, wherever the hunted animals would burrow into holes, the *schmaltzovnik* bloodhounds would find their spoor and search them out.

In the case of a male suspect, the *schmaltzovniks* had a sure way of determining nationality. They would pull their victim into a doorway or an alley and rip open his trousers, looking for the fateful sign of circumcision. There was at least one doctor who, for tremendous sums, performed plastic surgery to restore the appearance of a foreskin. The operation was extremely painful and dangerous, but some were desperate enough to try it.

Many times we asked the Polish underground to handle the *schmaltzovniks* as German collaborators, whom the underground used to condemn to death. We could not take any action ourselves. It was dangerous for Jewish faces to be seen on the street. Far more dangerous was the possibility that a Jew might be discovered in the act of killing a Gentile. Such an action might inflame the entire Polish community against us.

The illegal press often carried notices of trials of persons who collaborated with the Germans. They usually received a sentence of death which was carried out by the underground. Several times it printed warnings against the *schmaltzovniks*, but I did not hear of a single trial or of any punishment being meted out to them. Despite our appeals, the Polish underground refused to consider a serious campaign against these allies of the Germans.

It is remarkable that the *schmaltzovnik* plague was at its worst at a time when the entire Polish community was seized by a mystic religious zeal, as if in ecstatic prayer it could find deliverance and lighten the heavy burden of sorrow. In the evening at eight o'clock, when the gates of the courtyards were closed by the curfew, bells would ring throughout the city. Every resident, old and young, rich and poor, would stand in the courtyards in religious ecstasy before lighted candles, singing prayers and religious hymns, led by a priest or a layman versed in religious ritual. The Jews who lived as Christians joined their neighbors in these daily prayers. Literally every Pole throughout the entire city of Warsaw participated.

In such an atmosphere of religious dedication, which renewed itself each evening, such scoundrels as the *schmaltzovniks* operated freely and openly, without hindrance, without any signs of popular disapproval. How this was possible remains a psychological mystery.

I had moved back to the Chumatovskys' apartment at the Steyr arms factory. The Chumatovskys, always in danger of detection by the Poles and German officials who lived all around us, risked their lives to hide me.

One evening Mrs. Chumatovsky's father, Shcherbinsky, about whom I had some very serious doubts, came to visit them. They conferred all evening in low whispers I noticed that Mrs. Chumatovsky was extremely agitated, her eyes full of tears. I gathered that something terrible had happened. Shcherbinsky remained overnight.

Early in the morning I was awakened by a knock at the outside door. I heard a gruff unfriendly voice. "Does Malinovsky live here?"

"Yes," Mrs. Chumatovsky answered.

The door of my room flew open. Three young men in high boots entered. One, in a yellow leather jacket, who seemed to be the leader, said to me, "Get up!"

I tried to assume an attitude of innocent bewilderment. "What's wrong? What do you want?"

Leather-jacket tore off my blanket and directed his glance knowingly at the compromising part of my naked body. "Ah!" he half sniggered, and then more roughly, "Get up and be quick about it!"

"*Stehen Sie mal auf!*" one of the others ordered in transparently ungenuine German.

I realized I was lost. "Tell me, gentlemen, what will this cost?" I asked.

"No money. Get up! And stop acting foolish!"

"Tell me, how much do you want?" I asked again, getting out of bed.

"Twenty thousand zlotys."

My head swam. Where was I to get so much money? Through the open door I saw Mrs. Chumatovsky, red-eyed. I walked past her into the room where Shcherbinsky lay. I asked him to intercede, to get them to accept less. I had only six thousand zlotys. He seemed reluctant, but I pressed him.

He went in to talk to them and returned to tell me that they had agreed to accept ten thousand zlotys. I was to give them the six thousand now, and he would lend me four thousand, which I could repay later. He also promised to take me to his apartment on Zhelasna, an offer I had no intention of accepting.

The visitors took my six thousand zlotys and everything else I had. After warning me that if I were not gone in half an hour others would come for me, they left.

In deep melancholy, I went into the street. I felt alone, helpless, and completely beaten. Where was I to go in this teeming city where every man was an enemy, where I was carrion for all the vultures to pluck?

For several days I wandered about the city, seeking out our contacts and searching for a new hiding place. Several times I found temporary shelter—only to move again.

Finally Marisha Feinmesser and Inka Schweiger located an apartment for me in the Saska Kempa district. Although I was able to stay there for a longer period, it soon became unsafe. I left—one day before the police raided it.

At 29 Grzibovska Street, opposite the Community House, there had once been a photographic laboratory. This district had been part of the small ghetto and after its liquidation had been re-populated by non-Jews. The apartment which included the photographic laboratory had been occupied by a Gentile, his wife, and two small sons, the elder four years old and the other a baby of one year. The apartment consisted of two rooms, a kitchen, and the darkroom.

Until the ghetto uprising, this Christian family had sheltered Spichler with his wife and child, Moishel Kaufman, and Rabinowitz and his son-in-law, an engineer. Rabinowitz's wife and daughter had been killed earlier at Zhelasna when they had tried to escape from the ghetto after the first deportations.

Of all these tenants, none remained alive. Moishel Kaufman had entered the ghetto a few days before the uprising on an important mission and had remained there to die in battle. Spichler and his wife and child, as well as Rabinowitz and his son-in-law, were among the victims of the Hotel Polski fraud. They died in Hanover.

The landlord had lived through stark terror during the raids and shooting that accompanied the ghetto uprising. He was determined that his apartment would never again be used to conceal Jews.

But the apartment problem was extremely pressing for us. Many comrades wandered about with no place to stay, spending a day here and a night there, sometimes with no shelter at all. *Schmaltzovniks* were active everywhere. Marisha Feinmesser went to work on the landlord to persuade him to take us in. Although new to the movement, Marisha was already throwing all her youthful determination into the work of saving lives. She was a heavy-set girl in her twenties. She had been the sheltered child of a wealthy family until she was driven into the ghetto. There she went to work in the Children's Hospital, becoming a second mother to the homeless strays.

After their mother had been taken to Treblinka, Marisha and her sister drew closer to our movement. Marisha used her position in the hospital, which allowed her to leave the ghetto from time to time, to smuggle literature and establish contacts. The two girls managed to escape from the ghetto and they enlisted in the work of aiding Jews on the Aryan side. When her sister was captured and shot, Marisha became even more active, even more daring, even more determined.

By pleading and cajoling she finally persuaded the owner of the apartment at 29 Grzibovska to let us in. The price was high— 25,000 zlotys. The terms of our "lease" were hard, but essential: The Jews must remain completely hidden at all times and the apartment must be "covered" by a Christian tenant, Yanina Pavlitzka. She would carry complete responsibility for us, arrange for food, see that no one discovered the dangerous secret.

Yanina Pavlitzka was a sympathetic, kind, courageous woman, about thirty years old, who had long lived among Jews. She had grown up in Warsaw in the officers' colony near Cherniakov. Her father had been a janitor in the church of the colony. Before the war she had worked as a servant in the home of Rappoport of Zgerzh, a very pious Jew, owner of a textile factory. She had learned to speak Yiddish and became very much attached to the Rappoport family. Together with them she had moved from Lodz to the Warsaw ghetto, living as a Christian in the ghetto by permission of the authorities. She had helped the Rappoports in every way she could, even bringing them food from the Aryan side. She had gone to Zgerzh and Lodz to bring back their things. Even after the Rappoports had gone to Witel through the Hotel Polski, Pavlitzka corresponded with them.

Into the new apartment under Yanina's protection moved Mrs. Gurman, long an employee of the ORT, who after the war went to Czechoslovakia; Shierachek, a former Jewish policeman in the ghetto; an elderly woman of sixty-five whose children had gone from the Hotel Polski to Witel but had not had enough money to take their mother with them; and I. The neighbors knew that Yanina Pavlitzka lived in a dark room and made a living knitting sweaters. About the rest of us, of course, no one was permitted to have the least suspicion. Our apartment was the small room, the former darkroom of the photographic laboratory, in which there was space for only a small bed and a tiny table. We slept on the floor, crowded together. Pavlitzka gave up her bed to the old woman and slept on the floor with the rest of us. All of us, except Yanina, remained locked in our little dark hole, forbidden to see the light of day.

The most valuable feature of our hiding place was the bunker that Rabinowitz's son-in-law, the engineer, had painstakingly built long before. It had taken him many weeks. He had carried out the earth and bricks with great care in order not to arouse suspicion.

In the wall just above the floor was a small built-in cabinet which contained the usual odds and ends one expects to find in such places. When it was pulled away from the wall, it uncovered a hole large enough for a grown person to crawl through with great difficulty. The hole led down to a deep old cellar which was walled up on all sides. We got into the cellar by sliding down a sharply inclined board. Then we would replace the cabinet and lock it in place with a sliding iron bar. If Pavlitzka was at home, she would take care of that, but if she was out getting food or on other errands, we had to replace the cabinet ourselves, in the pitch-darkness, from our precarious position on the inclined board.

Sometimes we would make our expeditions through the hole and down the board into the cellar ten or fifteen times a day. The slightest tap on the apartment door was the signal for a painful pilgrimage, especially difficult for the old woman and for Mrs. Gurman. The difficult journey down and up would take their last ounce of strength.

We often sat in the cellar for hours, not speaking a word, not making the slightest movement. It was cold and dark; the walls and floor were crusted with mold and dirt. The damp, fetid air had a horrible smell; large rats raced around in the corners. When the danger was past, Pavlitzka, or in her absence the landlady, carefully tapped twice on the door of the cabinet as a sign that we could crawl out, often to go through the painful procedure again a few minutes later.

During the short period of the day when we were permitted to use the toilet, we waited in line. Only after everyone had finished was the bowl flushed.

The janitor's wife or other neighbors and relatives would often come to visit our landlord. While they sat for hours in friendly conversation, we crouched in the cellar.

Our greatest difficulty was to keep the secret from our host's four-year-old son. Four grown people lay day and night in a neighboring room of the same small apartment, but the boy was not permitted even to suspect it. Once each day, at dawn, we were allowed into the kitchen to wash, while the child was still asleep. His mother would lock the door of his room to be sure that he would not come out suddenly and discover us. In Yanina the boy found a pleasant companion, and he enjoyed visiting her. Besides, his mother would often take the child into the room, apparently casually, for an "inspection," to build up in his mind the certainty that the room was what it appeared to be and that only Yanina lived in it.

How many times each day this innocent little boy was the reason for our expedition into the cellar! How we suffered from this domestic "enemy"! Often the boy would decide that he wanted to play with Yanina precisely at the time we were sitting down to eat. We would hurriedly gather up the food and dishes and slide with them into our cellar hiding place.

Yanina had a difficult time buying food for five grown people. To do her marketing near Grzibovska would arouse suspicion. She was known to be a poor young woman who lived alone, and such heavy purchases of food would be sure to excite local curiosity. She had to do her shopping in the more distant parts of town, at illicit marketplaces, taking a chance on German raids against black marketeers.

Preparing and cooking the food presented a similar problem. Too large a pot or too heavily laden a platter of food could betray us. She was on her guard not only against the neighbors and chance visitors but also against the inquisitive little child who loved to follow her wherever she went. A pot of half-cooked food and our silverware and dishes would often descend into the cellar because someone had knocked at the apartment door.

Under the strain, Yanina became extremely nervous. Each new rumor about the arrest of hidden Jews threw her into an understandable fear about our own fate.

Once a Jewish woman was arrested in our building. While we cowered in the cellar, Yanina remained glued to the window of the landlady's room, watching the courtyard and the street with apprehension.

Our situation became more dangerous when the landlady began to quarrel violently with her husband for not giving her enough money for household expenses. After all, she complained, he had received from us the magnificent sum of 25,000 zlotys and had drunk and squandered it all. We tried to make peace, placating our landlady by offering to pay her a monthly rental, which finally ran as high as a thousand zlotys.

216

Such quarrels would often end with the landlady walking out of the apartment in a huff. She would stay away for days, leaving the house and the two children in Yanina's charge. Yanina had to care for us and for them, keeping us out of their sight, in addition to worrying about all the normal dangers. She carried her burden as though it were a holy religious duty. She contributed her share of all the expenses, categorically refusing to allow us to maintain her. We were horribly filthy, crawling with lice. We did not have enough clothing or underwear. Yanina washed, repaired, and patched our clothes. From her own things and from the proceeds of her knitting she would give presents to our landlady to keep her happy and would try to patch up the family quarrels.

In addition to all this, Yanina took care of an apartment at 17 Bratska Street where the brother of the Jewish policeman Shierachek lived. He was a chemist and manufactured perfumes, which his landlord peddled in the market while he himself lay hidden in a bunker together with his equipment. Yanina was his contact with his brother and with the outside world. She brought him food, clothing, and other necessities.

After the ghetto had been destroyed, we faced one urgent task: organizing help for those who were left on the Aryan side, providing them with apartments, hiding places, documents, and food. We began to get word of the liquidation of other ghettos, and of uprisings in labor camps and ghettos. We were asked for help, for weapons. Such requests came from the camps in Travniki, Poniatov, Skarzhisko, Plashuv, Belzhitz, and others.

Around Warsaw, hiding in the woods and in the open countryside, were possibly twenty thousand uprooted homeless wanderers. We estimated that the Bund alone was helping about three thousand of them. Until the outbreak of the Warsaw uprising, the organized help of all Jewish groups and organizations had reached about eight or nine thousand people. Generally each political party or group took care of its own members and periphery, but some centralization of the relief work was achieved through the Jewish Coordinating Committee, composed of the leaders of all the Jewish groups, and through the Council for Aid to Jews in which all the Polish underground parties were represented.

From the Polish government the Council received a small financial allotment, forged Aryan passports, work cards, and other necessary documents for Jews. There were two kinds of false identity papers: *litova*, blanks to be filled in with imaginary names, and *zhelasna*, iron passes, made out to actual people who were now dead. The iron passes were a great deal safer, since an inquiry into the police records would show that such a person had actually existed, but they had to be obtained through employees of the magistrates' offices or through other government officials who had some connection with the official records.

Above all we needed apartments to serve as bases for the necessary day-to-day activities. We had to have a center for our daredevil couriers who were so clever at getting to the scattered hiding places, to the conspiratorial apartments, to the labor camps, to the groups hiding in the forests—bringing sorely needed help, establishing contacts, and collecting accurate information.

Because of the *schmaltzovnik* plague, getting an apartment continued to be the most difficult of our problems, and one which, directly and indirectly, cost us many lives.

The Jews who managed to hide on the Aryan side after the total destruction of the ghetto were in spiritual torment during the North African campaign. The German press and the underground kept us informed of Rommel's march to the East. At Tobruk, Rommel gathered up a large number of Polish prisoners. As the German Army moved on Alexandria we trembled in helpless terror. Victory seemed so certainly theirs. British power in Africa was surely finished, and the fate of the Jewish community in Palestine certain. With leaden hearts we waited for the blow to fall on our brothers in the Holy Land.

When the British Army stopped Rommel at El Alamein we could not believe that it was more than a temporary halt. Each day we waited tensely for a Nazi breakthrough. If only something could transport us into the British lines! If only we, like the Poles at Tobruk, could strike a blow against the enemy! Our helplessness ate into our souls like a cancer.

After the Battle of El Alamein, the cloud lifted a little. We analyzed every report in the German press for a hidden admission of retreat. The turn of the tide had great importance for the entire world, but we felt first of all the end of our consuming anxiety over Palestine. I will never forget our gratitude to the British.

The Americans invaded Africa. When American and British troops landed in Sicily we held little parties of celebration. No counsel of caution could restrain our joy.

Zygmund Igla, a Bundist and Zukunftist, a member of the Warsaw Union of White Collar Workers, had been an active member of the fighting organization. A tall, broad-shouldered, well-built youth of completely Aryan appearance, he had distinguished himself by extraordinary heroism and courage. He refused to part with his loaded revolver. "They will never take me alive," he used to say.

Igla had escaped into the Wishkov forests. Several times he came to Warsaw for help, information, and advice. Later he moved to Shliska Street in Warsaw but had to leave after a short time because the *schmaltzovniks* were dogging his heels. Then he moved to 14 Pruzna into the apartment of the janitor, Yablonski, who was one of our agents active in the work of securing apartments.

We had bought arms through him even before the ghetto uprising. In an emergency one could always spend the night with him. His apartment soon became a rendezvous for our underground. Maintaining contact with him was the responsibility of Marisha Feinmesser.

A few days after Igla's arrival, during Yablonski's absence, gendarmes raided the apartment, which at that time also housed another man and woman, members of Hashomer, whose names I do not recall. They barricaded themselves and opened fire on the gendarmes. The fight lasted several hours. The gendarmes finally brought reinforcements in an armored car from which they sprayed the apartment with machine-gun fire and threw in a hand grenade. The ammunition of the defenders ran out, but before they were killed they wounded several of the gendarmes.

Yablonski, who was a member of General Sikorski's section of the underground, was caught and tortured but he betrayed no one.

In the same building, in an apartment owned by a friend of Yablonski, were hidden Rose Odes, who later came to America, her daughter and son-in-law, who escaped to Sweden, and several other Jews. The landlord of that apartment, fearing that Yablonski might betray him, locked them all in the apartment and ran away. They were without food. They lived in terrible fear, understanding the significance of Yablonski's arrest and their landlord's desertion. They could not go out, not only because the apartment was locked, but also because they were certain that the house was under police surveillance. Besides, they had nowhere to go.

Marisha, who was responsible for all of Yablonski's apartments, could not get to them because the neighbors in the building knew her too well. She came to me at Grzibovska for advice. We discussed a plan for finding a new apartment and then sending an armed expedition to free the prisoners. By this time it was urgent to calm their fears and let them know that we were taking steps to rescue them.

Yanina Pavlitzka agreed to take a note to them. As she walked into the building the new janitor followed her. He saw her push a note under the door and immediately seized her and the message. She claimed she had come to collect money due her for food. The janitor took her to the house administrator, who read the note and understood her mission immediately. He released her and told the janitor to drive the tenants out of the locked apartment. Yanina feared that if she were handed over to the police all of her charges would be caught. She arrived home half dead, unable to speak a word.

When Marisha came to see me in the morning, we learned what had happened on Pruzna. The janitor had forced the door and ordered the Jews to leave immediately. With the help of friendly Christians most of them managed to hide. Word was sent to Marisha and other comrades, who arranged for new apartments. One of the group, however, the elderly father-in-law of Rose Odes' daughter, killed himself immediately on being freed by throwing himself from a rooftop.

The torture of hunger, fright, and imprisonment in the apartment had lasted for twenty-seven days. What they lived through, listening to the gun-battle in the courtyard, and during the four weeks that followed, cannot be imagined.

Shortly afterward, we got a new addition to Yanina's little menage on Grzibovska, Marek Edelman. The *schmaltzovniks* had become very active on Panska where he had been living, and he had been born with a special handicap, an obviously Jewish face. Since it was difficult to find a new hiding place for him on the spur of the moment, we took him in with us.

Inka Schweiger brought him to us late one evening. We had not met since Marek had escorted me to the ghetto gate with the Okentche workers. His face was now much harder and more earnest. His experiences during the ghetto battles, the deaths of his friends, especially Abrasha Blum and Berek Snaidmil, to whom he had been closely attached, had embittered him greatly.

With a sarcastic smirk he talked of life and the world, always toying with the revolver in his pocket, his finger caressing the trigger. He listened with ironic bitterness to my instructions on how to let himself into the cellar, how to shinny out when the signal was given, and generally how to comply with the special rules of our cave-dwelling existence. He considered the whole business ridiculous.

For a few weeks we lived in peace. Then we were beset by new troubles. The janitor's wife reported to our landlady that our upstairs neighbor had told her that Yanina Pavlitzka probably kept "cats"—slang for hidden Jews—in her room. Our hosts were understandably alarmed and suggested that we move out for a few days. In the meantime, they would arrange to convince our neighbor that he was mistaken.

Marek and I went to stay with Wladka, a young girl who was one of our most active couriers, and who was able to pose as a Gentile. Our roommates found other temporary hiding places. While we were gone, the ceremony of reconciliation between Yanina and the neighbor was performed without a hitch. They invited the gossip, the janitor, and his wife in for a drink. Yanina played the role of insulted innocence beautifully and threatened to complain to the police. How dare he invent such slander against her! It was obvious that there were no "cats" in Yanina's room, and the neighbor begged her forgiveness. She could hardly conceal her joy at having things go so smoothly. We were able to return to the apartment, now more secure than ever.

When we had originally moved into the apartment on Grzibovska, our landlord had imposed the condition that only Yanina should be permitted to leave the house. We were to remain hidden at all times. The fear which inspired this stipulation was understandable. Enemies were all around us.

As a result, Wladka, Zelemainsky, Marisha, and other comrades had to come to see me for conferences.

Now I began a calculated campaign to get my landlord to agree to let me out at least once a week. Since he dearly loved liquor, I worked with bottles of whisky. When alcohol had ripened our friendship, he finally agreed.

My fellow-tenants were somewhat displeased at being placed in greater danger, but there was nothing they could do about it. My hosts considered me a member of their family.

On the first day of my newly acquired freedom, which happened to be my landlord's name-day, he took me to visit his family in Brudno, near Praga. My eyes squinted in pain at the strange flood of sunlight, and it seemed awkward to walk with such long strides.

At a gay little party in celebration of my landlord's anniversary, I met his father and mother, his brother Taddik, and his sister, all of whom were active in providing us with apartments. His mother even went to the length of maintaining a separate apartment on Franciskanska under the pretext that she could not get along with her husband and had had to move into separate quarters. In her second apartment, she concealed five Jews whom she even provided with food.

Taddik worked in the night shift at the Steyr arms factory in Wola, where I had once lived with the Chumatovskys. During the day he was the house administrator of the building in Brudno where his father lived. As a result he was able to obtain important documents for us, such as registrations, birth certificates, passes, and so forth. In whatever time he had left, Taddik also covered Wladka's apartment on Twarda. His sister, who also worked nights at Steyr, helped her mother cover the apartment on Franciskanska. The entire family were exceptional and likable people.

The old man, a railway worker, was a skeptic, a doubter, who always talked bitterly about the plagues that pestered mankind.

The mother was tall, slim, deeply religious, with the earnest face of a nun. Sadly she told me of mass killings of discovered Jews. She had not been able to sleep nights listening to the explosions and the gunfire in the ghetto.

"What kind of a world is this?" she murmured in a voice choked with tears.

I am reminded of an incident—one of hundreds—which occurred in the family of Shierachek, the former Jewish policeman, my fellow tenant on Grzibovska. His sister was a servant in a Christian home in Waver. Naturally she had to act the part of a Catholic. Regularly each Sunday she attended church and participated in the religious ceremonies with her neighbors. Her thirteen-year-old daughter lived with her, under the protection of her employers' daughter, a schoolteacher. Supposedly, the little girl's parents had been arrested by the Nazis, and she had been placed in the custody of the teacher. The girl was raised as a Christian.

The mother, although not at all religious, was deeply concerned about the child. She feared that in time the little girl would forget that she was a Jew and begin to feel truly like a Christian. She would thus be lost to the Jewish people.

Before her school examination, the little girl had to go to the priest for communion with all the other students. The teacher, a deeply religious woman, refused stubbornly to be a party to this deception. Her convictions would not permit her to send a Jewish child who had not been converted to such a holy ceremony. It would be a betrayal of her own religious faith.

The teacher consulted two other priests—the priest at the school was permitted to know nothing about it. One of them told her that his convictions would not permit him to baptize the girl under compulsion. The second, considering the desperate situation of the child, agreed to perform the ceremony.

Now the mother was assailed by doubts. She was afraid that

the impressiveness of the ritual would give her child the final push toward Catholicism. In her anxiety she came to Grzibovska to consult with her brother, Marek Edelman, and myself. Hard and bitter, Marek was inclined to oppose the whole idea on the ground that it was tantamount to capitulation. Child or adult, he was damned if he would recommend knuckling under to those Nazi bastards. To hell with them! But the more conservative counsel of Shierachek and myself prevailed. To save her life, the child must be baptized.

In addition to relief work, we concentrated on organizational contacts with the labor camps now holding the remnants of the ghettos, and on the areas where survivors were in hiding. We had to save and to keep alive the last bit of our blood, the last who remained after hell's fire had swallowed everything.

We lacked a central point where this work could be concentrated and where the threads of our underground system could be tied together in one way or another. The need for such a center had long plagued us.

Finally, in October 1943, we were able, for ten thousand zlotys, to buy an apartment at 24 Myodova Street in the former archives building of the Justice Department.

The building was ideal. The one-time offices now swarmed with tenants of all sorts. The long corridors were always crowded, alive with people coming and going. The busy traffic, the confused movement, made it difficult to keep track of the various people—who they were, where they went, what they did.

Into one of the former offices we moved Marisha Feinmesser and Inka Schweiger. Both held documents as employees of the Department of Child Welfare; both had faces which would not arouse suspicion. Here we knotted all the threads that led to the bunkers, the burrows, the forests, the labor camps, the towns and villages where our comrades were hiding.

Here you could often find Leon Feiner, the central figure in our contact with the Polish underground and the outside world, and Fishgrund, who specialized in the procurement of false documents. Here we had frequent meetings with Osubka-Morawski, representative of the RPPS (the left-wing faction of the Polish Socialist party) and later premier of the postwar Polish government; with Antek Zuckerman and Rifke Moshkowitz (Little Zoshka), representatives of the Chalutzim; and with leaders of the Jewish fighting organization.

We also had facilities for keeping overnight anyone who had suddenly lost his hiding place. We could take in newly arrived fugitives from the camps and forests, for whom there was no apartment immediately available.

From this headquarters our couriers, who also served the Jewish coordinating committee and the Jewish fighting organization, left to make their rounds. Through them we kept alive the little sparks of Jewish life which still flickered here and there. During that period, the end of 1943 and the beginning of 1944, the Jewish underground organizations cared for about ten thousand people scattered throughout the Warsaw area. The Bund alone had about three thousand besides those in the labor camps. Each courier was responsible for his own group. He had to provide for it everything within his power That meant documents, apartments, clothing, food, money, whatever was necessary in the particular situation. Each courier had to remain in constant touch with his charges, and see them once a month.

In their journeys across the length and breadth of the country, through strange towns and villages, along roads and on trains, the couriers often came face to face with the enemy. They were always in danger. Every moment was a desperate gamble with death. Their work required almost unbelievable courage, quickness of wit, and daring ingenuity. Into the lonely darkness of the hiding places, into the barracks of the condemned in labor camps, they brought a ray of hope; they inspired courage and a determination to hold out just a little longer. They brought news from

226

the great far-off world, cheered the broken spirits and reminded them that they were not alone in their suffering, that others, their comrades, thought about them and tried to help them and would never desert them.

While searching for Jews hidden in Warsaw, the Nazis did not neglect the towns and villages around the city.

During the last half of 1943 and the beginning of 1944 there were constant raids in the Otvotsk resort district and similar sections near Warsaw, like Podkova-Leshna, Bernardova, and Yablonna. These places, remote from the teeming city, surrounded by forests, with only isolated homes and villas, were well suited for concealment. Here were hidden most of the wealthier Jews, those completely assimilated and indistinguishable from Poles, and those who had the advantage of an Aryan appearance. Some owners of villas built special bunkers for those who had particularly Jewish faces. These had to remain in complete hiding. Everything had to be brought to them—for great sums of money, of course.

Here, too, lurked the *schmaltzovniks*, petty gangsters, and informers. And there was always danger from the unpaid Hitler agents, like the members of the Polish Falanga, who hunted Jews without any desire for monetary gain. They were a large group and even published an underground newspaper, *Shanyetz*. They organized partisan groups in the forest who hunted down and shot Jews in hiding.

In Shvider, not far from Warsaw, several Jewish families were concealed in the isolated villa of a Pole named Zavatzky, owner of a large wholesale drug company. He had constructed a special hiding place for a large store of drugs which he was saving for a more profitable moment.

Early one morning, the villa was surrounded by the Gestapo and gendarmes. They seized seven Jews, ordered them to dig their own graves and then strip; they were shot on the spot. Their clothes were distributed among the curious Gentile neighbors who had gathered to watch the execution. The only punishment inflicted upon the owner of the villa was the confiscation of his hidden store of drugs.

Tolla Kelson, sister of Dr. Kelson of the Medem Sanatorium, also lived in Shvider with her sick husband. Tolla had been a nurse in the Jewish Hospital on Chista Street and later in the Children's Hospital on Shliska. During the ghetto days she had had a pass for entering and leaving the ghetto and was therefore of great help to us in carrying out important and dangerous missions on the other side.

She and her husband had spotless Aryan documents. One day the Gestapo raided the villa. Tolla and her husband were discovered; their appearance and their documents were of no avail. The beasts examined her husband physically, discovered he was a Jew, and immediately shot both of them.

Dr. Kelson of the Medem Sanatorium, Tolla's sister, was arrested in a café on Myodova Street together with Anka Feinmesser, Marisha's sister. They were not suspected of being Jews but were accused of having connections with the underground. Anka was shot. Dr. Kelson was taken to Paviak Prison, held for some time, and finally sent to Oswiecim. We sent her packages of food from Warsaw, which, as a Gentile, she had the right to receive in Oswiecim. She was later rescued and went to Sweden.

The raids in and around Warsaw increased the fright not only of the hidden Jews but also of the handful of non-Jews who were disposed to help them. It became increasingly difficult to find new hiding places and to retain the old ones, and the succession of bad news deepened the despondency and hopelessness of the Jews.

At this time of extreme nervous tension and utter lack of hope, heartbreaking tragedies were enacted, touching everyone who knew of them, even in that time of human bestiality.

228

One of the victims was Mrs. Hechtman, the wife of one of the prewar leaders of the printers' union, and during the ghetto manager of the Bund's soup kitchen on Shliska Street. Her husband and one of their children had been killed during the deportations. She, with the second child, twelve years old, escaped to the Aryan side. She lived in Praga with the son and mother of Comrade Mirmelstein of Lodz, who had been killed on Prosta Street during the selection at Tebbens' factory.

Affected by fear for the safety of her child and by the constant danger of being exposed as Jews, suspicious of her landlord and her Gentile neighbors, suffocated by the miasma of death surrounding her, Mrs. Hechtman went out of her mind. Her mental illness became progressively more violent. She used to scream in wild hysteria and smash anything about her. Her neighbors lived through fearful moments, expecting her wild shrieks to bring death to all of them. They finally decided that the only way to save themselves and the Hechtman child was to do away with the mother. While the child watched, they administered the poison.

An especially staggering blow to all of us was the collapse of the large bunker on Gruyetzka Street which housed thirty-six people, among them the world-famous Jewish historian, Dr. Emanuel Ringelblum, and his family.

The bunker had been cleverly built in 1943 with the financial assistance of the American Joint Distribution Committee and the Jewish Coordinating Committee. In a large flower garden, there was a glass-enclosed greenhouse, warmed by steam pipes. Scores of people were accommodated in a large room under this greenhouse. The charge for admission, aside from maintenance, went as high as twenty thousand zlotys per person. The owner's sister opened a food store nearby, supplying food for the tenants of the bunker without arousing suspicion.

Everyone who entered the bunker had to be prepared to remain indefinitely. No one was permitted to leave. At night the residents were occasionally allowed into the garden for a little fresh air, since in the bunker itself the ventilation was very poor. The electric light and the heat of the steam pipes above made it uncomfortable, but it was, nevertheless, the best constructed and best camouflaged bunker in all Warsaw.

According to the original plan, space in the bunker had been reserved for me, but I decided against entering it because of the provision that, once in, I could never leave. It would have meant cutting myself off completely from all underground activity. Comrade Zelemainsky knew the gardener well and maintained contact with the bunker. He had permission to visit there from time to time to communicate with Dr. Ringelblum and with our comrade, Mrs. Mellman, formerly a teacher in the Medem School in Lodz and a lecturer in the illegal teachers' seminary of the Warsaw ghetto.

The bunker existed for more than a year, until March 1944, without arousing the slightest suspicion. How it was discovered we never did learn. It was rumored that the gardener had quarreled with his sweetheart, and she avenged herself by betraying the bunker.

One morning at dawn the garden was surrounded by soldiers and Gestapo; they went directly into the greenhouse and led out the thirty-six hidden people. They were taken to Paviak and shot.

It is hard to describe the impression which this mass tragedy made upon the city and upon our underground movement. It reinforced the feeling of despair and made the work of providing more bunkers and hiding places immensely more difficult.

At 24 Zhuravia in a large six-room apartment we set up headquarters for our party secretariat. There we kept our most important documents and our treasury. To protect this extremely important material, Chaim Ellenbogen, master craftsman, who later got to Sweden, constructed a wonderful hiding place in the floor.

He was a carpenter by trade, and specialized in laying intricate parquet flooring. Our vault was so carefully and expertly made that even a close examination of the floor would not reveal the secret of the removable boards.

In this apartment we conducted many of our important party activities, including meetings of our central committee.

Our efforts to find more, and yet more, apartments to house fugitive comrades received setbacks from time to time. An old apartment would fall under suspicion or a landlord, because of the intensified terror, would refuse to keep his tenants any longer.

The safety of the apartment on Panska, in which were hidden Zivia Lubetkin and Antek Zuckerman, and to which we had transferred Marek Edelman, all commanders of the Jewish fighting organization, became very doubtful. We decided to find a new apartment and to prepare it with every possible safety precaution so that these comrades and others would have a place more or less secure.

Marisha Feinmesser showed truly amazing heroism and perseverance. She already held the apartment at 24 Myodova in her own name. She was also responsible for keeping in touch with a number of other hiding places and with comrades in the forest. All this required constant attention during every waking hour. Constantly aware of her life-and-death responsibility for those in her care, exposed to the greatest danger, she worked tirelessly. In spite of her already heavy burdens she managed to find another apartment at 18 Leshno. She did not give up the old apartment at 24 Myodova. She got another passport and rented the new apartment under a new name.

Maria Savitzka and her brother, Gentiles, moved into the new apartment with Marisha. Supposedly Marisha was about to marry Maria's brother. Maria's pretended need for a dressmaking salon was the excuse for taking so large an apartment. It was a cheery, spacious apartment of three rooms, with a blind wall facing the Evangelical church. Parallel to this wall we built a second solid wall, providing a hiding place large enough to accommodate as many as ten people. Such a major construction operation required large quantities of building material, as well as a great deal of hammering and the removal of debris, it was difficult to do secretly. The work was carried on under the pretext that Marisha was putting in a bathroom in honor of her marriage and her new position in life. The wall was built by our wonderful comrades Chaim Ellenbogen, Simcha Roteiser, and Shwentochovsky, a Polish electrical worker who housed some of the partisan comrades in his own apartment.

Shwentochovsky used his electrical skill to set up a clever signal system at the apartment entrance. On the door he installed a well-concealed pinpoint, wired to the bell. If the pinpoint was pressed with a coin or other piece of metal the bell rang, indicating that a friend was coming and that we had no need to hide behind the double wall. Strangers had to knock because there was no doorbell. Whenever we heard a knock, we rushed behind the wall.

The comrades from Panska, Marek, Antek, and Zivia, moved into this apartment. Later Rifke Rosenstein and I moved in, too. We felt wonderfully secure with our hiding place behind the solidly constructed double wall. It was entered by lifting a board in the wardrobe wall.

Marisha or Maria would buy food across the street at 13 Leshno in a store owned by a Gentile friend of Marisha's. She herself kept some Jewish children and knew the secret of our apartment. Only those of us who had Aryan faces—Antek Zuckerman and myself—were permitted to leave the apartment. Zivia, Rifke, and Marek were not allowed to show themselves on the street at any time. Marek's Jewish face, his black hair, and his dark eyes had been a handicap in getting him moved into the apartment. Shwentochovsky belonged to the volunteer fire squad of the city electrical works and had managed to smuggle out an additional uniform. He and Marek arrived dressed as firemen.

For me the new apartment was a great relief after so many

months in the dark rooms and musty cellar on Grzibovska. Now I could go into town several times a week. Also I could be visited by other comrades in the underground like Feiner, Mushkat, Kazik, Zelemainsky, Little Zoshka, and Inka Schweiger.

Behind the security of the double wall we kept some of our more important documents, sums of money belonging to the party and to the fighting organization, and a store of guns, ammunition, and hand grenades. The cost of buying, rebuilding and maintaining the apartment was borne by both organizations—the Bund and the Jewish fighting organization.

Until the end of 1941, our connection with comrades abroad, especially those in the United States, had been more or less organized. In fact, it operated more easily than we had any right to hope. During that time we in the ghetto received various sums of money from abroad—naturally much less than we needed. The channels through which we received the money and maintained contact were not always entirely dependable. We had to take risks; otherwise we would have gotten nothing.

The following example is typical of the way such channels functioned.

In the summer of 1941 word came through the PPS that our comrades Shloime Mendelsohn and Emanuel Scherer had sent us and the PPS a sum of money from Stockholm to Berlin through an employee of the Japanese Embassy. A special messenger had to be dispatched to Berlin to pick up the American dollars. The PPS approached a Ukrainian who did business with the Germans and had the right to visit Germany. As our agent, he met the Japanese employee, obtained the money, and brought it back to Warsaw. Such transactions usually cost a 15 or 20 per cent commission.

A few months later we were to receive a second shipment through the same channels. The Ukrainian was sent to Berlin to meet the Japanese employee—but we never saw the money. On his return he reported that he had been arrested and searched; everything had been confiscated. He had barely managed to escape with his life. Naturally, we had no means of checking up. And, of course, we did not know, in other cases, how much money stuck to the hands through which it passed.

We tried to distribute whatever help we received as widely as possible throughout the entire country. For example, until the deportations from the Warsaw ghetto we managed to send help to Vilna through a PPS Pole to Mrs. Patye Kremer, seventy-five-year-old widow of one of the founders of the Bund, and to Comrade Grisha Jashunski, son of the vice-president of the Warsaw ghetto Judenrat. We sent money, passport blanks, and other necessary documents. When the deportations began, our contact with Vilna and other centers was broken.

Before the deportations, we found many people in the ghetto through whom we could arrange money transfers, especially from America. At that time we were burdened by heavy expenses, especially in preparation for the eventual uprising. When the deportations began, all the sources of money transfer were cut off. The expenses continued to increase, but no money was to be had. At the time of the last selection our entire capital consisted of three hundred dollars divided evenly among Abrasha Blum, Berek Snaidmil, and myself.

After the deportations, everything was concentrated on the Aryan side. We had to depend on help from abroad, especially on the Jewish Labor Committee in the United States, in which such men as Nathan Chanin of the Workmen's Circle, David Dubinsky of the International Ladies Garment Workers' Union, and other Americans were active. The funds now went through more dependable and precise channels. The Polish government-in-exile in London provided special couriers. Money and correspondence came by plane and parachute.

The accounting of income and outgo was conducted by our

old comrade Sigmund Mushkat. He kept his books with such precision that one would have thought he expected an audit at any moment. The bookkeeper's records lay in our central committee apartment at 24 Zhuravia in the tricky hiding place under the floor.

Through the official channels of the government-in-exile we were also able to send reports to our comrades abroad, to the representatives of the Bund in the United States, and to the Jewish Labor Committee. With their help, during 1943 and 1944, our contacts abroad were better organized and functioned fairly regularly. We were able to tell the world about the battles in the ghetto, about the situation of the rescued handful, about the crematoriums and the gas chambers.

I remember our great joy in July 1944 when the Polish government forwarded to us a microfilm which contained articles from *Unser Tsait*, the New York Bund magazine, and other documents, particularly declarations by the American Representation of the Bund on the question of the Eastern Polish provinces, which we were at that time discussing. Among us there were two points of view: a minority favored accepting the *fait accompli* and bowing to Soviet annexation; the majority stood for a plebiscite to settle the question. Our American comrades supported the position of the majority.

Our joy was boundless. The microfilm was a direct, almost a personal greeting from our comrades in America. We felt bound to them across the years of blood and suffering which divided us. Using a photographic enlarger, we transcribed all the documents, duplicated them on our machine, and distributed them among the comrades in the hiding places. This contact with America did much to raise our morale. It reminded us that we had friends. It gave us the feeling that if this wonderful miracle of communication could be accomplished, all was not yet lost.

The Polish underground was far from united. Indeed, it was split into various groups that fought each other politically. The illegal National Council within the country consisted of four parties—the PPS, the Peasant party, the National Democrats, and the Christian Democrats. These groups were represented in the London parliament-in-exile. So was the Bund, represented first by Artur Ziegelboim and then by Emanuel Scherer. But in Poland the National Council would not accept a representative of the Bund.

Aside from the Bund, the following groups, not counting the extreme fascist Falanga group, were also outside the National Council: (1) the RPPS, a split from the PPS led by Osubka-Morawski, (2) the Democrats, a group of intellectuals, and (3) two syndicalist trade-union groups.

As the front moved closer to Poland, it became clear that we would soon be free of the wild beasts who had raged over the land for five years. The three groups I have listed, together with the Bund, set up a central leadership to achieve unity among all underground democratic forces. They placed before the National Council the following proposals for a united platform: (1) Representation for all in the National Council. (2) Orientation on the basis of an understanding with Soviet Russia and a plebiscite to settle the question of the cession of Vilna to White Russia and the Eastern Ukraine to the Soviet Ukraine. (3) Orientation toward a socialist reconstruction after the war. (4) Agrarian reforms in a socialist spirit. (5) Full rights for national minorities. (6) Unity of the socialist movement. (7) Admission of the Communists into the National Council. (At that time they had set up their own People's Council.)

There were negotiations between the two leaderships, the National Council and our center. The Council was adamant. It refused any recognition of new groups which would require a change in its platform and orientation.

These discussions were interrupted when the Warsaw uprising

236

brushed aside all political considerations and orientations, sweeping up all forces in its dramatic impetus and tragic result.

The mood of the people had begun to change perceptibly. One could feel that the beginning of the end was approaching. As the fighting front drew nearer to Warsaw, the Germans became more nervous; the atmosphere became more strained from day to day. The Germans increased their campaign of terror, fearing outbreaks behind the fighting front. Sabotage was being stepped up. Attacks on military and ammunition trains were becoming more frequent. Evacuation transports were being harassed on the way back from the front.

There were strange and beautiful sights in the Warsaw streets. Long rows of horse-drawn wagons piled high with the paraphernalia of war moved in from the other side of the Vistula. They plodded along, manned by sloppy, worn-out, discouraged soldiers who kept their eyes lowered to hide their shame. Warsaw found it hard to conceal its joy as it watched this miserable retreat of the once haughty victors who had paraded through Warsaw with tanks, panzer cars, and well-polished, powerful weapons. Their heads had been high as they marched onward, onward, toward the east.

On the dirt roads and byways of the remote countryside, the Germans could no longer resist the temptations brought on by demoralization and the breakdown of discipline. They sold their horses, military uniforms, coats, underclothing, linens, blankets, and so forth. In some places they permitted themselves to be disarmed by soldiers of the underground armies. Occasionally small towns and military dumps were raided. The garrison would be overwhelmed; arms and stores of provisions would be carried off. Even in Warsaw there were some cases in which German soldiers were disarmed and humiliated. The military authorities issued orders that soldiers must not appear on the streets singly, but in groups, fully armed.

The underground organized an armed attack on the Paviak jail, which was crowded with political prisoners. Though the telephone wires had been cut, the German garrison succeeded in getting reinforcements. After a two-hour battle the attackers had to withdraw; both sides lost heavily in dead and wounded.

Some time later, several days before the Warsaw uprising, several Jews managed to escape from Paviak. They had been sent to repair sabotaged sewers and they used the sewers as an avenue to freedom.

The anxiety of the German civilians and Volksdeutsche, who during the occupation had sucked the blood of the helpless population like leeches, became more pronounced. They began to flee to the protection of the Fatherland. Since the railroads were glutted by the military evacuation, they used trucks and hand carts. They went accompanied by hostile, mocking looks from the Poles.

Even the mighty Gestapo began to tremble. Its offices in Lublin were evacuated. We had no difficulty in recognizing this gang as they moved with their trunks and equipment over the Vistula toward the west. The mighty had fallen after so many years of power, robbery, and murder.

For the most part the evacuation of the military took place at night, when the inhabitants were confined to their homes by the curfew.

We could already clearly hear the distant artillery fire from the front. It was heavenly music. Sweetly it caressed our hearts and lifted our spirits. The German governor, Fischer, as late as July 15, with typical Nazi insolence and obtuseness, posted flattering placards in the streets of Warsaw calling on the Poles to aid the army which was battling "the black might of bolshevism." He asked the people to build trenches for the defense of the city. Several assembly points were specified, but not a single person showed up. The brutal power which for five years had ruled with blood and iron was losing its grip. Similar treatment was given

238

an order to evacuate the large factories which produced supplies for the army. The underground hampered the evacuation and called upon its own militia and soldiers to protect such factories by every means as a national treasure.

Warsaw was now regularly bombed by Soviet planes. The people ran happily to the shelters. Unfortunately, it was a joy that the Jews could not completely share. They remained locked in their hiding places because their landlords feared that neighbors might inform. The bombing held a twofold danger for us—the danger of being hit and the danger of being disclosed.

As an uprising became more clearly the order of the day, we tried to assemble the remnants of our ghetto fighters from the forests where they lay hidden. We wanted our comrades closer to the city so that they would not be cut off from us when the front drew closer and fighting broke out in Warsaw. We managed to bring several to Warsaw. We also managed to take little Elsa Friedrych out of the convent near Cracow where she had been hidden. The child of our heroic Zalman Friedrych was now completely alone; her father had perished in a gun fight with the Gestapo, her mother had been killed in Maidanek. She was later brought to the United States and adopted by American comrades.

Jews, except those who looked unmistakably Aryan, could not take part in the military preparations for the uprising, since this involved being on the streets, going out to the countryside for military drill, and otherwise exposing oneself in public. Until the moment of battle we had to remain buried in our hiding places.

The city waited impatiently for the signal. No time had been set for the uprising, but everyone knew that it was inevitable and could come at any moment. The Soviet radio hammered away incessantly, stirring up the underground, asking if it was prepared to begin the last decisive battle, calling for help to annihilate the common enemy and win freedom.

.There were four underground military formations: (1) AK (Armia Kryova), the official underground army of the London

239

government; (2) The militia of the PPS; (3) AL (Armia Ludova), the communists; (4) PAL (Polska Armia Ludova), the center of left-wing democratic parties which has already been described. In the villages the peasants had organized "Green Battalions."

It is difficult to assess the relative strength of the various groups, but there is no doubt that the AK, under the command of General Bor-Komorowski, was by far the largest. In the end, all the groups united for the uprising and placed themselves under the over-all command of General Bor.

Three times the underground mobilized its forces and each time demobilized them again. Then, on August 1, 1944 . . .

EIGHT

WE WERE at 24 Zhuravia Street in the secret apartment of our central committee, discussing various pressing problems. It was four P.M. Suddenly our landlady, a courier in the underground, rushed in breathlessly and announced, "The uprising has been proclaimed. It starts at five o'clock."

We looked into the street and saw serious-faced, hurrying people, some with bundles under their arms, some with knapsacks on their shoulders. A little later we heard sporadic shooting from various parts of the city.

The radio, in Polish, called upon all Warsaw inhabitants to throw themselves into the final battle against the Nazi occupier. It announced in the name of the underground government that all men and women over sixteen were being mobilized and must immediately place themselves at the disposal of the anti-German military agencies. Everyone was asked to help build street barricades and fortify each house.

That night barricades sprouted over the entire city. They could be found at almost every corner stretching across the width of the street and reaching at least one story high. A small entrance way was left along the side. In each courtyard committees were formed to carry out the orders of the military command. Communication between courtyards was through tunnels dug between one cellar and the next.

At the outset the Germans concentrated on and held the strategic centers and communication lines. They controlled the

241

bridges over the Vistula, and could thus maintain uninterrupted contact with the centers on the other bank of the river—Praga, Yablonna, Waver, Grochov, and so forth. They divided the town into four sections and cut them off each from the other, making it impossible for the rebels to carry out a unified plan.

By dominating the railroad bridge and all the main roads leading through the city to the west, the Germans cut off the district of Zholibosh. Their grip on the Kerbedjia bridge and the roads through Theater Square, isolated the center of the city from Old Town. Their possession of Poniatovski bridge and Jerosolymska Avenue broke all communication between the center of the city and Mokotov. Each of the four sections—Zholibosh, Old Town, Mokotov, and the center of the city—became an isolated front.

The fiercest fighting took place in Povishle for the Kerbedjia and Poniatovski bridges; in the Old Town, around St. John's Cathedral; on Byelanski Street for the Bank Polski building; and in the center of the city on Napoleon Square around the Post Office building and the tall Prudential Insurance Company building. The skyscraper gave German machine guns command of the entire surrounding area. The rebels did not have the proper weapons to storm these important buildings.

We did seize the electric, gas, and water works at the beginning of the uprising, but were dislodged by the Germans. The lack of tanks and artillery soon proved to be an insurmountable handicap. The people could compensate for the lack of modern weapons and shortage of trained personnel only by a burning hate for the Nazis and by great devotion and sacrifice.

Underground newspapers were immediately established in captured printing plants. Placards on all the streets announced the formation of a national Polish government.

The Jews were scattered through the four isolated battle areas. Through the radio of the military command, in the name of the

Bund, we called upon all Jews, men and women, to join the socialist and democratic military groups fighting in their neighborhoods.
Over the same radio, the central committee of the underground
Bund appealed to the world to aid the fighters who were paying
with blood for the freedom of Poland and of all mankind.

Our comrades gave a good account of themselves in the fighting throughout the city. Men and women fought like demons,
afraid that a moment of rest would rob them of an opportunity
to strike at the enemy. They had so many accounts to settle.
They took desperate chances, exposing themselves recklessly to
come to closer grips with the Germans.

In the central committee's apartment at 24 Zhuravia, Feiner and
Leinkram lay deathly ill. As often as possible, Dr. Lipshitz would
rush back for a few moments from his post in the military hospital to bring them some sugar candy or a piece of bread from
his ration. Leon Feiner was suffering from cancer; it was already
in an advanced stage. Weak, lacking proper care and nourishment, his life flickered before our eyes. Leinkram, the lawyer from
Cracow, was dying of tuberculosis. During the final days of the
uprising, his wife managed to get him admitted to a hospital, but
he died as the hospital was being evacuated.

Dr. Lipshitz was remarkable. He always found some time to
be with them, to encourage them, to cheer them, to comfort
them with a friendly word or a smile.

On the first day of the uprising the military prison on Djika
Street was captured and all the prisoners freed. Most of them
were Jews, mainly from Greece, Hungary, and Rumania, with
a few from Poland. They were all slave laborers whom the Germans had been using to tear down the ruins of the ghetto.

I must confess that the attitude of the military command of
the uprising toward these most unfortunate of the unfortunate
Jews was far from proper, even considering the difficult times.
They were formed into labor brigades and immediately sent into
the front lines to dig trenches under the artillery fire of the

243

enemy. Toughs and hoodlums taunted and tormented them. Their difficulties were multiplied because they did not understand the language. We learned of the plight of these Jews and intervened on their behalf. We gave them what assistance we could and got a promise from the military command that their condition would be improved.

Some lawless underworld elements joined the uprising They often took it upon themselves to seize Aryan-looking Jews as German agents or spies. Even the average Pole showed hostility toward the Jews. Often our people were not allowed to enter the defense shelters. Foreign Jews were sometimes regarded with suspicion as Volksdeutsche. We had to find special shelters for Jews and provide them with food, money, and other necessities. The courtyard committees would refuse Jews ration cards for food from the commissaries or the public kitchens. We found ourselves constantly appealing to the authorities to win decent treatment for them. In the confusion we were not always able to check up on the promises we received.

The *Monitor Polski*, the official government gazette, published a communiqué abrogating the laws which the Germans had introduced during the occupation. They forgot one detail—to nullify the Nuremberg laws against the Jews. We promptly complained, and the government promised to correct the omission. A long time passed and many petitions were necessary before there was any action. And even then, instead of being printed in the space customarily reserved for such communiqués, the notice was tucked away in an inconspicuous corner.

The government agreed to ask the military to permit representatives of the Council for Aid to Jews to appear at investigations into accusations of spying and sabotage. It took a long time to arrange this, and in the meantime many innocent people perished. When the council finally managed to establish a special office to which Jews could bring their complaints, the uprising was in its last stages.

244

The fighting went on day and night. We suffered severe casualties. We did not possess the proper weapons to do battle with an enemy armed from head to foot with the most modern mechanized equipment.

The Germans hid time bombs in tanks and left them, supposedly abandoned, on the street. In their eagerness the rebels would seize such tanks, often bringing them behind the rebel lines, where they exploded with terrific destructive force. The Germans loosed self-propelled machines which crashed through walls and exploded inside the buildings. The merciless artillery fire continued to take its toll.

The dead lay about the streets for days. Under the constant hail of bullets, it was difficult to collect the bodies. The crude markers of hastily dug graves sprouted in the streets, squares, and courtyards.

Food became scarce. In the first days, we had captured the large German food warehouses on Zhelasna Street as well as the Haberbusch and Schille breweries. The people had carried out grain, all sorts of food products, and canned goods. Corn and wheat were milled with makeshift equipment and were baked in the shelters. But these supplies were soon requisitioned by the army. Each person was permitted to keep 10 per cent of what he had taken as a reward for his work.

The water situation was worse. In the early days of the uprising, after the rebels had been dislodged from the water, electric, and gas works, all utilities were completely shut off. Emergency wells were dug in some courtyards, but they supplied only a trickle. Racked by thirst, people hunted desperately for openings into the water mains.

We lay, then, in darkness and filth, without gas or water, unable to prepare what little food we had. The results were sickness and epidemics. The spirit of the fighters fell from day to day.

The entire uprising had of course been based on the prospect of help from the Soviet Army. It was close at hand, we expected it to enter the city at any moment. The long-suffering population had waited until the artillery fire from the front could be heard drawing steadily closer to the gates of Warsaw. For days the Soviet radio had been stirring up the underground, encouraging it to come out in open battle against the enemy.

The Russians were approaching from the direction of Praga. Two weeks after the uprising broke out the outlying sections of Praga were already in Russian hands, but the Germans still held the bridges over the Vistula. Expectations were high; liberation seemed imminent. At one time, when explosions were heard from the direction of the front, the people were sure that the bridges were being blown up, that the Germans were retreating, and that the Russians were entering the city. Spontaneously everyone rushed from cellars and bunkers. The balconies blossomed with Polish flags Crowds sang the "Rota," the traditional anti-German Polish hymn. But the fatal error was soon evident.

Everybody continued to wait with eager anticipation; but still help did not come. The Red Army remained in Praga, making no attempt to cross the Vistula. A few times Soviet planes dropped food, medical supplies, and arms. There were dogfights over the city between Russian and German fliers.

Two officers of the Russian command did cross to the rebel lines as observers. They promised assistance. And that was the end of that.

Then came exciting news. Our radio announced that Paris was in arms and that the American Army had entered the French capital. We felt a warm kinship with the Parisians whose success seemed to herald our own. But Warsaw was soon bitterly comparing its lot with that of Paris. If only the American Army were at *our* gates!

A few weeks after the outbreak of the uprising the Germans proposed through the Red Cross that women, children, and non-

combatants be permitted to leave the city. The rebels accepted
the offer. During the short truce, long rows of sick, of aged, of
tearful women carrying babes in their arms, trudged out of the
city to the safety of the German lines.

After this evacuation, the Germans intensified their artillery
bombardment. As the situation became progressively worse, the
knowledge that their loved ones were far behind the German
lines embittered the remaining fighters.

To buoy up the sinking spirit among the rebels, General Bor-
Komorowski announced over the radio and through the press
that the fight would go on, that help was coming soon. In truth,
a small number of Polish soldiers from the Red Army, commanded by a Colonel Berger, did cross from Praga in small boats
under heavy fire, suffering great losses. They told us that their
comrades were eager to break into Warsaw but that the Soviet
command refused to permit it.

Several times English planes dropped supplies. Many of them
were shot down and fell into German-controlled territory. The
appearance of airplanes was always greeted with cheers. But the
uprising dragged into its second month, and still there was no
real help.

The enthusiasm with which the people had rushed to battle
with the Germans waned and gradually flickered out. It was
replaced by a mounting disillusionment that ate its way into the
hearts of the population. The bitterness grew when the radio
announced that the Russians had refused to allow English planes
to use their bases. The British had to fly great distances over
enemy territory carrying full loads and then return without
landing. This made any substantial help from them impossible.
We knew that the planes were piloted by Poles from the Royal
Air Force and that they were straining every sinew to bring
us aid.

Among the comrades whom we had brought to Warsaw from the forests shortly before the uprising were Hanna Krishtal and Jan Bilak. Hanna's husband, Gabrish Frishdorf, had been one of the heroes of the last ghetto battle. He had been killed in a gun battle in the Wishkov Forest a few months before the Warsaw uprising. Hanna was a slight, twenty-two-year-old girl. She was at this time in her ninth month of pregnancy.

Hanna, Jan, and Mrs. Papierna, a Poale Zionist from Novidvor, were captured by the Germans and taken to Gestapo headquarters on Shucha Avenue. Jan Bilak was shot immediately. Hanna, Mrs. Papierna, and several other women were formed into a squad to retrieve German dead from the streets under fire. The Germans did not relish the idea of getting too close to the rebel barricades.

While engaged in this work Hanna and Mrs. Papierna escaped by dashing through a hail of bullets to the other side of the barricades. Hanna was of course shaken up by the experience. We were able to put her temporarily in a home for aged women, but we had to take her out after her labor pains began. We placed her in a cellar with several other maternity cases.

The battle raged everywhere. No one had time or patience for women in childbirth. I ran about like a madman trying to find the minimum necessities for the woman in labor and for the child she was about to bear.

I used my shirt to make diapers and somehow found a torn sheet, a nightgown, some cereal, some boiled water safe for drinking. I could not rest. I had known Hanna since she was a baby. She had grown up on my lap, gone through school with my own son. Now she writhed in pain in a dark cellar, a frail young girl grown old with experience, a veteran of the ghetto battle, burning with hunger and thirst, while around her the world flamed and crackled and paid no heed.

It was a miracle that the boy was born alive. We named him Gabrish after his heroic father.

248

Communication between various parts of the city was mostly through the sewers, and even this was finally interrupted. The Germans released poison gas into the sewers, trapping and killing hundreds.

Corpses accumulated in the streets. Burying them was no longer worth the effort or the risk. The rebels had to husband their dwindling resources.

One after another, Zholibosh, Mokotov, and Povishle fell. The fall of Old Town, where the battle had raged three weeks without interruption, was a hard blow. The Cathedral of St. John was completely destroyed. The Old Town Square with its ancient historic buildings was now a ruin.

Except for scattered, isolated strongholds, only the center of the city held out weakly. The battle was all but over. We heard frightful stories of how the Germans were treating the population in the captured districts. They burned homes with their occupants; they drove hundreds into the church on Wola and shot them all.

Warsaw was burning on all sides. All hope of help was gone. Our physical resources had run out. Embittered, disillusioned, hungry, and dispirited, the rebels were forced to capitulate in the face of the enemy's overwhelming power.

In tears the city heard the broken voice of its commander, General Bor-Komorowski, coming over the radio: "There is no more ammunition. We are exhausted. Help has not arrived and will not come. We must surrender to overwhelming force. Long live independent Poland!"

After sixty-three days and nights of heroic struggle against hopeless odds the Warsaw uprising was over.

Through the intervention of the Allies, the rebels were accorded the rights of prisoners of war. Civilians were to be evacuated to Prushkov and from there distributed among various camps. For the evacuation of the entire population of Warsaw, more than a million people, the Germans allowed only three days. The time was so impossibly short that they were forced to extend it by forty-eight hours.

The uprising ended six days after the birth of Hanna's child. She was still very weak, and the infant could scarcely breathe. If Hanna's Jewish face should attract notice, it would mean quick death for both of them. The Germans were still shooting Jews who fell into their hands. With a baby, her chances would be slim indeed. I decided that the only hope was to do away with the child and find a bunker for Hanna until the Russians took over the city.

All night I wrestled over my decision. In the morning I went to her cellar. It was damp and dark; I had to feel my way to her side. Hanna lit a candle which cast a faint glow on her deathly white face and on the little pile of rags beside her where the infant lay.

I picked up the week-old baby. Outside everyone was rushing around, preparing to leave, shouting and weeping. The noise from the street penetrated dimly into the dark cellar. I looked down at the shriveled little bundle in my hands. Surely it was condemned to death anyhow. While it lived it was a burden which might drag its mother to her death. A little pressure from my fingers, and all would be over.

Before me I seemed to see Gabrish Frishdorf, hero of the ghetto, rotting in an unknown grave. All that was left of him was this little flicker of life.

My fingers felt stiff. I laid the baby gently back on its little bed of rags.

I put Hanna and the child in the safe keeping of Jewish friends, gave her some money, and let her join the stream to Prushkov. They got through.

Eight months after the birth of the baby I met Hanna and little Gabrish in Lodz. Once again I held the child in my arms. Only then did I tell his mother the terrible secret I had carried in my heart.

After the war Hanna went to Sweden with her child.

With the capitulation of the rebels and the announcement that only three days were allowed for the complete evacuation of soldiers and civilians, the city became a madhouse. The chaos was unbelievable. Bewildered people raced in all directions trying to make last-minute preparations before leaving their homes.

Each soldier received thirty to fifty dollars from the Polish government. For both soldiers and civilians the Germans set a maximum limit on baggage of fifteen kilograms per person.

For the Jews the evacuation was a greater danger than for the Gentiles; for many it was too great a risk to run. It meant walking through the German lines, past soldiers and Gestapo officials who were certain to scan the stream of refugees closely. At the camps it meant examinations and re-examinations.

Some, who felt they could rely on their faces or their documents, and others, like Hanna Krishtal, who had no alternative, joined the refugees, hoping to get through in the confusion.

For the others, who elected to remain in the ruined city, bunkers had to be provided. They would need enough provisions to keep them alive until the Russians entered Warsaw. All this required a great deal of money. Fortunately, two or three weeks before the surrender we had received through the Polish government a large sum of money from the Jewish Labor Committee in New York. Thanks to that timely gift we were able to help those who left for Prushkov and those who remained in Warsaw.

Stocking the bunkers with food was not very difficult. The city became one tremendous market place. Since the evacuees were permitted to carry only fifteen kilograms, they sold and bartered their excess belongings in the streets. The only acceptable currency was the American dollar. No one would take Polish zlotys. Food of all sorts, clothing, jewelry, silver and gold were bought, traded, and sold. Many buried their most precious possessions deep under the cellars, hoping to dig them out after the war.

We were able to exchange our dollars for food and other necessities to provision the bunkers for the few Jews who remained in Warsaw. The accumulation of supplies seemed more than ample. If we had known how long we were to be buried alive!

Some Polish comrades advised me to accompany them to the prisoner-of-war camps. They promised to "cover" me. But I was extremely doubtful that their scheme would work. I decided to remain in the city and wait for the Russians. After all, in a few weeks the Russians would sweep through Warsaw, and I would be out of the Nazi grip.

Space was reserved for me in a bunker on Shenna Street which we had built and provisioned at a cost of a thousand dollars. It sheltered some of the ghetto fighters and partisans with Jewish faces—Belchatovsky, Spiegel, Marisha Chaitman, Miss Shefner, Mrs. Falk and her son, and others.

On my way to the bunker, as I was ready to move in, I met Mrs. Papierna, the woman who had escaped from the Germans with Hanna Krishtal. She was beside herself with terror, afraid to go to Prushkov, with no place to hide, no money, no friends. She pleaded with me to help her I invited her to come to the bunker with me. When we got there we discovered that there was room for only one more person. After having raised her hopes so high I could do only one thing. I gave up my own place to Mrs. Papierna and left.

Every road leading from Warsaw to Prushkov was crowded with the expelled citizens of the Polish capital. Long, dense rows trudged over the muddy roads in the cold October rain. Grimly, the refugees bowed under the weight of their fifteen kilograms, the distillate of a lifetime's accumulation. Behind them they left burned homes, streets strewn with debris, and squares littered with the bodies of their dead. Fires burned uncontrolled. A cloud of smoke hung over the weary marchers. The stench of ruin and desolation pursued them.

Warsaw lay broken and shattered. Her lifeblood flowed onto the roads to Prushkov.

It was the day before the evacuation deadline. On the street I ran into the Pole, Comrade Kaminsky, an active PPS leader of the underground. He drew me aside and whispered with suppressed excitement that an expedition of rebels was planning to cross the Vistula that night and enter the Russian lines. If I wished to join them I must decide immediately and we would stay together until the time for the rendezvous. I agreed.

Kaminsky outlined the general plan and told me that everything was arranged. When we reached the center of the river, Russian soldiers would meet us in small boats.

The meeting place was on Pyusa Street near Uyasdovsky Boulevard. Twenty-two people assembled, among them three women. Most were soldiers from the military formations of the PPS, AL, and PAL. A colonel was in command. We were to start at ten o'clock at night through the sewer opening at Three Cross Square. In the group were sanitation workers who knew the way well. The sewers led down to the banks of the Vistula. We would swim the river with the help of a small rubber boat and a long wire rope which we had wound on a small pulley.

At ten o'clock, without incident, we entered the sewer. Carefully we closed the opening behind us, leaving no trace. We were all partially undressed in order to move about more easily. Everyone wore a life preserver and carried a machine pistol. It was October—cold, wet, and unpleasant.

The sewer pipes were not very large. We had to stoop as we

walked. The course was downhill toward the Vistula. We moved slowly, slipping and sliding, half submerged in the stinking slime of dirt, garbage, and excrement. We bumped against dead bodies soaking in the filth—undoubtedly victims of the poison gas which the Germans had let into the sewers.

As we drew closer to the Vistula we came upon branching sewers which emptied into the large main through which we were moving. Here and there the way was blocked with barbed wire which the Germans had laid to make passage more difficult. We cut through the wire with a pair of military shears. It was not easy. In the dark we tore our skins on the barbs. Our flashlights were not much help.

At two in the morning we reached the opening which led directly to the Vistula near the Cherniakov docks. The colonel commanded everyone to strip. We set down the coil of wire rope, fastened it, inflated and prepared the rubber boat. We stripped and swabbed our bodies with benzine as protection against the cold water and the October night. We tied our machine pistols to our life preservers and slipped them on. Around my neck I carried a packet with a little money, my documents, and Sonya Novogrodsky's wallet.

The colonel whispered, "The first six, proceed."

They crawled toward the water. The end of the wire rope was tied around the waist of the leader. The other five stayed close to him. We lay on the ground and watched as, one after another, they dropped into the cold waves and began to swim.

The rope kept winding off the pulley—a sure sign that they were making progress. About three minutes later the colonel motioned the second six to get ready. They moved forward to let themselves into the water.

Suddenly a light blinded us. Powerful searchlights flashed on the river. A volley of bullets followed immediately. The pulley stopped turning. The colonel shouted, "Get back!"

We scrambled into the sewer and crawled frantically through

the filthy stream which poured into our faces as we climbed upward. The way back was a thousand times more difficult. We
slipped and slid and clawed our way, fighting to keep the current
from carrying us back to the river. From time to time we were
pounded by dead bodies carried downhill by the rush of slime.
"Faster, faster!" we urged each other. Perhaps the Germans had
already discovered the opening through which we had reached
the river. One gas grenade, and we would meet the same end
as the corpses under our feet.

It took all that was left of the night to reach the opening at
Three Cross Square. At six in the morning we emerged on the
street—sixteen naked people, three of them women, filthy,
smeared with excrement, bruised, with blood dripping from
wounds all over our bodies.

We stepped into the midst of a startled crowd of people rushing toward Prushkov with knapsacks on their backs. There was
no time to waste. We scattered into the side streets.

I covered my crotch with both hands, to hide the evidence of
my Jewishness, and ran toward Zhuravia Street. I was feverish
with excitment and shivering with cold. My body trembled, my
teeth chattered; my legs ached. Blood dripped from me at every
step.

At 24 Zhuravia Street I collapsed in the arms of my comrades.

Dr. Lipshitz stretched me out on a bed. He washed me with
some precious water and cleaned and dressed my wounds. He
rubbed me down with alcohol. I was suffering severely from
shock. It was several hours before I had recovered enough to
want to move on. Somehow, the comrades managed to assemble
some clothes—a suit, a shirt, a pair of shoes. I thanked them and
said good-by.

I still rejected the idea of going to Prushkov. Now that the
attempt to reach the Russian lines had failed, I returned to my
original determination to remain in Warsaw.

It was about noon. On the street I met Guzik of the Joint

255

Distribution Committee. He told me that he too intended to remain in the city and invited me to stay at his bunker. Six o'clock that evening was the final deadline for the evacuation of the entire Warsaw population. I had to make a decision quickly. I accepted.

At five-thirty I made my way through deserted side streets to the entrance of the bunker. It was already twilight A heavy rain was falling.

NINE

SOME twenty people stood in the rain at the entrance to the bunker on Vieyska Street near the Square of the Three Crosses, on the site of a former German school. Our bunker was the air-raid shelter constructed for the children. A bombing during the Warsaw uprising had destroyed the building, but the cellar was intact. The ruins provided excellent camouflage for our hiding place.

The group had been organized by Remba, an officer of the underground army who had escaped from the Paviak prison; Henrik Novogrodsky, a lawyer and former commissioner of the Jewish police in the ghetto, no relation to Sonya; and my friend Guzik. The people were a cross section of intellectuals, workers, and organizational leaders. One of them was badly wounded.

We let ourselves into the cellar through a narrow opening and then covered it carefully with broken pieces of wreckage. Inside, we took stock of our material and discovered that we had left a sack of onions outside. Bialer, a comrade who later got to New York, went out to get them, but, wandering in the dark, he lost his way in the ruins. After searching for some time, he stumbled on another entrance to the bunker, a long tunnel which the Germans had dug as an emergency exit. The tunnel later proved very useful.

Although the ventilation was poor, we found some advantages to the German construction. It was roomy, and there were

257

bunks for everyone. We lived communally. Each contributed whatever food he had to the general store. We figured that we had enough food to last two weeks if we used it sparingly. We also had a small supply of wood and coal.

The work was divided as equitably as possible, and everything was decided by majority vote. A commissary committee was in charge of the food supply. Two people, Bialer and Tishebov, formerly a druggist, were appointed cooks. One squad was organized for defense. They took charge of the submachine guns, revolvers, and hand grenades, and posted watch for the approach of the Germans. They put one guard at the main entrance, another at the tunnel entrance, and a group in the attic of a neighboring building with a good view of the entire surrounding area. I was elected manager of the bunker.

For more than a week everything went smoothly. Food was doled out twice a day—a small onion roll, a plate of soup, and a spoonful of sugar.

On the tenth day our water supply ran out. During the night we sent out searching parties. They finally found some water in the boiler of a heating system and two barrels of rain water. We brought this great treasure into our bunker through the tunnel.

When the food ran low we cut meals to one plate of soup a day. A few days later, our searching party stumbled on a second treasure, a sack of horse's oats. We dried the grain and milled it. The foul water was strained through a piece of cloth and used for making oatmeal.

But the food situation grew worse. Hunger made everyone irritable. Arguments began to break out. The cooks were accused of eating too much and there were angry demands that they be replaced. The hunger caused painful headaches. People lay passively in their bunks and thought about death by starvation. They began to lose confidence in their ability to hold out.

One man whom we knew only by his alias, Pyorun, a Jewish Catholic who looked like a typical Jew, huddled in his bunk and secretly said his prayers. He was ashamed to do it openly. He had come to us from the underground army, where he had served as a gendarme. Before the war, he had held a position in a large Polish firm. He had a Christian wife and two grown children. Under the Nuremberg Laws he was legally a Jew, and he had been forced to leave his home. Because of his Jewish appearance, he had been afraid to leave with the Polish Army for German prisoner-of-war camps. He had sent his family and joined our Jewish bunker.

He was torn by strange conflicts. He used to dwell on the fact that his father had been a very pious Jew and complained that Jews had lost their piety. "This great misfortune has struck the Jews because they have not been sufficiently devout," he would explain. Yet he remained a fervent Catholic. Some tried to convince him that his recent terrible experiences should bring him back to Judaism. He refused to consider such a thing. He insisted that he was a true Christian and would remain one. After the war I met him taking a peaceful walk in Warsaw with his wife and children.

While we still had food, many of us passed the time away by playing cards. When hunger began to gnaw at us, such games became too much of a strain. Besides, there was no longer any light. We sat in the darkness, burning a piece of wood for light only when necessary. It is small wonder that bad temper continued to mount. As the manager, I was constantly called upon to calm the irritated and hungry group. I had to intervene everywhere, settling petty arguments.

One day the group was seized by a mania of suspicion. There were charges that people had not given up all their food to the general store, and were eating surreptitiously. The loudest accusers were those who had put the largest contributions into the commissary. Every time someone gulped his dry spittle he was accused of swallowing a hidden morsel They demanded that I search everyone.

When some members loudly accused the food committee of playing favorites in doling food into the plates we were forced to change the personnel of the committee.

Now the members of the defense group demanded special food privileges for themselves on the ground that they were risking their lives in protecting the bunker. The wounded man demanded more to eat, insisting that his injuries were not healing properly because of his hunger. The atmosphere became more and more tense. It seemed that the group would inevitably destroy itself.

I searched for some way to calm the overwrought nerves. The best pacifier was food, but that was impossible. It occurred to me that perhaps a substitute would work—mental and spiritual food. If hunger could not be stilled through the stomach, perhaps it could be calmed through the mind and heart.

Since I was an experienced propagandist, I decided upon a series of lecture-discussions. After all, I had more than once been in a stormy mob which had fallen into wild, unreasoning rage and had been calmed by a few well-chosen words.

It was October. Every year at this time we had celebrated the anniversary of the Bund. We could start with that, especially since I saw around me some familiar Bundist faces.

The entire group sat on their bunks and listened as I spoke quietly, simply, and good-naturedly about various periods in the Bund's history, about the early difficult days and the triumphs we had won in the most hopeless situations. I took them from 1905 to 1945, from Warsaw to Siberia and back into our bunker. I told them of our long hunger strikes in Czarist prisons and of how we even refused to eat the food when it was piled temptingly before us by the guards. I lectured to them day after day. Memories poured out of my mind like water out of an open sluice gate. For hours my audience sat and listened, they began to feel ashamed of talking about a little more soup

One exception, however, was Zygmund, a lawyer, whose at-

260

tractive, quiet wife was with him in the bunker. Before the war he had been a peaceful, harmless collector of antiques. Here, however, he became wilder each day. He would walk back and forth all day, mumbling or crying aloud, "Food! Food! Food!" His shouting frightened us. Everyone else lay quietly in a sort of stupor, hardly able to bear Zygmund's shrieking. His constant refrain reminded us of the hunger we wanted so much to forget.

The situation became more serious when the half-crazed lawyer threatened to go out and tell the Germans everything. "I will not die of starvation!" he screamed.

No one could quiet him, neither his wife nor his personal friends. Everyone had the feeling that we must get rid of him. Otherwise we would all perish.

A secret trial was held. After a series of conversations and consultations, the court decided that the only course was to shoot him. They informed me of their decision and asked me, as manager, to have the sentence carried out

My stomach turned over. How could I possibly take the responsibility for such a murder, even in this situation? But what else was there to do? Surely the group, acting for the preservation of all, was well within its rights. I decided to make one last attempt to solve the problem without bloodshed.

I took Zygmund into another room and there, facing him, I began to talk. I knew immediately that my efforts were wasted. The words made no impression. Finally, as I was fumbling for something to say, a thought occurred to me. In a deadly serious tone I said to him, "Swear that you will not tell anyone. I have a very important secret to reveal to you."

He gave me his oath, and then I unfolded my "secret." "You know," I said in a whisper, "that the group has decided that you are to be shot. The supposed reason is that you are making so much noise, that you are shouting too much, and have threatened to reveal the bunker to the Germans. I want you to know the real reason. Your closest friend has arranged all this because he wants to see you killed. Do you know why? He wants to take away your wife."

I spoke quietly, with great seriousness. The lawyer looked at me with staring eyes, trying to control himself. In a trembling voice he said, "Comrade Bernard, it is true." He wept hysterically and fell to the ground. "Yes," he sobbed, "I felt it all the time. I have seen it happening with my own eyes."

He gave me his hand and swore that he would never reveal what I had told him and that from now on he would remain quiet. He would not permit himself to be tricked into being shot.

For a few days Zygmund avoided me and spoke to no one. He sat by himself, hunched over, throwing the others a guarded, sidelong glance from time to time. But from that time on he held himself carefully in check.

Our nightly expeditions continued. We searched the empty apartments of the abandoned buildings, now and then finding a bit of food—some dry bread or some cereal. We would immediately divide it. Each time food came into the bunker, hope for life suddenly rose.

Warsaw was now an empty city. Except for the few Jews in the underground bunkers, there were no inhabitants whatever. For a time Poland's capital became a Jewish city.

Our observers watched the ruins and reported what they saw. German patrols padded through the wreckage. At night there were only flames and smoke. By day we could see how the houses were being stripped by the Germans. Great trucks were loaded by gangs of Polish workers brought each day from Prushkov. Every item, every piece of furniture had some value to the Germans. Buildings were ransacked just as they had been after the deportations in the ghetto. From the warehouses of the *Wertverfassungstelle*, the stolen goods were transported to Germany to be divided among the members of the master race. After each building was emptied the Germans would play streams of benzine on it from large hoses and set it afire.

262

NOVEMBER 1944

We were in a no man's land between the Russian and the German front lines. Around us was the constant noise of cannonading, the whistling of shrapnel, the explosions of grenades, the near-by sound of the tank guns, the thunder of more distant artillery. We lived in the fear that, if German patrols did not find us, a stray shell might put an end to our little community.

One day, after we had been in the bunker about four weeks, we heard heavy blows over our heads. Someone was digging We could make out unmistakable voices speaking in German: "There must be a cellar under here. Someone must be here."

There was immediate panic. Everyone rushed into the tunnel. Our defense group, with their submachine guns, were the first to leave. They disappeared. The rest of us remained trembling in the tunnel all day. After dark I crawled carefully to the opening that led into the bunker. It was boarded up. The beasts had probably not pursued us into the tunnel for fear of an ambush, and had contented themselves with sealing up the opening. I tore some of the boards loose and entered the bunker. It was completely bare. They had taken everything we had.

We spent the night in the tunnel wondering how best to get away and find another hiding place.

Most of us decided to try to get to 9 Chozha where we had several times found food and hoped to find more. The others decided to look elsewhere for shelter.

To get to Chozha we had to cross the Square of the Three Crosses at night. This was very dangerous because the area was brilliantly lighted by the fiercely blazing School for the Deaf and Dumb.

We bound our feet in rags so that our steps would make less noise. In groups of three we moved along on hands and knees, close to the walls, until we reached the square. Then we crawled across it on our stomachs. One group moved while the others lay hidden in the ruins, waiting their turn. In this way twelve of us, including Guzik, Bialer, and Tishebov, finally reached 9 Chozha.

In the cellars of 9 Chozha we split up. We lay there until dawn, three or four people in each cellar. When day broke, we clambered up to the fourth floor. The steps were broken, hanging in the air, attached to pieces of broken floor.

For three days we lived peacefully at 9 Chozha, crawling up to the top floor each morning and back to the cellar each night. Then we decided to find a better place and get ourselves well settled for a long wait.

At one o'clock one night, with a twenty-six-year-old boy who had been a specialist in building bunkers in the ghetto, I started through the tunnels which connected 9 Chozha to the block of houses opening on Viltcha. I crawled ahead, holding a carbide lamp in front of me. Suddenly we heard a shout in German, *"Hande in die Hoch. Stehen bleiben!"*

We were caught in the blinding glare of a large searchlight. I saw two helmets. Submachine guns were pointing at us. For a second, I thought of reaching for my revolver, but I realized it was hopeless. I hurled my carbide lamp at the searchlight with all my strength. There was a crash and everything went dark. I scrambled back on all fours, toward a pile of coal we had passed. I burrowed into it, burying my entire body, and lay there for several hours with my heart pounding. I heard no footsteps. It was quiet, pitch-black.

At about four o'clock in the morning I crawled out of the coal pile and back to our hiding place at 9 Chozha. There I found four people sleeping, Guzik and Tishebov among them. The rest of the group had been scared away by the noise of our encounter with the Germans. My companion on the expedition was nowhere to be found. I never learned what happened to him.

Now we had to find some other place. Remaining here was too dangerous. Guzik, Tishebov and I crept through the cellars which stretched beneath the block of houses. In a courtyard at the corner of Viltcha and Krutcha we found a well which had been dug during the uprising. We decided to remain there in the hope that the Germans had not poisoned the water. Though foul and stinking, it was still water, and we could boil and use it.

One part of the cellar had exits in two directions—always a virtue in a bunker. We made ourselves comfortable.

All three of us were worn out, miserable, plagued by lice picked up in the constant crawling through ruins and cellars. Tishebov became sick of dysentery, which tortured him and us. He could hardly stand on his feet. He dripped constantly. Each morning, despite his pain, he had to climb several stories to be safe from the German patrols that constantly searched the cellars for signs of life. Leaving a trace of ourselves below could mean death.

Guzik was so completely exhausted and so agitated that I thought he was losing his mind. Once, lying on one of the upper stories of the ruin, we clearly heard heavy steps and shouts. We pressed deeper into our corners, but we heard them climbing upward. The voices came closer. It was clear that we had been discovered. They were coming after us. We began to climb higher. We reached the attic, but to get further we had to cross a wide hole that stretched all the way across the attic floor. A broken door lay nearby. I threw it across the opening, making a small bridge with broad deep holes on either side. Tishebov and I ran across. But Guzik simply stood there, his entire body trembling. He could not cross. His feet were rooted in terror.

Where I found the strength I will never know, but I raced back across the door, threw him over my shoulder, and carried him over the little bridge. We pulled the door to our side of the hole and crawled deeper into the attic, finally finding a dark place. We stayed there until the evening.

We hid in the cellars of the Viltcha-Krutcha block for two weeks. Guzik kept urging us to try to get to the bunker on

Vspulna where he had lived during the uprising. We finally agreed to make the attempt.

The block of houses was like a square. Unable to go through the wings, we had to cross a courtyard at some point to get to the other side of the square. From there we could get out to Vspulna Street.

We reached an opening into the courtyard. As I stepped through the door I suddenly saw a German and a group of Polish workers. I rushed back and all three of us raced to the opposite exit. Ahead of us we could hear shouts—we were trapped on both sides. From the courtyard we heard the loud explosion of a grenade. But the German had thrown it at the entrance on the other side of the court toward which he had seen me start. He had evidently not noticed that I had dashed back into the doorway.

We crawled into a small cellar and waited. We expected to be discovered at any moment. The building above us was burning. The heat began to penetrate into the small room and smoke filled it We lay there choking, but it might be fatal to move elsewhere We hardly dared breathe, listening intently for every sound, for every hint of a footfall.

Completely worn out, Guzik stretched out on the ground and went to sleep. He began to snore. In that deathly stillness, his snoring sounded like artillery fire. I shook him, trying to wake him.

"Go on alone," he moaned. "Leave me here. I am going to die anyhow."

His groaning and complaining made even more noise than his snoring. We could still hear sounds of activity in the courtyard.

I covered his mouth with my hand.

"Be quiet!" I whispered angrily. "Be still, or all three of us will be killed."

Tishebov lay deathly quiet. He was having a severe attack of dysentery.

266

NOVEMBER 1944

When it got dark we decided to make one more attempt to reach Guzik's bunker, this time through the streets. The buildings on every side were burning. Fragments fell all around us. We walked, crouching alongside the walls of the burning buildings, stumbling over burning timbers and doors, dodging chunks of masonry. Finally we reached the house on Vspulna where Guzik had had his bunker. It was completely demolished, burned out

After several days of wandering, we returned to our old hiding place on Viltcha-Krutcha near the precious well. The store of food we had left there was gone.

We searched through the neighboring cellars. In one we came upon a store of delicacies—pots of conserves and bottles of fruit syrups, including a large jug of blackberry syrup, precious medicine for dysentery. There was no bread or grain anywhere.

We made ourselves a meal of the preserves and fruit syrups We were all very weak, hardly able to keep our feet. All of us were beginning to swell from hunger. We could not even think of further expeditions for better hiding places or for food.

Guzik was certainly very near death.

In a weak voice he said, "Leave me here to die. I have no more strength. I am exhausted. Go on without me. I ask only one favor. Here is my will."

He held up a piece of paper.

"I have some property in Palestine and an only son. If you remain alive, tell him everything that happened to me. A part of my inheritance goes to you."

"I already carry one inheritance with me—Sonya's wallet for her son. I must carry that because Sonya no longer lives. I must obey the last wish of a murdered friend. You are alive and will go on living; I don't want either your will or your inheritance."

I tried to encourage him, but he had lost all hope. He did not dream that he would live to see the liberation and that soon after he would die in an airplane accident

267

It was the beginning of December. One night a heavy snow fell. We did not dare to go into the courtyard for water for fear our footprints would betray us.

We found a board long enough to reach the well. Using all our strength, the three of us would hold one end of the board and slowly edge it through the air over the threshhold until the other end reached the well wall. When the board rested firmly at both ends without touching the snow we could go after the water. Then we would pull the board back into our hole.

At night one of us stood guard while the other two slept. Once I heard footsteps close by. I put out the carbide lamp, and wakened my two comrades, but it was already too late to leave our little room. The sounds were too near. We were so frightened that we were seized by convulsions of trembling. This was surely the end.

"*Mietek, tu sohn ludje*" (Mietek, there are people here), we heard clearly in Polish.

As the footsteps and voices drew closer to our door, I lit the lamp and we stood with our revolvers poised.

"*Kto tam?*" (Who is there?) we heard someone ask and saw the barrel of a revolver pushing through the slightly open door.

"*Svoi*" (Friends), I answered, standing close to the wall alongside the door and pointing my revolver at the widening opening.

"*Amtcho?*" the person on the other side of the door asked in Yiddish.

This was a bit of gibberish which in the past few years had become a code for one person to ask another, "Are you a Jew?"

"Yes," I answered with a little more assurance.

The door opened wide and someone rushed in.

"Bernard!" He threw his arms around my neck and kissed me.

It was Yulek Smokovsky, Black Yulek. His father was a transport worker, a sympathizer of the Bund.

Mietek, the second member of the group, came from Lodz. He was a stocking worker. Mietek's wife was the third person.

DECEMBER 1944

They all talked excitedly at once. They lived in a bunker on Vspulna. They were on a food-hunting expedition, like all the rats in the cellars and bunkers. They had smelled our cooking and had entered our cellar.

That night we went with them to Vspulna. They left us in a cellar near their bunker, while they went to ask for permission to admit us. They reported that the people in the bunker were willing to take me in, but I refused to go without my two comrades. Later that night the manager of the bunker, accompanied by two others, came to see us. We talked things over and they agreed to admit us, but we had to wait in the cellar one more day. They undressed us completely, burned all our things, washed us and gave us new clothes. Guzik and I were taken to the main bunker at 26 Vspulna, Tishebov was placed in another bunker not far away.

There were twenty-nine people in our bunker, representing all classes of society. Among them was a Greek Jew with an unsavory reputation as an accomplished pickpocket. He entertained us by demonstrating his adroitness as a thief. There was also a Christian woman who had covered Jews in a bunker before and during the uprising and had decided to remain with them rather than leave for Prushkov.

Many of them knew me quite well because of the help they had received through me during the uprising and earlier. Some of them, including the two leaders of the bunker, I knew from prewar days and from the ghetto. One of the leaders was Matus Kulash, whose father had operated a well-known transport company on Grzibovska. Matus had his wife and child with him. The other was Tall Jacob from Praga. In the ghetto he had owned a large fleet of wagons in partnership with Matus under a contract for garbage removal. This had enabled him to carry on profitable smuggling on a broad scale.

269

Another member of the group was the sweater-maker Spiegelman, who had participated in the uprising in the Treblinka death camp with our comrade Yankel Viernik. They had escaped together. In the last days of the Warsaw uprising, when we were busy providing aid to hidden Jews, I had brought food and money to the cellar where Jacob's and Matus's families were concealed. That had undoubtedly played some part in the decision to admit us.

Everything in the bunker was well organized. The inhabitants were divided into teams for doing the various necessary tasks. The nightly search through the cellars for food and other necessities was performed by three groups in rotation. One committee maintained order and cleanliness in the bunker, another committee prepared and cooked the food.

The members of the little community, which represented all the strata of society, were of various characters and moral convictions. Most were good-hearted people, but they were sick, weak, irritable, unnerved because of their terrible experiences. Understandably, there was no lack of conflict and argument. Peculiar social tensions were revealed.

For example, the leaders, who came from the lowest social groups, maintained that the once-rich merchants, lawyers, and other intellectuals should now do the most menial work—like carrying out, each night, the filth and excrement collected during the day.

"You have lived your entire lives in ease," they jibed. "Now you can do a little of the dirty work."

Food was communal property: whatever the expeditions brought back went into the general store. But clothes or other valuables belonged to the individual or group who found them.

I learned that the families of the leaders had buried in various cellars great quantities of clothing, furs, silks, and even gold and silver articles which they had found on searching forays.

One night, while going through the cellars hunting for food, one group met several Poles from a village near Mokotov who had come to Warsaw to search the ruins for money, jewelry, and clothing. It was well known that many of Warsaw's citizens, before leaving the city for Prushkov, had buried their valuables in the hope of digging them out later. Some people were willing to risk their lives sneaking through the German patrols at night to look for these treasures. Such people were called *shabrovniks*, underworld argot for housebreakers.

Some members of our expedition were dressed in Polish military uniforms, and all spoke Polish well. They became friendly with the *shabrovniks*, and an agreement was made: the Poles would bring food from the village in exchange for the valuables we found. Of course they were not told the location of our bunker. A rendezvous was arranged far enough away to prevent detection.

A lively trade began between our bunker and the *shabrovniks*. Our contact with them put us in touch with the outside world. They brought us the news heard over the hidden radios in the villages, once they even brought a German newspaper. The barter was well worth while for both parties. We got good nourishing food, meat, butter, fats, and fresh bread, and saved ourselves the dangerous nightly expeditions through the cellars. The *shabrovniks* received all sorts of valuables without having to dig in the ruined buildings.

On the other hand, the shift in our economy ruined our commune and created bad blood among its members. We traded articles which, until then, had been considered the private property of the individuals who found them. They now insisted that the food so obtained was their private property also and did not belong to the community.

Besides goods, the *shabrovniks* were willing to accept American dollars, but not Polish zlotys. This also created conflict and suspicion among us. Some people accused Guzik of being loaded with dollars. After all, he was a finance director of the American

Joint Distribution Committee. Let him contribute some dollars. The accusers began to outdo themselves. Some complained that even in the ghetto Guzik had done little for the Jews. Others went so far as to accuse him of working with the Gestapo because of the tragic episode of the foreign visas at the Hotel Polski.

The campaign against him spread, and the atmosphere became more and more savage. Yulek Smokovsky whispered to me that he had overheard a conversation about Guzik. Some people intended to go out with him one night, take away all his dollars, and then do away with him.

I used every bit of influence I could muster, arguing with everyone who had been pushing the hate campaign against Guzik. Finally I called a meeting of the entire bunker and warned everyone of the consequences of such plotting. The atmosphere became somewhat less tense. The internal strife subsided.

The bunker was well camouflaged. The entrance was a small hole, big enough for a person to squirm through and then slide in. Before the sun rose each day two people would cover the opening carefully with earth and pieces of debris. They would light a small fire close to the opening, creating the impression that this was a smoldering ruin. Then they would go to their observation point a few houses away, high in a wrecked building. They would lie there the entire day, in rain and cold, exposed on all sides to the bitter wind. They watched the ceaseless Russian and German artillery fire. Each night we listened to their reports for signs of danger or of hope.

The inhabitants wove the most variegated and colorful plans for the future. They constantly complained against the American Jews for having given so little aid. Now that millions of Jews had been slaughtered there would be a greater share for those remaining. They harried poor Guzik with demands for information on which to base their calculations. How much money did the JDC customarily receive from America? How much did he think would be forthcoming after the war? They figured, reck-

272

oned and argued. Would they be able to make a better living than they had before the war, and what kind of a world would it be?

Life in the bunker continued its own normal course. We even lived through a funeral. Spiegelman caught a severe cold during a night expedition when he went out of a burning cellar into the December frost. He contracted pneumonia and died.

In the pitch-blackness of the winter night we labored to get his body through the bunker exit—a difficult passage even for the living who could twist and squirm and worm their way through. We buried him in a neighborhood ruin under a mountain of bricks and stones. For a moment we stood in silent mourning. Someone whispered a prayer.

We continued our unhappy life under the ground, living on the hope that the end must certainly be at hand. It was almost four months since the Warsaw uprising. Above us the battles between the Russians and Germans continued. Surely the beasts would be pushed out of Warsaw before long, and liberation would come. We lay in our little cavern, waiting and dreaming

In the middle of the night of January 16, 1945, our expedition returned to report strange activity on Marshalkovska Street. People were moving about and there were voices speaking Russian. We were doubtful at first. Conversations in Russian were no real sign. These could be Ukrainian bandits who worked with the Germans, or they could be followers of General Vlassov. We decided to wait till dawn before sticking our noses out of the bunker.

No one could sleep; we were in a fever of expectation. We suffered hot and cold flashes, and some of us actually had hallucinations.

At dawn our two regular observers went out and returned immediately in great excitement. "The Russian Army is marching down Marshalkovska!"

273

Weeping with joy, we hugged and kissed each other. Then at last we crawled out of our burrows into the light of day.

I hurried to Marshalkovska. It was filled with Russian soldiers. Tanks, cavalry, artillery rushed past, hurrying after the enemy. They moved in long rows through the littered streets, among the smoking ruins and burning buildings.

The city had been occupied the previous day, January 15.

TEN

I HURRIED to the bunker on Shenna where almost four months before I had given up my place to Mrs. Papierna. With some difficulty, I finally recognized the place where the bunker should be. I pounded on the walls and shouted. There was no answer. I moved through the wreckage, hammering and calling into all the openings, but got no response. For three days I returned to repeat the pounding and shouting. I dared not dig into the bunker. If anyone were left alive he would certainly shoot first and investigate afterward.

On the fourth day I succeeded in bringing them out of the bunker. They were all practically naked, half dead, impossible to recognize. They had heard my clamor from the start, but were sure that Germans or Poles were coming after them. In their fright they had crawled deeper into the ground, reaching a sewer where they had stood for twenty-four hours up to their knees in cold scum, paralyzed with fear, while freedom awaited them above ground.

On the third night Little Jacob, Masha Claitman's husband, had crawled out. Near the bunker he had met two Poles and covered them with his machine gun.

They had shouted to him, "What are you afraid of? Why are you still buried? You have been free for three days."

He had refused to believe them, had opened fire, wounding one of them, and had "escaped."

Each day I saw more civilians in the city, mostly Poles, with a scattering of Jews. Of the five hundred Jews who had crawled into bunkers after the uprising there were only two hundred left alive. Many bunkers had been uncovered by digging machines or detected by the specially trained bloodhounds and the listening devices of the Germans. Some Jews had been killed by fire and explosions; many had died of hunger and disease.

Of the few who now crawled out of the bunkers many were sick. We could not provide medical help or even a decent place to lay them down. The filthy human skeletons, miraculous testimony to the obstinacy of life, moved in the streets like shadows.

A few days later a transport of food and some medicine arrived from Lublin, and we were able to care for the most desperate cases. In Praga the Jewish Committee began to function, registering all arrivals and doling out to everyone a pound of bread a day.

Jews began to arrive from camps, still in their striped prison garb; from villages and forests; from partisan groups in Lithuania and around Bialystok; and some from Russia, with military travel permits. Poles began to stream back from Prushkov and from all around Warsaw. Everyone hunted for the valuables he had buried in the earth or hidden in his apartment. Most of them were gone—burned, destroyed, or stolen.

Sharp conflicts broke out between Poles and Jews over apartments and bunkers. The Poles found the few buildings that remained standing occupied by Jews, who, having been in the city, were first-comers and had taken possession of the better quarters. The previous landlords returned and ordered them back to their cellars or into the streets. Many did go back to the bunkers, unable to find other places to live. Landlords who evicted Jews insisted that they leave behind whatever valuables and food they had accumulated.

I contracted dysentery, and this, in my already weakened physical condition, made it impossible for me to drag myself around. My feet were still extremely painful. Comrade Luba Byelitzka, wife of Abrasha Blum, and her sister Riva took me to live with them in Shvider. For two weeks they cared for me tenderly, until some of my strength returned.

In the meantime more people returned to Warsaw. Jews besieged the Jewish Committee, crying, shouting, complaining, begging for a suit of clothes, a crust of bread, a place to sleep. The committee had very limited resources and was not in a position to satisfy even the most elementary needs of the unfortunate.

The great majority of Poles were hostile to the surviving Jews. Constantly one would hear, "Still so many Jews? Where did they come from?" Anti-Semitism was evident everywhere. The returning Jews were made to feel that they were superfluous, that every piece of bread they ate was food taken from the mouths of their betters.

On the streets booths began to appear with goods of various kinds. Commerce was carried on exclusively by Poles. In such an atmosphere Jews did not dare enter into trade. The black market and the black bourse were exclusively reserved to the Poles. On the busy streets they would call out in clear Polish, "I buy dollars. I buy gold and diamonds. I need manufactured goods. I need textiles."

Jews were afraid to speak Yiddish in public. One day I was walking with Comrade Poppover in Grochov, conversing in Yiddish. Someone stopped us with a curt insult, and we answered him sharply. On his complaint, a policeman led us to the local police commissariat. There we were loftily told that it was "inadvisable" for Jews to provoke Poles by speaking Yiddish on the public streets.

With my good friends of the underground—Communists as well as others—I discussed the painful evidences of the rising anti-Semitic wave. Some put the blame on Hitler—"So many years of poisoning with hate"; others on the fear of Communism—"You know the old saying of the Polish reactionaries: all Bolsheviks are Jews."

Our complaints were received sympathetically by Polish friends but there was no action against the anti-Jewish campaign. There were too many other problems. After so many years of blood-letting and terror, during which every humanitarian instinct had been crushed, the morale of the liberated people of Poland was at a low ebb. And the conduct of the liberators, the rank-and-file soldiers of the Red Army who did not shrink from robbery and rape, further demoralized the population.

The chaos and anarchy of Polish economic life and the dis-satisfaction and disappointment of the Polish population were in-creased by the economic policies of the new rulers. They began to remove the machines and equipment from the factories at Lodz and other industrial centers. The ruin which the Nazis had spread in five years of pillage now increased. Unemployment mounted.

We found that the liberators had brought political demoraliza-tion, too. With the Russian Army came those who claimed to speak for the Bund. Without consulting the membership, they proceeded to reverse many of the Bund's policies, tying it to the kite of the Russian-sponsored Lublin government. Through all the difficult days of the occupation we had tried to maintain our organization as a democratic political party. We had arrived at our political decisions only after consultation and discussion, often in the shadow of death. The newcomers, with the help of Soviet authority, set themselves up as "the Bund," and the declarations they issued in our name mocked those who had stood fast through the long years of suffering.

The NKVD, the Soviet secret police, was carrying out mass arrests of those suspected of belonging to the Armia Kryova, the military organization of the London Polish government. They imprisoned members of other sections of the underground, such as the PPS and the Peasant party—any, indeed, who refused to

278

be *"gleichgeschaltet"* and who rejected the "line" of the temporary Lublin government. This wave of political terror further increased the chaos.

With almost physical pain, I received the tragic news that our beloved Leon Feiner had died in a Lublin hospital. After the liberation of Warsaw I had been able to arrange a visit to Lublin for a political conference and had seen Feiner. Once again I had seen the pale, sunken, ghostly white face tortured by disease, the blue eyes staring listlessly. Until his last moment this almost legendary hero of the underground had struggled with the painful problems of his people. Racked by physical and mental torment for five years he had lived just long enough to see the liberation and then had found his peace.

Comrade Herman Kirshenbaum, a leader of the Bund in Kutno and active in the Warsaw underground, had fallen in the uprising. He was buried with others somewhere in a courtyard in Zholibosh. A wooden board marked his grave. Now, his wife, Eva, a member of the Kutno City Council, asked that we disinter his body and transfer it to the Jewish cemetery on Gensha.

Communication with Zholibosh was not yet re-established. The roads were littered with masonry and broken by craters and trenches. It took several weeks to make the necessary arrangements. Finally, on a foggy March morning in 1945, we went for the body of our fallen comrade. In an automobile provided by the Jewish Central Aid Committee, sat the widow, Mrs. Shefner, Comrade Fishgrund, a cousin of Comrade Kirshenbaum, and myself. The road was deserted. We bounced over the debris, through ruts and holes. At the tunnel near the Danzig Station, Eva Kirshenbaum had a heart attack.

We took her, unconscious, to the home of a doctor in Zholibosh, left Mrs. Shefner to care for her, and continued to the courtyard to find the grave.

With great difficulty we located the wooden marker which identified Comrade Kirshenbaum's last resting place among the scores of snow-covered graves. Some Christian neighbors helped us to exhume the body and pay tribute to our fallen comrade.

It took a long time to negotiate the fields and pitted roads on the way to the Gensha cemetery. When we got there, everything was desolate. There were many open graves. Holes had been dug under broken tombstones where ghouls had searched for the gold teeth of the dead. Close to the cemetery fence, near the ceremonial hall, I passed a half-decomposed body in rags which lay partly submerged in the loose mud. The sex organ was completely exposed. The murderers had had a simple way to determine the nationality of their victim.

We walked along the rusted tracks of the railroad spur over which the Nazis had carried the loot from the destroyed ghetto after the uprising. I turned into the first row of graves. Here lay our dear comrades, Yanek Yankelevitch, Kalman Kamashenmacher, and others whose graves we had tended for many years, and whose memories we had cherished. As I passed a stone mausoleum, several huge cats sprang out, almost on top of me. With a sickening feeling I realized that they had suffered no shortage of food.

We found a plot of ground not far from the grave of Beynish Michalevitch. There we buried one of his best students, Herman Kirshenbaum, who until his last breath had been loyal to the spiritual heritage of his great teacher.

We hurried back over the difficult road to Zholibosh, anxious about the condition of Comrade Eva. Deathly pale, Mrs. Shefner told us that Eva was dead. The doctor insisted that we move her from his house immediately. We were dumfounded. We had nowhere to leave the body even for a night. It was an insult to the dead to take her still-warm body to its grave, but we had no alternative. We returned to the cemetery to place Comrade Eva at the side of her beloved husband.

In April 1945 the Polish government organized a memorial meeting in Praga at a hall on Enginierska Street to commemorate the second anniversary of the ghetto uprising. I went to the meeting with Riva Byelitzka.

On the way we met Major Rugg who, during the Warsaw uprising, had been in charge of the commissary on Koshikova Street and had helped us distribute aid to needy Jews. He made a great show of being happy to see me, asking about various comrades and about the state of our organization. He introduced me to his companion, who, he said, was a Polish engineer and an active leader of the underground peasant movement. All four of us went to the meeting together.

Rugg wanted to see me again. He insisted that we fix a definite appointment. We decided to meet at eleven one morning in a café in Praga.

At the railway station on my way to Praga on the appointed day I met Rugg's friend, the engineer, with four others, one of them in the uniform of a captain of the Polish Army. They too, it seemed, were on their way to Praga. When I arrived at the café to meet Rugg, I found the same group of people. They explained that Rugg had arranged to meet them in the same café at the same hour.

We sat down together and ordered tea. Rugg came late, profusely apologetic. Suddenly through the window we saw a truck drive up carrying officers of the NKVD. With a great deal of shouting they rushed past the startled patrons directly to our table. Waving their revolvers, they demanded our documents. The papers were confiscated, and we were ordered into the truck.

It was all very strange, particularly Major Rugg's calm, unconcerned air.

As we walked side by side toward the truck I said to him, "What is all this?"

"Be calm," he whispered. "Just tell them that you are my cousin. Nothing will happen to you."

They took us to the NKVD building and locked us in a bare room without even a single chair. The guards who remained with us forbade us to talk to each other or to put our hands in our pockets. We stood silently for several hours, waiting.

Finally we were called out, one at a time, at long intervals. No one who was taken out returned to the room. I was the last to go.

They took me to a simply furnished room. At a table sat two officers. A third paced back and forth in the background. Every few minutes a soldier, usually with a revolver displayed where I could not miss it, walked into the room, studied my face silently, and then walked out. After a long silence, the inquiry began.

They asked the usual questions.

I told them that I was a Jew, that the name on the Polish passport was an alias, and that my real name was Bernard Goldstein.

"Why do you have a false passport?"

I explained that under Hitler many Jews had tried to save themselves with forged papers.

"Ah-h!" my interrogator answered in a tone evidently intended to convey his complete disbelief "Who were the people with whom you were sitting?"

"I know only the name of the one to whom I was introduced by Major Rugg."

"How do you know Major Rugg?"

"He is a friend of mine. I have known him since the uprising."

"What were you discussing in the café? What kind of conference was it?"

"We had no opportunity to talk about anything. It was not a conference. As soon as I sat down with Rugg, you came in and arrested us."

"To which party do you belong?"

282

"To the Bund."

"What bund? Are you stirring up rebellion?" He was punning in Russian on the word bund.

I tried to explain. "The Bund is the name of the Jewish Labor party."

"Ah-h!" he said, as if he had just learned something strange and interesting.

My interrogator rang the bell. A soldier walked in and led me back to the empty room. I was called back several times for questioning. We covered the same ground over and over again.

Late in the evening a soldier came in and ordered me to follow him. He led me through dark corridors to the door of the building and said, "You are free. You may go."

"But my passport!" I cried in despair. "They did not return my passport!"

"Why didn't you tell me earlier?" shouted the soldier irritably. He took me back inside, got my passport, and ordered me to leave.

I was seized with a feeling of disgust and nausea at myself and at the entire world. My heart was heavy and my body trembled. My throat was choked with angry sobs.

On the street I found Rugg waiting for me. "You see! I told you nothing would happen to you. I told you they would set you free."

He wanted to arrange to see me again. I told him to leave me alone, that I was too upset to talk now.

I learned later that all those who had been arrested with me at the café were active in the underground peasant movement. They were never seen again. I heard rumors in Warsaw that they had somehow disappeared.

I made a special trip to Podkova-Leshna to the headquarters of the opposition PPS to inquire about Major Rugg. There I was given indisputable evidence that Rugg was now an agent of the NKVD and served as an informer on Polish political parties, using the information that he had acquired in the underground during the Nazi occupation.

It was clear that the NKVD was playing a cat-and-mouse game with me. They knew what the Bund was, and who I was. The Polish Communist party had once passed an official sentence of death against me. That honor was not accorded to many. Surely the NKVD had that in their records.

Some of my comrades who had returned from Russia had told me that in the course of their "interrogations" by the NKVD they had been asked about me. They urged me to get out of Poland and clear of Soviet authority as quickly as possible. I firmly rejected all such suggestions—at first.

At meetings of the Bund I spoke openly and bitterly about the murders of Erlich and Alter. I made no secret of my resentment at the "new course" of the Bund. I knew that some of the new "comrades" were noting all this for the dossier of the NKVD. I felt surrounded by spies and police agents. My arrest, it seemed to me, was only a teaser. They hoped to compromise me a little, to prepare the ground for a second arrest. For the moment, I could go free. Such things did not have to be rushed. I was safely in their grasp.

But to me freedom meant activity. I found that I no longer dared to meet my comrades of the Polish underground. I could not get rid of Rugg. Wherever I went he would suddenly appear. He was always offering to spend time with me, always asking friendly questions about various comrades.

Whatever my opinion of Rugg, he must have been one of the NKVD's more valuable agents. I learned later that he engineered the widely reported arrest of the sixteen Polish underground leaders aboard a Soviet plane on the way to a Moscow "conference."

It was clear that this creature wanted to involve me in his espionage. Any persons with whom I might meet would be in danger of investigation or arrest. I tried to isolate myself as much as possible, to deny Rugg every thread which would lead to comrades in the Socialist and peasant underground. I decided that they had not finished me once and for all because they hoped I would be more useful free. I was determined not to help them. But deliberately avoiding old comrades, deliberately remaining politically inactive, became more and more distasteful. And I did not like waiting for the inevitable arrest. If Henryk Erlich and Victor Alter could be executed as "Nazi agents," what hope was there for me? Many Socialist comrades were already in the Polish prisons. I was only waiting for my turn.

Rugg's attentions, the unconcealed anti-Semitism of the Polish people, the atmosphere of political and intellectual asphyxiation generated by the police regime all made Warsaw and Poland intolerable for me. This was not the liberation for which I had waited five long, heartbreaking years, for which I had degraded myself to the level of the meanest animal in order to remain alive.

Under the Nazis we had lost our homes, we had lost the lives of millions upon millions of men, women, and children—an entire people, victims of a crime against humanity so vast, so staggering that beside it the bestiality of the darkest ages of humanity grows pale. But now we had lost the faith that, after all the pain and suffering, after the nightmare of helplessness in the murderers' grasp, would come a new day of justice, of human decency and brotherhood. That faith, that longing to stand upright once more with our faces toward the light, had given us the will to live during the blackest hours of the Nazi terror.

The decision to leave Poland was the most painful of my entire life. I arrived at it only after long hours of tortured deliberation. But once I had made it I felt a weight lift from my heart, and I was eager to go as quickly as possible.

Before quitting Warsaw I attended a memorial meeting for the ghetto, arranged by the Jewish fighting organization. On the ruins near the former jail on Zamenhof, the only recognizable portion of a building still standing, I stood among a group of close comrades who had participated in the uprising and in the Jewish underground. Around us, over a wide area, there was nothing but powdered rubble—ruins, ruins, ruins. It was impossible to believe that destruction could be so complete.

My entire life had been part of the lively rushing stream that had poured through these streets and alleys. I had known every corner, every house, every cobblestone. Where was it all? Where were Nalefky, Franciskanska, Zamenhof, Novolipya, Karmelitzka? Where were the countless streets and alleys filled with the exciting noise of life, sometimes happy, sometimes sad, but always vibrant and animated? Now all was dust. I could not even tell where the streets had been. One patch of rubble was exactly like the next.

I felt a deep and bitter sorrow. The blue sky and bright spring day mocked me. I felt the lonely emptiness of a disembodied spirit who wanders aimlessly over the deserted ruins after the cataclysm.

Who had cheated the Nazis? Those who rotted beneath the broken stones or were ashes in some charnel pit, or I, sentenced to live out my days and nights with the tortured memories of what had been?

This was the end. This was the sum total of hundreds of generations of living and building, of religion, of Torah, of piety, of free thinking, of Zionism, of Bundism, of struggles and battles, of the hopes of an entire people—this, this empty desert.

I looked around me at what had been the Jews of Warsaw. I felt one hope, and I feel it now. May this sea of emptiness bubble and boil, may it cry out eternal condemnation of the murderers and pillagers, may it be forever the shame of the civilized world which saw and heard and chose to remain silent.

Like a thief, I crept out of the city which had been my life and which still holds my soul imprisoned beneath its ashes and rubble.

Carrying a forged Czech passport in the name of Malinovsky, I made my way to Prague. I had no plan. I was driven only by the conviction that whatever will to live had brought me through five years of hell would not sustain me through another moment of the mocking frustration called "liberation."

In Prague I asked the secretary of the Czech Social Democratic party to wire my comrades in New York informing them of my situation. He was very understanding and sympathetic but pointed out that martial law still prevailed. Only the most urgent private telegrams were permitted to go through and even those were carefully scanned by the Russian authorities. He advised me to wait until controls relaxed somewhat and promised he would then do everything he could to help.

I could not wait. My restlessness would not permit it, nor would the uneasy feeling that I might be picked up by the NKVD. What explanation could cover the false name and false passport?

The hopes and fears of the expatriates and refugees who wandered homeless in the streets of Prague rose and fell on a flood of rumors and misinformation. I heard of two repatriation centers in the American Army zone of Czechoslovakia, near Pilsen—one for Eastern Europeans, principally Poles, and the other for Western Europeans. This was vouched for by some who claimed to have seen the camps.

The idea was appealing. I had little to lose. If I could manage to get into the camp for Western Europeans, I would have a much better opportunity to contact comrades who had succeeded in leaving Poland at the outbreak of the war. They were now the only ones I could turn to for aid.

With the help of a Soviet officer I negotiated the military demarcation line without documents and without difficulty.

In Pilsen I ran into a stone wall. The incredulous officials at the American repatriation office rejected my applications in amazement. This was too much! A Czech in his own country applying for admission to a repatriation camp for displaced foreigners! I pleaded that all my family and friends had been killed, that I no longer had anyone left in Czechoslovakia, that the only ones I could turn to were relatives in—in Holland. I was turned down by various interviewers in turn, but I kept trying someone else, hoping to improve my luck. One of them suggested that if I were really alone and needed help he might be able to arrange admission to the camp for Eastern Europeans. I declined hastily, with thanks.

Finally I got the ear of an American Army sergeant. He was Jewish and could understand just enough Yiddish to hear me out. He was very sympathetic. It was irregular, but he was willing to discuss the matter with his superiors.

I waited an eternity until he came back waving a little slip of paper. This would admit me to the camp, he explained, but the trip to Holland was strictly a matter for the Dutch authorities. They would examine my case and decide.

Once inside the camp, there was nothing to do but wait. Applying to the Dutch was out of the question. That might precipitate a thorough investigation ending with a trip back to Poland.

It was a good place to rest. I was tired of running and hiding, of listening for the sound of footsteps. My body cried out for rest. Walking was painful, the swelling had not yet left my feet.

The repatriation camp accommodated perhaps five hundred men and women assigned to barracks according to their nationalities. I was put in a small dormitory with about fifteen men awaiting repatriation to Holland. Good food, rest, and the friendly Czech sun poured strength into minds and bodies slowly finding their way back to health.

Except for the few who had smuggled themselves in, all were Western Europeans who had been conscripted for forced labor by the Nazis. They waited eagerly and fearfully for the return to homes and families from which they had been separated for long years.

I could not suppress a feeling of envy at those around me who were busy with happy preparations for their journeys. Their dreams were coming true. They filled out forms, wrote letters, cheerfully wondered out loud how familiar people and places would look after years of war. Everyone was in a pleasant state of impatient anticipation. Around the dining-room tables and the barrack bunks the talk was all of home and family. In his mind's eye each one embraced his own, unable to slow his fervid imagination to the plodding pace of the repatriation machinery.

Everyone was hurrying home. I was hurrying away from home. Extraordinary good luck had got me into the Pilsen camp, under American jurisdiction, only two weeks after I left Warsaw. I was grateful, but I could not escape the feeling that it was an empty accomplishment. It was difficult to see what could come next. For the others, this was the road back. For me it was a dead end.

I struck up an acquaintance with Pierre, a friendly young Belgian about thirty years old who had spent several years in Nazi forced labor camps. He had already gone through the repatriation procedure. His papers were all in order and he was waiting impatiently for transportation home.

It was pleasant to sit on the ground and talk, looking out past the barbed-wire fence and the precisely spaced guard towers at the warm green Czech countryside stretching into the distance. There was no feeling of confinement. The guard towers seemed almost to be friendly sentinels.

We would sit and talk for hours in broken German, helping each other while away the days.

I discovered that Pierre too was a Socialist. Years of prison had not made him cynical. He was going home to rebuild. I listened with painful nostalgia as he talked eagerly about the world that could be if we willed it and worked for it. Could I ever recapture such hope, such faith in the future?

Our friendship ripened. I asked him to deliver letters for me to Paul Henri Spaak, later Belgium's prime minister, and to Pro-

289

fessor Allar, Victor Alter's brother-in-law, then in the Belgian Foreign Ministry. He agreed readily.

Pierre did not have long to wait. One morning early in July we were awakened by the roar of many airplanes directly over the camp grounds. We dressed and rushed out to find the entire camp bustling. Overhead a dozen large American transports were circling to land at the near-by airfield. The lucky repatriates were already assembling in small groups surrounded by their luggage. There was a holiday spirit in the air. Those who were remaining dashed about to wish their friends good luck.

I finally spotted Pierre between two large suitcases in a knot of beaming compatriots. He waved happily to me. We shook hands, and he assured me solemnly that my letters would be delivered.

The loudspeaker shouted instructions, and the groups began to move toward the camp gate. Pierre leaned over to pick up his bags. I put a restraining hand on his arm and without a word he let me take one suitcase while he picked up the other. We walked along side by side. I was already beginning to feel lonely, thinking of the long days of waiting for the results of my letters.

I wanted to prolong the farewell, to warm myself just a little longer in the atmosphere of unalloyed happiness which radiated from exiles going home. I wanted to be with them until the last moment, to hear the motors roar and watch the planes rise and fade away toward the west.

The joy of the repatriates was contagious. I held up my worthless documents and tried to look as much as possible like a happy Belgian DP. The guards simply smiled their congratulations and waved us through the gate. We walked to the airport. The bright sun sparkling off the giant airplanes made my mind race. They were so close, those planes, so close . . . perhaps . . . perhaps . . .

My belongings were back in the barrack, but my most valuable possession was in a little pouch hanging from a string around my neck—the little leather wallet given to me by Sonya Novogrodsky while we waited together for death. It never left me day or night.

My comrade smiled at me. We said nothing. He understood the crazy thoughts running through my head. Our little group was escorted to a waiting plane. I followed Pierre into it and sat down beside him. He reached over casually and took back his suitcase.

I was wet with perspiration. My beard burned my face. It had disguised me for five years; now it marked me as a stranger, an impostor.

An American Army officer stepped into the airplane and slowly went around, examining documents in turn. I handed him my Czech passport. His puzzled expression changed to one of amazement and displeasure. He took me roughly by the arm and led me out of the plane and across the field to the administration building. Behind me the door of the airplane slammed and the roar of the motors increased.

We walked into a large hall toward two other officers, one of whom I took to be the commandant, engaged in earnest conversation. My escort told me in a tone that crossed boundaries of language that I was to wait there until the commandant was free to deal with me. He then returned to his duties.

I watched unhappily through the windows as, one after another, the planes took on their passengers and rose into the air. Soon there was only one airplane left, with a cluster of people standing alongside it, waiting to get on board. It was now or never.

The commandant was still engrossed in conversation, apparently not even aware of my presence. As nonchalantly as my quaking heart permitted, I walked behind him and toward the exit. Once through, I raced to the last waiting group, reaching them as they started to climb into the airplane.

Everyone ahead of me was in, and still I hung back hesitantly. The soldier standing at the door of the airplane shouted at me impatiently. He pointed insistently toward the doorway. I stepped in, and he closed the door behind me. I found a place to sit. The plane was already vibrating, and the roar of the motors was deafening.

We were moving. I had never been in an airplane before. I looked out of the window. We were off the ground.

For a moment I was seized by a sickening doubt. Perhaps I had been tricked. Perhaps we were flying east after all.

I shouted into the ear of the passenger alongside me. He looked startled and incredulous. "We are going home, of course!"

"Home?"

"Home—to Belgium!"

In Brussels the airport officials, after one look at my Czech passport, whisked me off to the nearest prison. But I was free in a matter of hours, and in a matter of days I had a new passport issued by the Polish government-in-exile in my rightful name.

A few days after I arrived in Brussels, United States Army Sergeant Mark Novogrodsky came to visit me. He was released from the front on a short furlough to hear, after years of uncertainty, the story of his mother's death. Tall, lanky, with the thin white face I remembered so well, he looked strange to me in his American Army uniform.

Before I spoke, he knew what I had to tell him. He told me that the message we had sent through the Polish underground about Sonya's death had reached New York, but the family had refused to believe it.

Without a word, with tears glistening in his eyes, he listened as I told him of Sonya's life in the ghetto and during the deportations, of her devotion and heroism, and of her final acceptance of death. Then from the pouch hung around my neck I took the small Mexican wallet which Sonya had placed in my care so many months before. I had carried it with me always, through the dark hiding places on the Aryan side, through the sewers and the cellars of abandoned Warsaw, through liberation and escape from liberation.

With a feeling of unreality, like an actor in a bizarre opera, I handed the wallet to the sobbing boy.

Months later I came to America. It is, perhaps, the end of my journey. While I wait for the immigration authorities to decide whether I shall be permitted to remain, my thoughts cannot stay still. In Poland, miles away, where we once made our life, there is now a void. We could have remade that life if we had had a chance. But there was no chance.

At the end of the war there were perhaps 250,000 Polish Jews. This surviving fragment of a prewar population of more than three and a half million had a strong loyalty to the traditions of Polish Jewry. They had lived through the war, either in Soviet Russia, in Nazi death camps, or in Poland, under assumed names and in constant fear of death. Yet they still had energy and drive; they had come home to rebuild. Almost immediately they organized political parties, schools, producer cooperatives, theater groups. They re-created in miniature the flourishing Jewish community of old.

These Jews had returned to ruins of which every stone, every bit of rubble reminded them of their own heartbreak. They were prepared, at least to some extent, to live with their sorrow. In a few generations that fragment of 250,000 could have grown in numbers sufficient to guarantee a continuation of its past. In spite of all the desolation, the destruction, they wanted to go on, to insure that Polish Jewry, with its nine-hundred-year history, would not be destroyed.

But there were two things for which they were not prepared: anti-Semitism and communism.

Never in all the years before 1939 did Polish Jews feel so insecure, so fearful for their lives as they did after World War II. Anti-Semitism was more pronounced, more virulent, more blood-thirsty than it had been before the war. In the old days, when Jews made up about 10 per cent of the Polish population, "cultured" anti-Semites had urged as justification that there were too many Jews in the country. Yet when the Jews were reduced to a tiny fraction of their former number, the worst anti-Semitic wave of all swept across Poland.

And many Jews who would have clung stubbornly to their homes despite anti-Semitism felt that they had to flee communism. In postwar Poland the early hopes born of the working agreement between Mikolayczyk and the Russian masters of the country were soon extinguished. Mass arrests, the appearance of police agents in all organizations, the swift use of terroristic methods against dissenters, quickly opened the eyes of Jews who had lived under communism in Russia. About a quarter of a million of them had fled to the Soviet Union as refugees during the war; approximately 150,000 returned. When the Russian government offered them Soviet citizenship very few had accepted—not because the old life in Poland had been perfect, but because, in comparison with life under the Soviet regime, it seemed like a beautiful, lost dream. And when, after their return, they began to see Soviet methods used in Poland, they did not wait for a dictatorship to materialize; the first signs were enough. Every institution and political party in Poland, including the Bund, was perverted to serve the purpose of the new masters. Under labels which the people had learned to respect, the rulers peddled the quack slogans of dictatorship. As the regime became more secure, even the appearance of political freedom was cast aside. The PPS, having served its purpose, was liquidated. The Bund has since suffered the same fate.

The people had only one way to vote against conditions—with their feet. The revived Jewish community began to melt away. It filtered out of the country, to displaced persons' camps in Germany, to Palestine, or to a wandering, homeless existence—anything to escape.

Now there are only sixty or seventy thousand left, and even these are trying to get away. As a cultural and national entity, the small community is going through its death throes; the Jewish Yishuv in Poland, once the most important segment of world Jewry, no longer exists. Those who are left are too few to revive it again. It is true that Jews like Minc, Berman, Zambrovski, Boreisza, and others occupy high places in the Communist ruling caste. But the power of these men does not indicate strength in the Jewish community. They are hired stooges for a dictatorship. Thus the remaining Jews of Poland act out the epilogue to the great national tragedy which began in September 1939.

Those of us who survived that holocaust are freaks of nature, testimony to the dogged human will to live. But we are as surely dead as our more fortunate brothers who have found peace. We have our lives, but our life is gone.

If there is any purpose in our survival, perhaps it is to give testimony. It is a debt we owe, not alone to the millions who were dragged to death in crematoriums and gas chambers, but to all our fellow human beings who want to live in brotherhood—and who must find a way.

Lightning Source UK Ltd.
Milton Keynes UK
UKHW022059030921
389864UK00006B/1429